HISTORY
OF RUSSIA

Sergei Mikhailovich Soloviev

The *Academic International Press* Edition of *Sergei M. Soloviev's* History
of Russia From Earliest Times. *Peter von Wahlde, General Editor.*

Contributing Editors:

HUGH F. GRAHAM

JOHN D. WINDHAUSEN

ALEXANDER V. MULLER

K. A. PAPMEHL

RICHARD HANTULA

WALTER J. GLEASON, JR.

WILLIAM H. HILL

G. EDWARD ORCHARD

LINDSEY A.J. HUGHES

NICKOLAS LUPININ

SERGEI M. SOLOVIEV

History of Russia

Volume 42

A New Empress

Peter III and Catherine II, 1761 – 1762

Edited, Translated and With an
Introduction by

Nicholas Lupinin

Academic International Press

1990

The Academic International Press Edition of S.M. Soloviev's
History of Russia from Earliest Times in fifty volumes.

Volume 42. *A New Empress. Peter III and Catherine II, 1761–1762.*
Unabridged translation of the text of Volume 25, Chapters 1–2 of
S.M. Soloviev's *Istoriia Rossii s drevneishikh vremen* as found in
Volume XIII of this work published in Moscow in 1965.

Library of Congress Card Number:
ISBN: 0-87569-117-X

Composition by Lois Dugas and Barbara Knoelke

Printed in the United States of America

A list of Academic International Press publications is found at the
end of this volume.

ACADEMIC INTERNATIONAL PRESS
POB 1111 Gulf Breeze FL 32562

CONTENTS

First Days—The New Council—New Measures Before the Senate—Freedom of the Nobility—Administrative Changes—Ecclesiastical Problems—The Peasants Stir—Finances and Military Preparation—Peter and Frederick the Great—Peace and Alliance with Prussia—Trouble with Denmark—When Friends Fence: Austria and Russia—Relations with France—Communications with England—Sweden, Poland—Obrezkov in Turkey—Reversal of Foreign Policy—Dissatisfaction—Dissatisfaction in the Church, the Army, and the Guards—General Discontent and Prussian Fears—The Russian Army Abroad—The Prisoner of Schlüsselburg—Catherine's Difficult Position—Panin, Razumovsky, the Guards—Princess Dashkova and the Growing Conspiracy—Catherine Takes the Throne—The Last Efforts of Peter III

Rewards and Returns—The Fate of the Favorites—Catherine and the Senate—The Death of Peter III—Economic Measures and Domestic Affairs—Catherine's Coronation—A Problem from the Past—Capitals, Provinces, Peasants—The Questions of an Imperial Council—Foreign Policy—The Prussian Response—Relief in Denmark—Sweden Observes—Poland and Courland—Turkey and Austria—France and England

Illustrations

WEIGHTS AND MEASURES

Linear Measure

Verst: 500 sazhen, 1166 yards and 2 feet, .663 miles, 1.0668 km.
Sazhen: 3 arshins, 7 feet, 2.133 m
Arshin: 16 vershoks, 28in. (diuims) 72.12 cm
Chetvert: 1/4 arshin
Fut: 12 diuims, 1 foot, 30.48 cm
Vershok: 1.75 in., 4.445 cm, 1/16 arshin
Diuim: 1 inch, 2.54 cm
Desiatina: 2400 square sazhens, 2.7 acres, 1.0925 hectare
Chetvert (quarter): 1/2 desiatine, 1.35 acre (sometimes 1.5 desiatinas or ca. 4.1 acres)

Liquid Measure

Stof: Kruzhka (cup), 1/10 vedro, ca. 1.3 quarts, 1.23 liters
Kufa: 30 stofy
Vedro (paid): 3.25 gallons, 12.3 liters, 10 stofy
Bochka (barrel): 40 vedros, 121 gallons, 492 liters
Chetvert (quarter): 1.4 bochka, 32.5 gallons

Weights

Berkovets: 361 olbs., 10 puds
Pud: 40 funts, 36,113 lbs. (US), 40 lbs. (Russian), 16.38 kg
Funt: 96 zolotniks, .903 lb., 14.4 ozs., 408.24 grams
Grivenka: 205 grams
Korob (basket): 7 puds, 252 lbs.
Rad: 14 puds, 505.58 lbs
Chetvert (grain measure): 1/4 rad, 3.5 puds, 126.39 lbs., ca. 8 bushels
Chetverik (grain measure dating from 16th century): 1/8 chetvert, 15.8 lbs.
Zolotnik: 1/96 lb., 4.26 grams

Money

Chervonets (chervonny): A gold coin minted in the first half of the 18th century worth
    about 3 rubles
Muscovite Denga: 200 equals 1 ruble
Novgorod Denga: 100 equals 1 ruble
Ruble: 100 copecks, 200 dengas
Altyn: 6 Muscovite dengas, 3 copecks
Grivna: 20 Muscovite dengas, 100 grivnas equals 1 ruble, 10 copecks
Poltina (Poltinnik): 50 copecks, 100 dengas
Polupoltina (-nik): 25 copecks, 50 dengas
Poltora: 1 1/2 rubles
Peniaz: 10 equals one grosh (Lithuania)
Kopa grosh: 60 groshas, one Muscovite poltina
Chetvertak: silver coin equal to 25 copecks or 1/4 rubles (18-19th centuries)
Copeck: two Muscovite dengas
Foreign Denominations: 1 efimok or 1 thaler (Joachimsthaler)-about 1 ruble, 1 chervonets
    or chervonnyi—a ducat, about 3 rubles
Levok—Dutch silver lion dollar

Note: Weights and measures often changed values over time and sometimes held more than
    one value at the same time. For details consult Sergei G. Pushkarev, *Dictionary of
    Russian Historical Terms from the Eleventh Century to 1917* (Yale, 1970).

Empress Catherine II, 1729–1796

Painting by Lévitsky

Count Nikita Ivanovich Panin, 1718–1785
Painting by Rostin

PREFACE

The translator's task is often a thankless one. Whatever translation "method" is used, it has its adherents as well as opponents who claim other "methods" are better fitted for the translator's craft. It frequently helps if the critic has more than a passing knowledge of the language from which the translation is being made. I find that such arguments should best be saved for works of literature and poetry where the demands on the translator might lend themselves better to argumentation regarding method. My translating procedure has been to attempt a rendition that is above all a proper mixture of fidelity to the text and good English.

This book is an unabridged translation of Volume 25, Chapters 1-2, which are pp. 7-190 in Volume XIII of the multi-volume edition of *Istoriia Rossii s drevneishikh vremen* (History of Russia From Earliest Times, 29 vols., St. Petersburgh, 1851-1879) published from 1962 through 1966 in Moscow. Soloviev's work is one of serious scholarship, very thorough, and expository in nature. It ranks with the classics of nineteenth-century historiography and laid the groundwork for the Russian historical writing that followed.

Its reputation as a scholarly foundation piece is well deserved. Soloviev utilized an immense body of archival material previously untapped. This material is quite impressive, and quite in keeping with Soloviev's emphasis on the history of the Russian State, both political and diplomatic. It may be instructive to note some of this vast array of sources: the Journals and the Protocols of the Senate, the Vorontsov Archives, the Shakhovskoy Archives, the diplomatic papers of Russian relations with Prussia, Denmark, Austria, France, England, Sweden, Courland, Turkey, and others. Utilized as well are the memoirs of Princess Dashkova, of A.T. Bolotov, and the diary of A.V. Khrapovitsky. Official and unofficial collections of documents, historical journals, holdings of historical societies and archives and the Complete Collection of Russian Laws are cited. And Soloviev did not limit his research to Russian sources. Some of the foreign sources used are *Oevres de Frederic* (Works of Frederick the Great), *Memoires de Frederic II, roi de Prussie,* and *Correspondence secrete inedite de Louis XV sur la politique* (Paris, 1866). This is not to cite secondary works by such European historians as E. Hermann's *Geschichte der europäischen Staaten,* F. Raumer's *Beiträge zur neuren Geschichte aus dem britischen Museum und Reichsarchive,* and J.H. Castera's *Histoire de Catherine II, imperatrice de Russie.* This is truly an impressive list, especially when we consider that it is a partial one.

The present translation endeavors to render the text and Soloviev's thought as accurately as possible. No attempt has been made to reproduce his style and text word for word, for this would have yielded a bizarre Russianized text. The main consideration has been to make his history as readable as possible consistent with accuracy, while retaining at least something of the flavor of the language of the era. An effort has been made to find English-language equivalents for all technical terms Soloviev employs (ranks, offices, titles, legal, administrative and so forth) in the belief that English is no less rich in such terms than other languages. This is intended to smooth the flow of the narrative for the reader and to avoid marring the pages with annoying untranslated words. The exception involves Russian words which have become common in English—boyar, tsar, cossack. In all of this the translator remains painfully aware of the inevitable shortcomings that may remain.

Soloviev's pages are monotonous and interminable, one long and complex sentence marching after the last. To make the text easier to follow for today's readers, long paragraphs and sentences have been broken into shorter ones. Most of the subtitles are based on the descriptive topic headings clustered at the beginnings of the chapters in the Russian edition. These headings have been moved into the body of the text as subtitles to mark and ease for the reader the transition from one subject to another. In some cases, to even the frequency of breaks in the text or to show topics not listed by Soloviev at the beginning of chapters, new subtitles have been added. Soloviev's arrangement of the material has been followed strictly.

Brief explanatory or interpretive materials have been inserted into the text enclosed in brackets, or added as footnotes to each chapter at the end of the book. All material enclosed in brackets has been added by the present editor and all material in parenthesis is the author's. Emphasized words or phrases in italics are the author's.

The general policy followed in annotating has been to identify prominent personalities at first mention and to give explanation and elucidations of less common or obscure terms and passages, assuming the typical reader to have relatively little familiarity with Russian history. If brief, these have been included in the text in brackets; otherwise they appear as numbered footnotes found at the back of the book by chapters. Most of the author's own notes are not included because their highly specialized archival, documentary and bibliographic nature is of value solely to specialists who, in any case, will prefer to consult the original Russian text. In addition, most of the notes added by the editors of the edition published in the Soviet Union are technical in nature—and fuller bibliographic citations than those in Soloviev's notes—have not been included. When the author's notes and those of the Soviet editors are included, they are so designated. All other notes are those of the present editor.

Russian personal names are preserved in their Russian form except for Alexander, Alexis, Michael, Nicholas, Catherine and Peter, which English usage has made familiar with respect to Russian historical figures, and important ecclesiastics whose names largely have been recast into Latin or Greek equivalents, especially for the earlier period of Russian history. This applies to prominent individuals; Russian forms usually are used for the less prominent. Certain other names and terms have been anglicized for the sake of clarity and because they are used widely—Casimir, Sophia, Danzig, rubles, versts, Dnieper river, and others.

The editors of the edition published in the USSR frequently have added patronymics and other names, and these have been retained without brackets; patronymics appearing in the original edition also have been included. Plural forms for names and terms which might be confusing have been anglicized—Vologdians rather than Vologzhane, Voguls not Vogulichi, the Dolgorukys not Dolgorukie, and so forth. Even so, in a few cases the Russian plural form is used when this form is common. Most Slavic surnames show gender, and this has been preserved. Since an "a" at the word end usually indicates a female, Golovkin would have a wife or daughter, Golovkina. The final "iia" in feminine personal names has been shortened to "ia"—"Maria" and "Evdokia" instead of "Mariia" and "Evdokiia."

Non-Russian names, locations, terms, ranks and so on are spelled according to the language native to the person or particular to the city, region or culture when this can be determined. Confusion arises at times because the text is not clear about nationalities. An excruciating example is Lithuania where at least three languages intermingle. In such cases the context is the guide used and as a last resort the Russian spelling in the text is accepted. Individuals whose families were once non-Russian but had been in Russian service for generations are named by the original spelling of the family name. Turkish, Tatar, Persian and other names and terms are spelled in the original according to accepted forms in scholarly books. In some instances, if not otherwise ascertainable, they are transliterated from the Russian as given by Soloviev. The names of geographical locations conform to commonly accepted English usage—Podolia, Moscow, Copenhagen, Saxony, and so forth.

Finally, with respect to transliteration, this translation follows a modified Library of Congress system omitting diacritical marks and ligatures, rendering the initial "ia" and "iu" as "ya" and "yu"("Yasnaia" and "Yury"), the suffixes "ii", "skii","skaia" and "skoe" as "Dmitry Poliansky", "Polianskaia" and "Polianskoe", and the form "oi" has been replaced by "oy" ("Tolstoy" not "Tolstoi") for certain family names familiar in this form in English. In some cases "i" has been inserted in place of hard and soft signs, or apostrophes indicating these signs. Hence Soloviev and not Solov'ev. The soft sign is not indicated by an apostrophe, as in some transliteration systems, but is dropped completely.

All dates, as in the original, except where otherwise specified, are according to the Julian calendar ("Old Style"); that is, for the sixteenth and seventeenth centuries, ten days behind the Gregorian calendar used in the West.

A table of weights and measures is included at the front of this volume for the convenience of the reader.

In conclusion I would like to thank Peter von Wahlde, the general editor, for his assistance and suggestions. Professor George Pahomov of Bryn Mawr College, who read the manuscript, deserves particular credit for his masterful and astute aid. His superb knowledge of both Russian and English and their many nuances made me especially aware of the benefits of excellent editing and the constant need for such in all of the scholarly pursuits that rely heavily on writing. I am no less grateful to John T. Alexander, whose suggestions have improved this volume materially. Needless to say, any errors that may appear in the text are wholly my responsibility.

Nickolas Lupinin

INTRODUCTION

George Vernadsky, the dean of historians studying Russia in the West, wrote that Sergei M. Soloviev (1820-1879) "laid the channel for the major course of Russian historical thought in the second half of the nineteenth century." This assessment is not new but after more than a century since Soloviev's death it is still accurate. It echoes some much earlier reflections that bear the same thought. Vasily Kliuchevsky, a student of Soloviev and possibly the most outstanding Russian historian of all, noted in a ceremony commemorating the twenty-fifth year of Soloviev's death that Soloviev "deserved just merit for the clearing of the path and the first working of the raw material." This was a reference to Soloviev's colossal use of archival sources, his immense documentation. It is no wonder that his work served as the essential background for more than a generation of Russian scholars and why it is still indispensable to this day. Kliuchevsky, in discussing Soloviev's history course, said that "it produced a powerful methodological influence on us. It awakened and formed historical thinking. We recognized that we were not only learning the new but that we also understood what we were learning. Together, we learned how we should understand that which we were coming to know."

Soloviev was the son of a priest and the influence of a religious background stayed with him. His father also taught and, thanks to a good home library, Soloviev developed the habit of reading and studying at an early age. By the age of thirteen he had read Karamzin's *History* (twelve volumes, and up to that time the leading Russian historical work) several times.

His youthful passion for history remained with him at the University of Moscow. Upon completion of his studies, he spent two years abroad as a tutor in Count Stroganov's family. Among the historians whose lectures he attended while abroad were Ranke, Ritter, Guizot, Michelet, and others. It was valuable schooling. Upon his return to Russia in 1845 he was appointed professor of Russian history at the University of

Moscow. He remained in this post until his retirement. He attained the rectorship in 1870 and in 1859-1860 he was tutor to the heir. The latter responsibility is interesting in that it shows the trust of the tsar in the scholar. When Soloviev asked Alexander II for permission to examine secret archives during his research, he was allowed to do so. In some cases, Alexander II acted as the censor. In a problem directly pertaining to Peter III's death, Alexander II read Soloviev's treatment and let it stand.

It is on the immensity of his historical investigation that Soloviev's reputation stands. Aside from two earlier works, his primary contribution is the *History of Russia From Earliest Times*. The first volume appeared in 1851 and then, like clockwork, succeeding volumes appeared yearly. Kliuchevsky noted that the difficulty of the task was reduced by two traits Soloviev possessed in abundance: indomitable industriousness and an ability to utilize every minute of each day. Vernadsky said: "Soloviev considered the basic factors of the Russian historical process to be the government and the people. He did not contrast them but attempted to clarify the mutual connection between them."

The many subjects and themes which Soloviev treated are those that are related to the history of the Russian state. By this I mean to say that the overwhelming emphasis is on diplomacy, administration, and politics. We find very little that can be considered social, economic, or religious history. Thus, when Soloviev discusses certain church problems, it is in terms of its administration and relation to the state. For example, he writes of the problems attendant to Peter III's secularization of church lands. Or, he discusses the difficulties engendered by this or that method of collecting church tithes or, conversely, of providing money for the ecclesiastical establishment. Historians such as Fedotov are quite correct in asserting that Soloviev was essentially a historian of the state. It might be added that this has a twofold explanation: a personal proclivity for that line of research, and the historical style of the day which leaned in this direction.

Soloviev was a groundbreaker and an excellent historian who retained his personal humility despite the magnitude of his work. In this, of course, others may be less humble in appreciating his achievement. Kliuchevsky remarked of him: "In the absence of firm bases, he preferred to evade a problem and open himself to criticism rather than to solve the problem by a witty conjecture. This might lead to a false self-assurance

which would only place an obstacle in the path of other researchers."
Moreover, continued Kliuchevsky, "a Russian through and through, he
never closed his eyes so as not to see the dark sides of the past and the
present of the Russian people. More than many, many patriots he felt the
great powers of his own people and believed in their future more firmly
than others. But he did not sanctify them. To the degree that it was possible, he was above that crude disregard for the people which is frequently
hidden by intemperate and unnecessary glorification of valor or by a supercilious and indifferent condescension to their faults. He loved and
respected the Russian people too deeply to flatter them and considered
them to be too mature to tell them children's tales of national knighthood
under the guise of national history."

Late in 1761 a woman born in 1709 lay dying in Russia. This was
nothing unusual in view of the life expectancy of the eighteenth century,
even if the woman was Elizabeth of Russia, empress, tsarina, and daughter
of Peter the Great. She had ruled over her vast domain since 1741 and
some, like the historian Miliukov, consider her reign one of great accom-
plishment, a reign with a minimum of conflict and shock, few histrionics,
and one preparing the way for many measures undertaken by Catherine
the Great.

Elizabeth had been sick before and in some of these illnesses her hypo-
chondriac tendencies were evident. But this time her illness was real. And
the problem being created was real as well. Being childless, she faced the
stark choice of a successor. The choice was stark because of the character
and person of Grand Duke Peter, soon to become Peter III, emperor of
Russia. He was Elizabeth's nephew, son of her older sister Anne. In a moment of candor, Elizabeth had said: "My nephew is a monster, a scarecrow... I do not know what to do with him." Now the problem of what
to do with him had to be solved.

Peter III was from Holstein, a north German province. His father,
Charles Friedrich, duke of Holstein, had married Anne, daughter of Peter
the Great. His father was a nephew of Charles XII of Sweden. Thus Peter
had been in line for the Swedish throne until, in 1742, he was summoned
to Petersburg by Elizabeth. He was named heir apparent, an act he never
forgave. He would much have preferred the Swedish throne, which ultimately went to Adolph Friedrich, bishop of Lübeck and Peter's guardian
after his father died.

In 1745 Peter was given a consort. He was married to Catherine, his cousin, who had come to Russia the year before from the German principality of Anhalt-Zerbst where she had been born in 1729. In fact, she had been brought expressly to Russia for the conjugal tie. It cannot be said that the marriage was a success, or that it was a happy one. But, probably, neither was fully expected. Because they were so different, the two were not compatible. From the beginning Catherine followed her own course. She learned Russian. She became Orthodox. She read and studied the latest books and political treatises. She showed much interest in her new people and their country, her country. She learned intrigue at court. In a word, she did everything that Peter did not do; Peter disdained Russia and everything about it, and mocked the Orthodox faith. Catherine knew that power was harder to hold than to attain. She built her influence slowly, carefully, consciously. In her memoirs she said of Peter and the crown: "I myself felt little more than indifference towards him, though I was not indifferent to the Russian crown."

A brief look at Peter's character will make his indifference understandable. He was, in Kliuchevsky's words, an "eternal child," a mental invalid, lost in Russia. He played with toy soldiers. Once, having caught a rat in his chamber, he court-martialed it. The penalty was death by hanging. In church he made grimaces, laughed at priests, joked. He had an inordinate love for everything Prussian. Frederick II was an object of adoration. He brought out Frederick's portrait constantly, once falling on his knees before it in public. His love of music and playing the violin was matched by a propensity for drunkenness in which state he would speak of secret state affairs. There were many revelries and much carousing. And, he was much taken with drilling his own pride and joy—a contingent of Holstein guards, his own personal unit of guards, who had the run of the palace. This unit Princess Dashkova inelegantly described as "a bunch of swine consisting of sons of German shoemakers."

Yet fairness demands another view as well. There are few good sources on Peter III. Soloviev's treatment is still the best and most complete. The others? Catherine's famous memoirs are very negative regarding Peter III. So are those of most of the ambassadors of the time. The Prussians liked him but that in itself became a black mark against him. In the absence of much else, these factors and interpretations came to dominate historians' assessments and became standard in textbooks. Additional information may be gleaned from more general studies such as Isabel de Madariaga's *Russia in the Age of Catherine the Great* (1981), Carol Leonard's unpublished dissertation (Indiana, 1976), and John T. Alexander's *Catherine the Great. Life and Legend* (1989).

If boorish and obnoxious in behavior and character (which further colored his image), he was not uneducated. His initial upbringing in Holstein was of a kind to prepare him for the Swedish throne, for he was the grandson of Charles XII. And he had the largest personal library in St. Petersburg. Catherine even admitted that he was lenient with her and far from stupid.

Elizabeth died on December 25, 1761 and Peter became tsar. His six-month reign is more interesting and intriguing than one might suspect, for it raises some problems. One is the degree to which Peter III was responsible for the decrees promulgated in his reign. These decrees were not the work of a demented "scarecrow," though it has been suggested that his officials were primarily responsible since they were interested in promoting their own positions. The more negative aspects of Peter's character appear more prevalent in day to day affairs and, although he was educated, it is hard to say which side of his character dominated any specific occasion.

Peter ascended the throne with no real opposition or support. The decrees which he quickly promulgated are instructive. He began by recalling from exile those banished in previous reigns. Among these were Münnich, and Biron. He cut the tax on salt on January 17 and announced that the salt monopoly would be abolished as soon as possible. Import duties were reduced. The decree of January 19, 1762 allowed the return of Old Believers. This showed his toleration but also may have stemmed from his own mocking attitude toward Orthodoxy.

The decree of February 21 which abolished the remnants of the security police also noted that no legal action by the state against anyone could be instituted without full appraisal by the Senate. Conceivably this decree may have played a role in the coup which deposed him, for he had no advance knowledge about it from any quarter. The sale of serfs to industrial enterprises, was forbidden and Soloviev gives considerable attention to this question. Having also abolished the Conference of Ten, Peter created a situation wherein during his brief reign few favorites played unduly large roles. It is curious that the official court journals ceased by early March, 1762 and did not resume until August—a gap in documentation not unfamiliar in our own times.

What is more, Peter emancipated the nobility from service to the state in peacetime, a measure announced on January 17 and confirmed by decree on February 10. Among many of its provisions, service to the state was made voluntary. Some of the other provisions allowed nobles to enter foreign service and resign from civil and military service except in wartime. If the decree ignored some issues, notably freedom from confiscation of inherited estates, it was received very joyously.

These were not the measures that led to Catherine's coup. Nor were they the decrees of a madman. More direct elements were responsible and Peter III's mistakes were along other lines. He offended the court nobility. He made enemies of the guards regiments, which he tried to convert forcibly to the Prussian model. He drew the ire of the church hierarchy by forcing revenues to go through a newly established College of Economy rather than through the normal channel of the Holy Synod. Money to the church thus would be distributed by the College, in effect putting the churchmen on salary. Catherine, who was to rescind this measure temporarily, later did the very same thing. He offended everybody by his incredible concern for Holstein, a concern which preempted any other matter of state. Not long before Catherine's coup on June 28, 1762, Peter actually was about to send a Russian army against Denmark in order to reclaim Schleswig to Holstein. This was totally repugnant to Russia since just previously Peter had ended Russian participation in the Seven Years War in a most casual way.

Russia's military record was outstanding in this war and, as never before, Europe took sharp notice of its powerful Eastern neighbor. Of all Frederick's opponents, Russia did the most damage. In 1758 East Prussia was taken. In 1759 Frankfurt on the Oder fell. In 1760 the Russians entered Berlin briefly. Yet, it was all for naught, for Peter simply surrendered everything Russia had won. Even Frederick II, knowing well Peter's tremendous love for everything Prussian, did not expect such generosity. Frederick had offered East Prussia in compensation to the victorious Russians, only to be rejected; thus he benefited inordinately from Peter III's act. The whole Russo-Prussian relationship is brought out by Soloviev. How might the history of Europe have proceeded had Russia taken East Prussia and, pursuing its advantage, totally defeated Frederick II?

So Peter was removed. We would be wrong to assume that he fell because of widespread national resentment. This was beginning, as Soloviev implies, but it is doubtful that it took hold in a mere six months given the communication capabilities of the eighteenth century. Had the so-called "resentment" spread deeply, it is unlikely that ten years later Pugachev, in leading the rebellion that bears his name, would have passed himself off as Peter III. As it was, he drew considerable support from the peasantry which, among other things, was impressed by his claim of being the legitimate heir to the throne. Professor L. Jay Oliva has suggested that insofar as the attitude of Peter III to Orthodoxy is concerned, it was not instrumental in the coup when viewed in terms of the people as a whole, for only a relatively small circle of people knew of Peter's derogatory attitude to the faith. In a sense, the qualifications themselves should be qualified, for it wasn't necessary to ignite national resentment to be overthrown in the eighteenth century. The right enemies had to be made in the right spheres. This Peter did not fail to do being, as Kliuchevsky said, "an active conspirator against himself; he fanned the smouldering flame."

In the six months of Peter III's reign Catherine was quiet. Quiet and busy. She was cultivating ground for the upcoming coup and building a party. At the same time this party was cultivating her as the likely choice to replace Peter. The coup itself might have occurred sooner were it not for Catherine's pregnancy. On April 11, 1762 she bore Grigory Orlov's son, the future Count Bobrinsky. Among the very active members of Catherine's party were Nikita Panin, Kirill Razumovsky, Archbishop Dmitry of Novgorod, the Orlov brothers, Prince Volkonsky, Baron Korff and others. These, along with their activities in Catherine's behalf, are ably treated in the text. It is interesting to note how quietly all this occurred. Catherine's position was becoming increasingly precarious, for her relations with Peter III had deteriorated. He had threatened her with incarceration or the convent, neither very conducive to political maneuvering. It appears that the coup itself, which occurred on June 29, 1762, was a complete surprise to Peter and his staff. It was a well kept secret in foreign ambassadorial circles as well for, although it was known and feared that much opposition was building against Peter, the nature, extent, and the personnel of the opposition was not known. This is readily seen in the example of the Prussian ministry, which feared for Peter's position but which, in dispatches to Frederick II, pointed to the wrong men as being the alleged conspirators. The Prussians greatly feared losing the peace they had attained so easily with Russia, and signed, just that very April.

Although the coup may have been a surprise to Peter, it was augmented considerably by pressure which he himself created. Four items might be mentioned: (1) an alert to the army went out in May and was unpopular; (2) his public insult to Catherine when he stated that he would not have to put up with her much longer; (3) the arrest of Captain Passek of the Preobrazhensky Regiment on June 27; and (4) continuous preparations for the guards to participate in the Danish war.

The arrest of Passek was especially disturbing since it was feared that Passek, who had been taken while drunk and making disparaging remarks about Peter, might be forced to reveal what he knew. As a member of Catherine's circle and party, the whole coup might be jeopardized.

Action had to be taken quickly. Alexis Orlov arrived at Peterhof where Catherine was staying on the morning of June 28. He and his brother Grigory then led Catherine to the assemblages of the three guards regiments, the Izmailovsky, the Semenovsky, and the Preobrazhensky. She was hailed as empress by all and pledges were taken. A third Orlov brother went to Kirill Razumovsky, who then issued the manifesto of accession. An assembly of clergy marched to the Kazan cathedral. Razumovsky had assembled the Holy Synod, the Senate, and the collegial heads at the Winter Palace. Nikita Panin arrived with Grand Duke Paul. And Catherine appeared on the balcony to accept her new role. The manifesto of accession was issued immediately. A public reception ensued and after Peter III's deposition the next day a triumphal re-entry into St. Petersburg occurred on June 30.

Peter III knew nothing of this at Oranienbaum, where he was staying, on June 28. When finally apprised of the events, he sent three envoys to Catherine. These were Count Vorontsov, Peter Shuvalov, and Count Trubetskoi. She refused his offer to rule with him. When arrested, Peter did not seem to be depressed as he did not expect anything bad to happen. He asked for three things: (1) his mistress, Elizabeth Vorontsova, (2) his dog, and (3) his violin. His suffocation occurred on July 6 (the Orlov brothers had been assigned as his guards) and the public announcement of his "accidental" death was made. A second manifesto regarding Catherine's accession was issued as well.

Soloviev ably and in much detail treats the actual coup and we shall defer to his analysis. Suffice it to say that it was masterfully and bloodlessly executed. The only victim as such was Peter III who, after the coup, was killed (on July 6, 1762). Officially, death was attributed to apoplexy from a "hemorrhoidal colic;" most historical scholarship prefers the former explanation. "An accidental guest on the Russian throne, he flashed briefly, like a falling star, across the Russian horizon, and left everyone in a quandary as to why he had appeared."

Catherine, ultimately to be called "the Great," was much more than a mere flash, reigning as she did for thirty-four years and achieving not only personal glory and prestige, but presiding over the substantial rise of the same for the Russian empire.

Her early days on the throne began to demonstrate her ability. She had much to deal with, including her own insecurity and fear of losing the newly attained throne. Breteuil, the French ambassador, wrote to Paris: "The fear of losing what she had the audacity to take is constantly manifested in the Tsarina's behavior." Perhaps this was so, although she continued to act according to her own reasoning and aided by her unquestioned ability to work with people. Catherine had to counter support for her son Paul, who was deemed by some, including the redoubtable Panin, to be the legal ruler by right of birth. The same Panin also thought that an imperial council to aid Catherine would be in order. Catherine disagreed, although six years later a council did emerge. Soon after her accession she repealed the secularization of church lands, the unpopular measure of Peter III. Yet, two years later, in 1764, she re-secularized them. Her position was stronger; she could more readily proceed with her own program.

In the meantime, in Miliukov's phrase, Catherine II was "assaulted by the outrageous demands of those who had worked for her accession and now claimed their rewards, deserved or otherwise." She withstood this assault as she did the others. She distributed favors and rewards generously. This too was an element of her consolidation of power, matching her decrees and actions in government affairs. In addition to the examples cited above, many others could be mentioned. A decree of July 1, 1762, just two days after the coup, forbade further recruitment for the service of Holstein. This, as has been seen, was an extremely volatile point. On July 15 a decree was issued again permitting domestic churches and chapels. It was, as others had been and others were to be, a measure designed to make her popular, to consolidate her position, to differentiate her from the anti-Russian behavior of her husband and predecessor.

Three days later a decree was issued to warn against the widespread use of bribery and extortion by public officials, promising that, if improvement did not occur, strong measures would be taken.

Catherine also proved to be a hard worker. She began to attend Senate sessions immediately and was appalled at their disarray inherited from the two preceding reigns. She occupied herself with the affairs of the army, provincial administration, and state finances. She found great disparities and errors. She tried to be a monarch who was not alien to any legitimate concerns of her state. She continued, as before, in the attempt to build a bond with her people. And, her frequently cited love life was always, with very few exceptions, divorced from political concerns. In September of her first year as ruler Catherine was crowned officially in Moscow, the old Russian capital in the heart of the nation. After the coronation she stayed in Moscow for eight months, building her influence there as well. In 1763 she traveled to Rostov the Great; a year later, to the Baltic provinces. But, we are getting ahead of the text. Catherine came to rule, and she ruled. Her early days on the throne set the pattern for the future. That future could not have been realized without the ability exercised in the present. In this volume Soloviev describes the tribulations and the successes of an empress on the rise, an empress who had learned well the lessons of court and state, frequently by herself. It is an intriguing and an illuminating story.

History of Russia

Volume 42

A New Empress

Peter III and Catherine II, 1761 – 1762

TO MY DEAR WIFE, YILDIZ

I

THE REIGN OF EMPEROR PETER III
25 December 1761-28 June 1762

FIRST DAYS

The majority of people greeted the new reign gloomily. They knew the character of the new sovereign and expected nothing good. The minority of people who aspired to prominence in the reign of Peter III had, understandably, to attempt to dispel the melancholy disposition of the majority and prove that the latter were being fooled by their dark forebodings.

"Immortal will be the memory in God of the sovereign empress who has passed away. Unending also are our thanks to the giver of all good when we see that his imperial majesty, having ascended the throne of the forefathers, pours forth mercy and bounty to all just as kindhearted Elizabeth did. He turns quickly and assiduously to the labors of government like an indefatigable Peter the Great. Her imperial majesty [Catherine II], in continuously attending the body of her beloved aunt and mixing her tears with the tears of mourners, takes up the burden which nature and a sincere love for the name and blood of Peter the Great impose."

With these words Conference Secretary Volkov ended his description of Elizabeth's death. The new emperor here is compared to his deceased aunt in charity and generosity. But what charitable acts could be cited? Kindness to those in disfavor in the preceding reign is usually expected from a new ruler. On December 26, the day after Peter's accession to the throne, an imperial decree ended the investigation of governors Saltykov and Pushkin. But this might be seen as the intercession of powerful men on behalf of their friends. Only later was the freeing of people who had long suffered in confinement announced. But foreign, and even hated names interfered with this positive impression. On January 17 [1762] decrees were signed concerning the return from exile of Mengden's [member of the College of Justice] son, the wife, son and daughter of Lilienfeld [the chamberlain], Natalia Lopukhina, and Münnich and his son. The latter two could return to Petersburg. The rest were forbidden to appear in the area of the emperor's residence. Zhukov, the voevoda[1] of Penza, who was notorious for the complexity and magnitude of the investigative proceeding against him, was freed from arrest. By a decree of March 4 Duke Biron returned from Yaroslavl to Petersburg with his family.

It is easy to imagine the curiosity with which both old and young looked at Biron and Münnich, formerly sworn enemies who now appeared at court and in society.[2] Münnich, despite his age and ill fortune, distinguished himself by his great liveliness and was able to gain proximity to the emperor. On May 6 a decree was issued. In place of the stone house on Vasiliev island taken from General Field Marshal Count Münnich, and now occupied by the Naval Cadet Corps, another stone house by the Admiralty near the Semenovsky bridge, bought for 25,000 rubles from the master of the horse, Naryshkin, was to be given to the count in perpetuity.

Along with Münnich and Biron, another pair of similarly sworn enemies, also exiled in Elizabeth's reign, were returned. This was Lestocq and Bestuzhev-Riumin.[3] On December 25, the first day of the accession to the throne, the chancellor, Count Vorontsov, submitted a report to the emperor in which, among other things, was an item "On Pardoning and Freeing from Exile the Unfortunate Count Lestocq." But it is understandable why in Vorontsov's reports nothing was found concerning the return of the unfortunate Count Bestuzhev. Furthermore, besides Vorontsov, none of those having access to and influence on the emperor had any motivation to ask for Bestuzhev's pardon. At the side of Peter III there was not one person favorably disposed toward the former chancellor. Peter himself was biased strongly against him. From foreigners there is information that, allegedly, Peter told Vorontsov, Volkov, and Glebov [head of the War College] about Bestuzhev: "I suspect this man of secret complicity with my wife and, besides, I recall what my deceased aunt said to me on her deathbed about Bestuzhev. She firmly instructed me never to free him from exile."

To be sure, one cannot be assured completely by this information because the witnesses, Vorontsov, Volkov, and Glebov, are suspect. Be that as it may, Lestocq was returned and Bestuzhev remained in exile. It is easy to imagine the impression made by this on the uninvolved majority. Lestocq was returned; Biron was returned; and others with foreign names were returned. Only one Russian who had worked long and energetically for Russian interests was not returned.

Perhaps other favors blotted out the unpleasant impression. Perhaps people were pleased by the growing closeness to the sovereign of worthy men and the removal of those deemed disloyal?

On December 25, when Elizabeth was breathing her last, Nikita Yurievich Trubetskoy, the former procurator general, and Alexander Ivanovich Glebov, the former senior procurator[4] of the Senate and now quartermaster general, took quarters two rooms away from the bedroom of the dying empress. Having situated themselves at a desk, they called in first one then another of the men close to the heir. They whispered back and forth, wrote things down, and then went to the grand duke, seemingly with reports or to obtain instructions. The latter mostly was to be found at the bedroom of his dying aunt. Here, among other courtiers two old men staggered like shadows in great sorrow. One was the fledgling of Peter the Great, the famous senator and conference minister, Ivan Ivanovich Nepliuev; the other was the procurator general, Prince Yakov Shakhovskoy. But the presence of these two old men was offensive to the persons reporting to the heir and in the name of the grand duke it was suggested to them that they leave.

Soon after this Shakhovskoy had to visit the court again, for he received notice of the empress's death. Expecting nothing good for himself in the new reign, he asked Lev Naryshkin, a member of the emperor's retinue, that he make known to Peter his request to be relieved of all duties. The request was granted. On that very same day, December 25, Shakhovskoy was relieved of all duties. Glebov, while retaining his position as head of the War College, a profitable post he did not wish to relinquish, was appointed procurator general.

The same day the Vorontsovs, one of the most favored families, were granted awards. Ivan Larionovich Vorontsov, the brother of the chancellor and the uncle of the [emperor's] favorite, Elizabeth Romanovna Vorontsova, was appointed senator and sent to Moscow to assume the chief senatorial post there, the directorship of the Senate Office. Two days later, on December 28, other awards were issued. Prince and Field Marshal Nikita Trubetskoy was made lieutenant colonel of the Preobrazhensky Regiment (the tsar himself was colonel).[5] The Shuvalovs,[6] Peter and

Alexander, were promoted to the rank of field marshal. Count Peter did not long enjoy the honors of his new title. His days were already numbered. But, despite the serious illness which drained his strength, he hungered for governmental activity and ordered that he be carried from his own house to that of his friend, Glebov, whom he had brought into the public eye, the new procurator general, because it was closer to court. The emperor not only kept in touch with him via Glebov but frequently came to discuss various matters. Such mental strain, as it was then thought, speeded the demise of Count Peter, which followed on January 4.

In his hands Ivan Shuvalov held the directorships of the three military corps, the army, navy, and artillery. At the same time he remained the rector of Moscow University. Thus, in a fashion, he was the minister of the newly born Russian enlightenment. Only the Academy of Sciences remained, as previously, under the presidency of Count Kirill Razumovsky. A decree of March 6 regarding the elder Razumovsky, Count Alexis, stated: "General, Field Marshal, and Count Razumovsky is released and forever freed of all military and civil service in order that at court, or wherever he may choose to live, he be honored according to his rank. His imperial majesty pledges to maintain good will and to keep him in favor."

THE NEW COUNCIL

In the fifth month of the reign men enjoying the emperor's special favor and trust were enumerated. A decree read in the Senate on May 20, said: "In order that many of his imperial majesty's resolutions for the glory and the good of his empire and for the welfare of faithful subjects be put most quickly and in the best fashion into practice, his imperial majesty has chosen the following men to work under his personal supervision on many matters previously subject to his highness Duke George; his highness the prince of Holstein-Beck; General and Field Marshal Münnich; General and Field Marshal Trubetskoy; Chancellor and Count Vorontsov; General and Master of the Horse Villebois; Lieutenant General Melgunov, and the State Councillor and Privy Secretary Volkov."

In the top positions on this council we see the relatives of the emperor on the paternal side of the Holstein princes. The first one, Duke George, uncle of Peter III by marriage, was a general in the Prussian army. Upon Peter's accession to the throne he was summoned immediately to Russia, for Peter was very attached to him. He promoted him to general field marshal, and colonel of the [Emperor's own] private cavalry Life Guards

Horse Regiment at a salary of 48,000 rubles per year. The other prince, Peter August Friedrich of Holstein-Beck, was made field marshal, governor general of Petersburg, and the commander of all field and garrison regiments in Petersburg, Finland, Reval, Estland, and Narva. The next three members of the council, Münnich, Trubetskoy, and Vorontsov, are familiar to us.

Lieutenant General Villebois received the post of master of the horse, vacant since the death of Count Peter Shuvalov [in January, 1762]. As seen in the responses of contemporaries, Villebois had a good reputation. Prince Volkonsky was especially known as an envoy to Poland. Lieutenant General Alexis Melgunov rose from the ranks with the help of Ivan Shuvalov. He became close to Peter during Elizabeth's rule when he directed the cadet corps, of which the grand duke was chief. Volkov gained fame as a most accomplished writer of rescripts during his tenure as head of the chancellery. Furthermore, both Shuvalov and Vorontsov could attest that he was a dedicated man. In the new council his place was the same as the one he had held in the now abolished Conference. Volkov was made privy secretary after January 31.

Procurator General Glebov and Ivan Shuvalov complete the list of the new Council members who could influence important government decisions at the beginning of Peter's reign. People close to the tsar such as the generals and aides-de-camp, Andrei Gudovich and Ungern-Sternberg, and the master of the horse, Lev Naryshkin, did not have this influence.

NEW MEASURES BEFORE THE SENATE

On the seventeenth of January the emperor visited the Senate from ten to twelve o'clock. He signed decrees which returned Mengden, the Lilienfelds, the Münnichs, and Lopukhina from exile. Then he decreed that the price of salt at least be lowered if trade in it could not be made totally free. The Senate was to consider this.

Kronstadt harbor, which had been damaged so severely that ships had difficulty docking, was to be repaired without delay, deepened, and finished in stone. The Senate was to consider completion of the Rogervik harbor by free labor and to shift convict labor to Nerchinsk. The proposal of the deceased Count Peter Shuvalov concerning water communications from the Volkhov river to the settlement of Rybny was reported to Peter. It said that the route from Rybny through Tver, the Borovitsky rapids, and Novgorod to Novaia Ladoga was 1120 versts.[7] But that from

Rybny to Noaoia Ladoga there was another route: from Rybny by the Volga, Mologa, Chagodashchaia, and Goriun rivers, Lake Sominskoe, the Somina and Bolchinsky rivers, Lake Krupinoe, the Tikhvin river, and Sias. From the Sias a canal of seven versts was needed to reach the Volkhov river opposite the Ladoga canal. This route was in all 592 versts. The Senate further reported that Lieutenant General Riazanov had been sent to examine and describe this route and had completed his mission. The emperor considered the plans, approved them, and ordered that all work be done by free labor.

At the same session the emperor ordered the Senate to attend to Petersburg, the construction of which, primarily in wood, was proceeding extensively. Efforts had to be made to limit this and try to build in stone. This was to be done less extensively, but more regularly and more vertically than horizontally. The emperor also ordered the Senate to confer with the Holy Synod[8] concerning monastic peasants. In conclusion, Peter announced his decision regarding the service of the nobility.[9] "Nobles may continue their service voluntarily wherever and as long as they wish. In time of war, they must all appear on the same basis as the nobility in Lifland [Livonia]."[10]

On the following day, January 18, Procurator General Glebov orally submitted the following: should not the Senate build, as a sign of gratitude of the nobility for the imperial favor regarding the continuance of service on voluntary terms at a place of their choosing, a golden statue of his imperial majesty in the name of the entire nobility and so report it to him? The proposal was not confirmed. There is information that the emperor answered: "The Senate can put the gold to better use. Through my reign I intend to erect a more permanent monument in the hearts of my subjects."

FREEDOM OF THE NOBILITY

It was a month later, on February 18, that the manifesto on the nobility's freedom was promulgated. In it the emperor noted that under Peter the Great and his successors the nobility had to be forced to learn and to serve. Incalculable good had resulted. Among the negligent, notions contrary to the common good had been overcome; ignorance had been replaced by common sense. In military affairs, knowledge and diligence had increased the number of skilled and brave generals. In civil and political matters, experienced and suitable men had found work. In a word, "noble thoughts in the hearts of all true Russian patriots have been rooted firmly.

Thus, in view of the boundless love shown to us and the great dedication to duty, we do not find it necessary to speak of service in terms that have been used up to this time."

The entire nobility, regardless, of their place of service civil or military, might continue such service or retire. But the military might not petition for retirement or take leave three months prior to and during a campaign. A noble who was not in service might, without hindrance, travel abroad and enter the service of foreign rulers. But he was obligated to return in all due haste at the first call of the government.

"We hope," the manifesto read, "that the well-born Russian nobility, in feeling the favor shown by us to them and their heirs will, in all faith and diligence, be moved not to refrain or hide from service but will, with desire and passion, enter the service and honorably and honestly continue to execute their duties. No less do we trust, that they zealously and assiduously will teach the useful sciences to their children. For those who have never served anywhere and, instead, have spent their time in inactivity and idleness, will set quite similarly an example to their children, who otherwise will not be able to utilize any of the useful arts for the good of the fatherland. We will enjoin our loyal subjects and true sons to hold such people, who are negligent of the common good, in contempt and scorn. Neither their presence at court nor at public meetings and celebrations will be tolerated."

The circumstance is striking that the manifesto on the freedom of the nobility appeared a month after the emperor announced his wish in the Senate. Knowing Peter's character, it is not a surprise. The men close to Peter, who wished to keep their importance in the new regime, wanted to cultivate a popularity and brilliance that would dissipate the gloomy thoughts of those who knew in whose hands the fate of Russia now rested. These men attempted to impress on Peter the necessity of undertaking certain measures that would alleviate some of the people's burdens. Among these measures, and one that was desired by many, was the freeing of the nobility from compulsory service. The emperor announced all these measures in one appearance before the Senate. However, having stated his will regarding the freedom of the nobility from service, he did not charge the Senate to take action but to think the problem over carefully and present it for imperial confirmation.

The emperor's intention was announced. The Senate presented the report on the golden statue, received a not very humble answer, and there the entire matter ended. The emperor took up other affairs. Understandably, the people to whom the glory of the reign was dear and who wished to announce and carry out the popular measures as soon as possible, were very worried, seeing that they were forgotten. Prince Shcherbatov, in his famous *On the Corruption of Morals in Russia*, tells a story he heard from Dmitry Volkov. The emperor, wishing to hide his nightly pleasures from his favorite, Countess Elizabeth Vorontsova, told her in the presence of Volkov that he wished to spend the whole night with him on an important matter of government organization. Night came and Peter went to amuse himself, telling Volkov that by morning he should write some important decree. Volkov was locked into an empty room with a Danish hound. The poor secretary did not know what to write, but something had to be written. Finally he remembered what Count Roman Larionovich Vorontsov most often reiterated to the tsar, the matter of the nobility's freedom. Volkov wrote a manifesto which was approved by the emperor on the following day.

It is clear that the story of Shcherbatov or Volkov relates to the writing of the manifesto, not to the initial idea concerning the freedom of the nobility. That thought had been announced a month earlier. The story is important because it identifies the man who constantly repeated to the emperor the point about freedom of the nobility. This was Count Roman Vorontsov, who was especially interested in the popularity of the new reign because of the relationship of his family to the emperor. There are, however, doubts regarding the veracity of Shcherbatov's story. Citing Staehlin's [Jacob von Staehlin was a professor at the Academy of Sciences] evidence, it is said that the manifesto was written by Glebov, not Volkov. But why should one believe Staehlin more than Shcherbatov or Volkov himself? It is said that Volkov, in his apologia written upon the accession to the throne of Catherine II, says nothing of the fact that he wrote the manifesto on the freedom of the nobility in that part of his statement where he boasts of the works of his pen. While Volkov does not say that he wrote the manifesto, he does not say that he did not write it. Consequently, he in no way contradicts the story told to Shcherbatov. Volkov said: "In domestic affairs, my three main works deal with (1) monastic estates,[11] (2) the Secret Office, and (3) the far-reaching decree on commerce." He had good reason for not including the manifesto on the freedom of the nobility among his chief works.

As a very intelligent man, Volkov could not but realize that the manifesto was poorly written. It was hard to write a better version without lengthy and comprehensive discussion. There were strong complaints that the nobility, in being obligated to lifetime service, could not manage their estates. Yet the shortage of men and the government's need to support itself by means of a large regular army did not permit it to free the nobles from compulsory service. Measures had been adopted long since to reconcile the interests of the government with those of the landowners: long leaves of absence under Catherine I [1725-1727] and shortening of the terms of service under Anne [1730-1740].

The manifesto of 1736 obligated a noble to serve only twenty-five years, beginning in his twentieth year. When it developed that too many were willing to take advantage of the twenty-five-year term, the government, in 1740, in view of the war,[12] was forced to delay retirement. Thus, evidently, the twenty-five-year term remained only on paper, for Ivan Shuvalov, in his proposal to Empress Elizabeth regarding fundamental laws, states: "A noble should serve twenty-six years, counting from the time of his actual service, that is from his twentieth year."

This twenty-six-year term mentioned by Shuvalov illustrates the care with which the most educated and liberal people treated the question of the nobility's freedom from service. They were frightened by the thought that the multitude of nobles would retire, some to their households, others to live in idleness on their estates. Many army positions would become vacant and, of necessity, be filled by foreigners. Fear of strengthening the foreign element in the army led the very same Shuvalov to propose, as a fundamental law, that three quarters of the generals in the guards, the army, and the navy be Russian, and one fourth be Livonians, Estonians, and foreigners.

In the manifesto of February 18 not only was there no mention of any measures against an excessive exodus into retirement and negligence of the education of nobles, there was no mention even of the order to the nobility to serve which the emperor made in the Senate: "In time of war they must all appear on the same basis as the nobility of Livonia." The manifesto of February 18 was greeted with wide satisfaction. But this satisfaction could not be shared in the same degree by the nobles who occupied the higher positions and who were prompted to continue the service which gave them importance and advantage. These men were far more preoccupied by other privileges such as exemption from corporal punishment and ending confiscation of a noble's property.

Into his project of fundamental laws Ivan Shuvalov entered the following: "Noblemen who have fallen into wrongdoing lose by confiscation only the estate personally gained, not the hereditary holding. The nobility is to be exempted from dishonorable political punishment." The nobility was not given these more desirable privileges. Without them, freedom from service was not particularly significant, especially for the nobles comprising the higher circle in Petersburg to whom Volkov was responsible. In this circle it was awkward to boast of the manifesto of February 18 and Volkov adroitly ignored it, failing to include it among his major works.

ADMINISTRATIVE CHANGES

Among the three main works of which Volkov boasts there was one that dealt with the Secret Office. On February 7 the emperor announced to the Senate that henceforth the Secret Office of the political police would be no more. On February 21 a manifesto was issued in which it was stated: "It is known to all that in the creation of the secret police offices, regardless of the names given them by our dear grandfather, Emperor Peter the Great, a generous and philanthropic monarch, was moved by the circumstances of the time and by the still unreformed manners of the people. Since that time the need for the aforementioned offices has lessened constantly. But the Secret Office has remained powerful. Evil, base, and idle men, be it by lies, extended sentences and punishments, could always falsely accuse their superiors or their enemies. The above named Secret Office of the political police is forever abolished from this day hence. Its files are to be sealed in the archives of the Senate and forever forgotten. The hated expression "word and deed" henceforth must signify nothing. We forbid it. It is not to be used by anybody. Whosoever shall use it when drunk or in a fight, or to escape beating or punishment, shall be punished by the police in the manner reserved for the malicious and the scandalous.

"On the other hand, anyone who really and truly does have information against someone according to points one or two, must immediately report it to the nearest judicial office or the closest military commander. He must present the denunciation in writing. If he is illiterate, he must give it verbally. All arrested for robbery, murder, or other capital crimes and sentenced to exile, like those in penal servitude, are not permitted to submit denunciations of any kind. If an informer appears regarding the first two points, he is to be taken into custody immediately and questioned as to whether he is aware of these points. If he is unaware of them yet testifies to an important matter, he is to be released instantly. If it is found that the accuser is aware of the first two points, he is to be questioned about his complaint. If he describes his information but presents no witnesses and has no truthful document, he is to be queried about making an unfounded complaint. If the informer does not disavow his information, he is to be placed under strong guard, without bread and water for two days. He will spend this entire time in reflection. When the two days are up, he should be questioned and exhorted about the truth of his information and, if it is still so maintained, the informer should be sent under strict guard, if he be close to Petersburg or Moscow, to the Senate or the Senate offices. If not, he should be taken to the nearest provincial office. Those on whom he informs without witnesses or written proof should not be detained, to ward off suspicion until the matter can be reviewed in a higher office and a warrant issued against those who are accused. If the accuser has both witnesses and proof that his denunciation is correct, he, the witnesses, and the accused party are to be taken into strict custody, the case reported to the Senate, and a decree awaited.

"If a noble, officer, or a distinguished merchant be the accuser and the case is confirmed in the nearest court, he must be sent immediately to the Senate under strong guard. There he is to be investigated. However, those who are accused are not to be taken into custody without a Senate decree. This is to allay suspicion. Concerning the crown, the conduct of the case that touches the first two points is left to us in order to exemplify how the investigation can be handled gently and to show how truth can be determined without bloodshed and distinguished from perfidy and calumny. Methods are to be sought by which charity may be used to bring evildoers to confess and to show them the path to their own atonement. Not everyone, even with a fair accusation, can reach us as quickly as need warrants. Besides, with free access given everyone, we must avert the possibility of people sharpening their desire to inform. It is our will that anyone who has anything of importance to report to us come forth without fear with the information to our lieutenants, Lev Naryshkin and Alexis Melgunov, and to Privy Secretary Volkov, appointed and entrusted by the monarch for this purpose."

For a long time there had been complaints that the Senate was burdened with appellate cases and had no time for government affairs. Ivan Shuvalov had proposed that Empress Elizabeth "place several senators in the Senate office in Moscow and give them capable aides so that appellate petitions be dealt with, thereby leaving the Senate time for affairs of state."

Now this suggestion hurriedly was put into practice. A special department was set up, although not in Moscow, but in Petersburg. On January 29 the Senate heard a signed imperial decree. "His imperial majesty is aware that the number of unresolved cases in the Senate, the Colleges of Justice and of Hereditary Estates, and in the high courts has increased. Thus, for greater order and quicker decisions, the Colleges of Justice and Hereditary Estates and the high courts are each to establish three departments for petitioners. The Senate must create a special department to deal with questions of land, justice, and other matters in much the same way. In the Senate three or four senators must staff this department. In the colleges and the courts members are to be assigned and authority delegated to the provinces as well."

On the same day a decree followed to the effect that the Conference be dissolved and its business assumed by the Senate and to the Chancellory of Foreign Affairs. But we have seen that on May 20, a nameless body was established "better and more quickly to bring the emperor's wishes into reality." Only two senators were members of this nameless establishment, Chancellor Count Vorontsov and Field Marshal Prince Trubetskoy. The Senate at this time consisted of thirteen members in addition to the procurator general. These were Count Michael Vorontsov, Count Roman Vorontsov, Prince Nikita Trubetskoy, Prince Peter Trubetskoy, Prince Michael Golitsyn, Count Alexis Golitsyn, Count Alexander Shuvalov, Prince Ivan Odoevsky, Ivan Nepliuev, Alexander Buturlin, Alexander Zherebtsov, Peter Sumarokov, and Ivan Kastiurin.

ECCLESIASTICAL PROBLEMS

The Senate rushed to complete a matter that had dragged on since 1757, the question of church estates. On January 7 it re-examined the matter and decided to confer with the Synod on the basis that monastic peasants pay fifty copecks into the state treasury and fifty to the monastery or diocese to which they belonged. On January 17 the emperor personally ordered the Senate to meet with the Synod. But his intention was not carried out. It was thought necessary to hasten this matter and on February 16 an imperial decree was issued. It read:

"Her majesty, Empress Elizabeth, combined piety with the good of the country and wisely distinguished between the abuses and prejudices that had crept into practice and the true dogmas and foundations of faith of the Eastern Church. She found it useful to free monastic inhabitants, they having given up this temporal world, from worldly, everyday needs. Consequently, appearing personally before the Conference on September 30, 1757, she ordered the necessary measures for the regulation of episcopal and monastic estates. This by itself, apart from her other great and kind deeds, would be enough to insure her glory forever.

"His imperial majesty recently visited the Senate and ordered that the cited statute be placed immediately into effect by the Senate and the Synod. In discussing the importance of this matter, and to prevent fruitless decisions and wasting of time, his imperial majesty wishes to impress upon the Senate that the above cited law of Empress Elizabeth enter immediately into effect without changes. It is always to be enforced without fail. His imperial majesty also finds needful the decree of Peter the Great forbidding the taking of monastic vows without special imperial decrees. This is to be adhered to and enforced to the letter."

According to this decree, Elizabeth's original idea that monastic estates be managed by retired officers of higher rank and not by monastic servants, likewise was to be implemented. The Senate ordered that (1) a college be formed to manage all synodal, diocesan, monastic, and church lands; a president with members and a procurator were to be assigned to it. It was to be under the Senate's rule. (2) The peasants were to pay one ruble. The land which they formerly worked for bishops, monasteries, and the church was to be returned to them. (3) All income was to be collected for the monasteries but only that portion allowed in the statutes was to be used. The rest was to be saved and exact balances kept so as to provide construction money for the monasteries.

The College of Church Landed Property was to tabulate all monasteries and hermitages according to classes. Thereupon it was to pay monks six rubles in cash and five quarters of bread, deacons eight rubles and seven quarters, treasurers eighteen rubles and eight quarters, deputies twenty-four rubles and eight quarters, preachers thirty rubles and thirty quarters, the father superior fifty rubles and eight quarters, and the abbot one hundred rubles and eight quarters. Monasteries of the second class were to receive one half of this scale for their support. Retired officers and soldiers in monasteries, some 1358 in all, were to be supported by the college according to a previously determined scale. Privy Councillor Prince Obolensky was appointed chairman of the College of Church Landed Property.

This order was announced in the decree of March 21. Three bishops, those of Moscow, Novgorod, and Petersburg, were given 5000 rubles yearly, the rest of the bishops, 3000. Three thousand more was alloted for the support of seminaries. Abbots of the "ten autonomous monasteries[13] are to receive 500 rubles, others of the second class, 200 rubles, and the remaining, 150 rubles per year. In this fashion, according to statute, the funding of three classes of monasteries is determined." When nothing was done to separate the monasteries into classes, and when nothing was done to give the new institution proper direction, an imperial decree was announced to the Senate on April 4: "Commencing with the time of the decrees of February 16 and March 21 (precisely what time is meant?) all monies collected are to be returned. Support in the future is to be according to the allotments given to the dioceses in that decree. No collections are to be made from the peasants in those dioceses and agents sent there to make collections are to be sent back."

In his apologia, Volkov noted: "In domestic affairs my three main achievements dealt with monastic estates, the Secret Office, and an extensive decree on commerce. I took up the first all the more willingly for the matter seemed equitable to me. I was happy for the occasion to give due glory to the memory of the empress. But, unfortunately, this whole thing was ruined in the Senate."

Volkov does not tell us in what way it was ruined. It is known that the Senate was to present the emperor a report on June 1. Payment from monastic and diocesan peasants was fixed at one ruble per soul.[14] It had been decreed by the crown that collections be started beginning in the second half of the current year.

"This tax is to take effect no later than this year. Meanwhile, there are no funds from which to grant sums assigned to the monasteries. Since these estates were removed from control of bishops and monastic heads at the start of this year, beginning in March, and the lands returned to the peasants, will not the emperor deign to order that a ruble be taken from monastic and diocesan peasants to cover all of this year, 1762, when the first payment is due?" The emperor confirmed this memorandum.

Volkov's rival in the intense labor of drafting manifestos, Procurator General Glebov, announced an imperial decree to the Senate on January

29 which stated that schismatics[15] who had fled to Poland and other countries might return to Russia. They could settle in Siberia in the Barabin steppe and other such places. There were to be no obstacles placed in the way of their adherence to their rules and old books. "In the Russian Empire there are believers of heterodox faiths also, such as Muslims and pagans. The schismatics, although Christians, are alone in the ancient prejudice and stubborness held against them. This must be alleviated but not by compulsion and the distress which made them flee across the borders where they now live fruitlessly."

Then the Senate issued an order to determine whether there were any schismatic groups that practiced self-immolation. Were such loathsome gatherings found, worthy people should be sent there immediately. They should urge them in every way to abstain from such pernicious intentions and ask them why they wished to commit such deeds. Should it become evident that these intentions were caused by repression and arrest, they were to be assured that orders had been given to stop such investigations. They were to be truly left alone. Those currently under arrest were to be released. New arrests were not to be made.

Afanasy Ivanov, the trustee of the registered schismatics and hermits of the many forests of Nizhegorod Province and the districts of Balakhonsk and Yurevets, arrived in Petersburg. Ivanov presented a petition to the Senate in which the schismatics complained of suffering repression in the form of graft paid to church leaders. In 1716, he noted, there were, according to the census, some 40,000 schismatics of both sexes in Nizhegorod Province. Among these were up to 8000 anchorites. But, due to repression, there were only about 5000 persons left. The schismatics requested that the money alloted them be paid directly into the Bureau for Schismatics' Affairs. For defense against injury they wished to be assigned in perpetuity to the Verkhiset ironworks of Count Roman Vorontsov. The Senate ordered that a retired senior officer be appointed to defend these schismatics. He was to be a man of a high repute who could be trusted. Funds were to be paid directly to the Bureau for Schismatics' Affairs.

The schismatics asked that they be assigned to a plant. But peasants registered to the factories of the merchant Pokhodiashin from Verkhoturie petitioned against the owner and the Senate conducted an investigation. After a month and a half the peasants belonging to the factories of Count Ivan Chernyshev and Nicholas and Evdokim Demidov [famed merchants and factory owners] complained that the stewards and bailliffs oppressed them, beat them, and even had killed some. The Senate assigned the investigation to Major General Kokoshkin and Colonel Lopatin. Since to this point the peasants who were creating disturbance were primarily those assigned to factories and plants, the factory and plant owners were forbidden to buy villages that is, serfs, with or without land. Until confirmation of a new code they had to be satisfied with hired labor.

THE PEASANTS STIR

Soon, however, there came news of stirrings of borderland peasants as well. On the lands of State Councillor Evgraf Tatishchev (son of the famous Vasily Nikitich)[16] and lieutenant of the guards Peter Khlopov, in the districts of Tver and Klin, the peasants rebelled against the landowners according to the teachings of the retired scribe from Tver, Ivan Sobakin. They razed Tatishchev's mansion and Khlopov's house and granaries. They stole the peasants' payment money, ordered their landowners to stay away, and wanted to kill the bailiffs and manor serfs but wound up chasing them away. Then followed reports from the procurator of the Moscow provincial chancellery, Zybin, about the revolt of his own Belevsk peasants; from Princess Elena Dolgoruky about her Galitsk peasants; from Captain Balk-Polev about peasants of the Kashira; from Collegial Councillor Afrosimov about the Tula and Epifan peasants, from the wife of Colonel Dmitriev-Mamonov about the Volokolamsk peasants.[17]

The number of those who mutinied were 700 at Tatishchev's estate, 800 at Khlopov's, 340 at Zybin's, 2000 at Princess Dolgoruky's, 959 at Balk-Polev's, 650 at Afrosimov's, 400 at Dmitriev-Mamonov's. Moreover, in the district of Volokolamsk, in the village of Vishensk, the elder and the peasants came with clubs to the house of the landowner Erchakova, abused her verbally and chased her out of the village. Four peasants belonging to Tatishchev came to the Senate with a complaint against him. They claimed that he had sent a good number of them to his other villages and made them house servants.[18] Others worked for him and he penalized them by raising their annual payments and military levies.[19] The Senate ordered these peasants to be lashed mercilessly. Sobakin was to be chased down and an army detachment was to be sent against the rebellious peasants. But Tatishchev's and Khlopov's peasants attacked the detachment, wounded one officer, and beat or wounded all of the soldiers, sixty-four of whom vanished. No one knew where they were.

Later, more detailed news was received. The peasants smashed the detachment because it had killed three of them and wounded up to twenty others. The peasants seized sixty-four soldiers and held them under guard for three days. They then sent them to Tver with an officer who was not immediately involved. Five peasants along with women and children were sent to return the horses. The Senate directed that a detachment of 400 men and four cannon be sent against them. Instead, Major General Witten was sent with a regiment of cuirassiers by decree of the emperor. Finally, in the district of Viazemsk-Voskresensk, 1000 peasants belonging to the Dolgoruky princes beat and robbed the bailiffs and sent a request to the Senate that they be registered to crown lands.

Uprisings also were occurring in Moscow among the factory workers. The owner of the leading Moscow textile mill, Vasily Surovshchikov, reported that the artisans and workers, together with the sons of military men assigned to the plant because of their inabilities in school, began to rebel as they had done in 1746 and 1749. In the last days of February the textile manufacturer Fedor Andreev reported important news and was sent to the College of Manufactures. At the same time some of the soldiers' sons complained to the Main Commissariat that money earned by them was being held back and that poor wool was being given them for making cloth.

On February 22 Prince Meshchersky and two soldiers brought the textile manufacturer Andreev from the College of Manufactures in order to punish him for false information. When they wished to punish him in front of all the factory help, he began to protest. The sons of the soldiers yelled fiercely and did not allow him to be punished. Meshchersky returned Andreev to the College of Manufactures. The soldiers beat up the sergeant in charge of them. Then, in fairly large groups, they began to stop work. Some claimed that the exiles of 1749 had been returned and that Surovshchikov, the owner, was under arrest in Petersburg at their request.

FINANCES AND MILITARY PREPARATION

Finances troubled the Senate most of all. It was noted that Volkov boasted of "an extensive decree on commerce" as being one of his creations. This decree was written as a result of the plea of Shemiakin and Savva Yakovlev [a collegial assessor] that the customs duties be farmed out to them for another ten years.[20] This was done, but at the same time it was ordered that grain be exported freely from all ports, including those on the Caspian and Black seas. Furthermore, the customs collected were to be levied at half the rate of the ports of Riga, Reval, and Pernau. The reason was that commerce was long established in these ports and the import and export of grain was not so difficult.

Also allowed was the export, from all ports, not only of salted meat but livestock as well. The export of goods from the port of Archangel was duty-free while the customs fee on imports was equal to that of Petersburg and other ports. Some goods which, by stretching the interpretation of previous decrees, were duty-free, were subjected to customs duty. Among these were sugar and cotton. The benefits of these measures lay in the future, whereas for the present the treasury was empty.

The Senate was forced into an ominous decision on May 8. Commencement of work on the new water route from Rybny settlement to the Volkhov was to be suspended until further notice due to lack of funds. It was reported to the emperor that there was a total of 15,350,636 rubles and ninety three and one quarter copecks in government funds. Spending was accounted for as follows: (1) 10,418,747 rubles and seventy and three quarter copecks on the army; (2) 1.5 million rubles—emperor's funds from salt and custom duties; (3) 603,333 rubles and thirty three and one quarter copecks for the upkeep of the court and the Chancellery of Buildings; (4) 98,147 rubles and eighty five copecks for the hetman of Little Russia;[21] (5) 4,232,432 rubles—base pay, the extraordinary allotments and grants of the College of State Accounts, plus the debts of this office. The total came to 16,502,023 rubles. Consequently, the deficit was 1,152,023 rubles. This deficit could be met from salt and liquor sales of 1.4 million rubles and from the new peasant assessments. The surplus would be used to pay the army abroad.

The Senate pointed out that the deficit was caused by the cost of maintaining the army abroad but it did not contemplate avoiding this expense. Therefore it resorted to a measure which had been avoided so carefully under Elizabeth. On May 25, the third day after the report was given to the emperor, an imperial decree was read in the Senate regarding the establishment of a bank. "Upon our accession to the throne our first care was for urgent matters which demanded correction and solution. The recoinage of copper money, its lightening and multiplication according to a project previously drawn up and approved by the Senate seemed to be one of the most important government matters. The Senate presented it to us in this light. For this reason we did not delay in assenting to it.

"But, as we stipulated then, the measure adopted, although producing some relief, did not avert all the related disparities. Experience and time convinced us all the more of this truth. Therefore we did not stop thinking about the simplest and most reliable means to ease the circulation of copper money in order to make it convenient and useful in commerce. The establishment of a state bank for the use of all at moderate interest rates according to their capital, and the circulation of bank notes, seemed the best means to achieve this. European experience has shown this. Time will make people accustomed to it and lead them to participate with their capital. This will bring benefit to the whole realm. We shall now do a good deed for the country, and especially for the merchants and for commerce; namely, to issue as soon as possible bank notes in the sum of five million rubles. These are to be in denominations of 10, 50, 100, 500, and 1000 rubles.

"Upon issuance of these five million they immediately will be divided among the government offices that distribute the most money in order that they be used as cash. We wish that these notes actually be used like cash. From this moment and henceforth we establish this bank with our own resources in the sum of five million rubles. The bank will be operated by two equal offices, one here and one in Moscow. We now entrust to these two offices two million rubles, one million in silver and one million in copper. The remaining three million rubles will be deposited over a period of three years at the rate of one million per year. The offices and the designated capital are assigned for the sole purpose that should a note holder wish cash instead of notes he will be given cash immediately without signatures and paper accounting, and especially without delay. If cash is presented in exchange for an equivalent bank note, the purchaser shall be satisfied as well."

Assigned as directors of the Petersburg office were Rogovikov as chief director and as aides the Petersburg merchants Barmin and Yamshchikov, the merchants Pastukhov of Tula and Gubkin of Kaluga, and the English merchant, Ritter. In the Moscow office the directors were customs officers Zemsky, Zhuravlev, and Sitnikov, Luginin of Tula, Ivan Zatrapeznov of Yaroslavl, and the foreign merchant Wolf. The conclusion of the bank decree states: "The recoinage of copper money from heavy to light coinage is to continue without change. In the future no new copper coinage is to be minted and none is to be accepted by the Treasury. Factory owners should dispose of it abroad and sell it for Joachimsthalers."[22] One day before the rule ended the Senate heard an imperial decree: loans made to merchants and banks of the nobility were to be granted no further extensions; they were to be collected actively.

Money was needed because the major expenses for the army could not be reduced. Rather, they must be increased because of heightened military preparations. An imperial decree was read to the Senate on March 6. "Since the time that regular soldiers and military discipline were introduced into our army, our empire has grown and achieved far greater renown. Since, especially recently, almost all European rulers are making indefatigable efforts to bring their forces into the best possible condition, two incontestable truths must be recognized. First, the military profession has changed in many ways and has reached much greater perfection. Second, our duty obliges us. We feel justified in applying every effort and labor to make our empire flower and, to building our armed forces into the best possible condition so that friends will respect it and enemies will fear it.

"For the attainment of this goal we have judged it necessary to form a special military commission which will be directed principally by us. Members will be His Highness Prince George of Holstein, our dear uncle who will be general and field marshal, Field Marshal Prince Trubetskoy, General and Field Marshal Prince of Holstein-Beck, General and Master of Ordnance Villebois, Procurator General and Quartermaster Glebov, Lieutenant General Melgunov, and our adjutant general, Baron Ungern." Previously, on February 16, an imperial decree had ordered the formation of a special commission to bring the navy into a state necessary to satisfy the security and honor of the empire. According to the emperor's order of March 1, the entire fleet must be armed. On May 11 the emperor ordered that all public stone construction be halted. This was applicable also to the building projects receiving extra-budgetary allotments pending increase of revenues. This was because of the large sums given to the army.

Apart from the Russian forces Peter intended to create a special Holstinian force. Recruiters were sent to Livonia and Estonia with orders to recruit free men but not subjects of his imperial majesty. They also were sent to Little Russia to recruit among the Poles and the Wallachians but not among the Little Russians.

PETER AND FREDERICK THE GREAT

Why was there need to strengthen the army and navy and why so many expenses for the maintenance of an army abroad? Was this necessary for a final effort to end the war with Prussia and reach an honorable peace for Russia and its allies? It has been observed that Peter had great respect for Frederick II and no sympathy for the political system that had prevailed under his aunt. We can accept with only the greatest caution the various reports regarding secret dealings of the heir to the Russian throne with Frederick II. Conclusions concerning these dealings were drawn from Peter's own words. But we know how childishly he could be absorbed in his own stories and what incredible things he could attribute to himself.

The following two stories related by Princess Dashkova, placed one right after the other, as if purposely, best determines our view of this matter. Once Peter III was eating at the home of Chancellor Vorontsov. Dashkova was next to the emperor and heard his conversation with Count Mercy, the Austrian ambassador. Peter was describing how his father, the duke of Holstein, had entrusted to him an expedition against the gypsies and how he had beaten them in one minute. Dashkova then tells how at another time Peter during a holiday at court, while speaking at length about his favorite subject, the king of Prussia, suddenly turned to Volkov with a question: "Isn't it true that many times you and I laughed at the secret orders Empress Elizabeth sent to her forces in Prussia?"

Volkov was very embarrassed by this remark. Princess Dashkova, ill-disposed toward Peter and Volkov and considering the gypsy story a fabrication, accepted the words about relations with Frederick II as truth and accused Volkov of sending copies of rescripts to the Prussian king as a sign of good will. Removed as we are from these persons and events by more than one hundred years, we cannot be satisfied by these contradictions and must depend solely on indisputable evidence.

If table talk similar to that about the victory over the gypsies in Holstein is not to be believed, one still must admit that Peter's Prussian ties did not lessen during the Seven Years War. They were supported especially by the Holstein officers in whose circle Peter most liked to spend his time. Some of these Holsteiners had served in the Prussian army. All of them, in their north German patriotism, revered their national hero, Frederick II.

Staehlin tells us that the more the Seven Years War raged, the stronger were Peter's sallies against Russia's political system. He said that the empress was being fooled about the Prussian king and that her advisers were bribed by Austria and duped by France. Reading of allied victories in the newspapers, Peter would say: "These are all lies. My sources say something different." It was deduced from these words that Peter received information from Prussia. If he personally led people to believe he had some kind of secret contacts, the story of the gypsies comes to mind willy-nilly. But, most likely, these words were completely true. Peter received Prussian newspapers, believed only the news therein, and thus called this news his own in contrast to that received from the opposition.

In this connection the report to his court by the Saxon diplomatic counselor Prasse in the fall of 1758 is interesting. Colonel Rosen brought news of the battle of Zorndorf to Petersburg. The servant who came with him told everyone that the battle had been lost by the Russians. For this he was sent to the court guard house. Upon hearing this, the grand duke ordered that the servant be brought to him and said: "You have acted honestly. Tell me everything, even though I know full well that the Russians can never beat the Prussians." When Rosen's servant told all that he could or wanted, Peter, pointing to the Holstein officers, said: "Be careful! All these men are Prussians. Can such people be beaten by the Russians?" Peter sent the story-teller away, giving him five rubles and assuring him of his favor.

Hence it is easy to understand what was in Peter's head regarding the war and change in the political system at the time of Elizabeth's death. On the day of the empress's death the chancellor, Vorontsov, submitted a report which asked in passing: "Will not his imperial majesty, if it so pleases him, order one of the court cavaliers sent to his relatives, the king of Sweden , and an officer of the guards to the reigning prince of Anhalt-Zerbst with an announcement of his accession to the throne? And, in what manner shall we send news of this to the king of Prussia, through General Field Marshal Buturlin via Count Chernyshev who is with the Austrian army, or by that ruler's own example, via the ministers of Russia and Prussia living in Warsaw?"

The report was executed without delay, but it was done not through Buturlin, Chernyshev, or the Russian minister in Warsaw. That very day, December 25, a favorite of the new emperor, the brigadier and courtier, Andrei Gudovich, was sent to the prince of Anhalt-Zerbst with notification of Peter's accession to the throne. At the same time he took the emperor's note to Frederick II.

After providing information on the death of Elizabeth and of Peter's accession, the note stated: "We did not wish to delay reporting this, your royal highness, being confident that your highness, by means of the friendship established by our imperial predecessors, will take part in this new enterprise. This is especially so in matters that relate to renewal, expansion, and continuous maintenance between both courts of friendship and accord to their mutual benefit. It would please us that you be of common interest and disposition to us. For we, being of most excellent opinion of your highness, always will make a special effort in this regard and to inform your highness of our true and inviolable inclination, and are pleased to testify to it in every way."

Gudovich found the Prussian court and its foreign minister, Count Finckenstein, in Magdeburg. But, Frederick II was in Breslau. He received his first notification of Elizabeth's death from Warsaw on January 19. It is not difficult to understand what thoughts and hopes were stirred in him by this news since he was in such desperate straits at the time. Still, he could not count on the great gift of fortune that was being prepared for him in Petersburg.

He did not think that the first step toward direct relations would be made from Petersburg. Therefore he entrusted Keith, the English ambassador in Petersburg, to congratulate the emperor and the empress in the name of their "old friend." Frederick received news from Magdeburg of Gudovich's arrival on January 31 and of the letter he brought from Peter. "Thank heaven," wrote the king to his brother Heinrich, "our rear is free." "The dove that brought the olive branch to the ark," Gudovich, was invited to Breslau and was received with open arms.

Frederick wrote to Peter on January 28: "I am particularly happy that your imperial majesty now has received the throne which long belonged to you not so much by heredity as by virtue, and to which you will add new luster. My pleasure at the event is deepened by the fact that your imperial majesty has been pleased to give me hope of certain friendship and inclination toward the renewal and expansion of an accord beneficial to both courts. I had indulged myself always with the hope that your imperial majesty would not change your favorable attitude toward me and that again I would find in you a former friend. And, a friend for whom I, for my part, have an unchanging, and most sincere and special respect and faithfulness. I wish to assure you that I most truly desire to keep your exceptionally valuable friendship. And in re-establishing the previous accord, so beneficial to both courts, we should expand and confirm it on solid foundations. This I am willing to facilitate in any possible manner."

PEACE AND ALLIANCE WITH PRUSSIA

These words were put into effect rapidly. Prisoners of war on both sides were released. On the very day of his accession to the throne Peter released two important Prussian prisoners. They were General Werner and Colonel Count Hordt (a Swede by birth). They appeared at court and entered the ranks of the emperor's favorite companions. On February 15 Peter wrote to Frederick: "I have given the necessary instructions quickly that the prisoners of war who belong to your majesty and are currently under my control be released and returned immediately. This is contingent on receipt of reports that your majesty, in releasing my prisoners, ardently desires to confirm that tie which long has united us and which soon will unite our peoples.

"In accordance with our mutual inclinations, I can no longer keep Werner, your general lieutenant, and Count Hordt, even though I would like to see them constantly at my court. I cannot refrain from commending their behavior and the zeal which they continued to exhibit in your service. I have not hesitated to entrust my opinions to the former and thus request that your majesty hear and credit his report to you on my behalf. Your majesty will oblige me greatly if he, in addition to the proofs of friendship offered to me, will add one more. This is to assign Werner to my service and grant Hordt the excellent and singular kindness which he deserves, changing his regiment to the rank of a field regiment. One serving here and one in your majesty's army will serve as a guarantee of your friendship and as witness to the world of the sentiments of faithfulness and respect with which I, my brother, am, in turn, your brother and friend, Peter."

Frederick replied: "You request General Werner. He is at your disposal. But as I am completely without generals currently and have a difficult war on my hands, will you not allow him to serve me in one more campaign? In any case, should you wish to take him earlier, he will be at your feet at the appointed time."

General Prince Volkonsky, then in Pomerania, informed the emperor on January 28 that the duke of Bevern, governor of Stettin, had offered to conclude a general truce. Peter immediately ordered Volkonsky to accede to the duke's request and the truce was concluded on March 5. The Russians retained their quarters in Pomerania and Neumark. The Oder, up to the Warta, served as the border.

Volkov relates the following concerning this incident: "The prince of Bevern offered a truce to Prince Michael Volkonsky. But the latter refused to act without permission. For this he was called ill-intentioned and a fool. But I, unafraid of his possible dismissal, replied to him with truce conditions that honored our government and our forces. Many marvelled that I dared to lay down such strictures to the king of Prussia. But I recall that Trubetskoy, among others, told me that he would build me a statue for this. It must be admitted that at the time it was still not that difficult to serve the fatherland and meet one's oath. Goltz and Steben were not here yet and our celebrated embassy had not yet returned from Breslau. The arrival of these men soon gave matters, and my own situation, a different form."

Who were these men whose arrival gave matters a different form?

Volkov mockingly calls Gudovich's embassy "celebrated," pointing out the insignificance of the envoy. But inconsequential people become powerful through the passions and weaknesses of the strong. Gudovich was sent to Frederick as a man in complete possession of his ruler's sympathies. The reception of "the dove" in Magdeburg, and especially in Breslau, was such that upon his return the dove was unlimited in his enthusiasm for the king of Prussia. Such zeal was advantageous because it was so admired. For this faithful and zealous service Gudovich received six villages[23] in the Starodub and Chernigov regimental districts.

Gudovich remained in Breslau until the twelfth of February. During this time the king of Prussia received news that Chernyshev had been ordered to leave the Austrian forces and proceed to the Vistula. Therefore, in the letter that Gudovich took back, Frederick wrote to Peter: "I have learned that Count Chernyshev's corps has received instructions to separate from the Austrians. One would be completely callous not to feel eternally grateful to your majesty. I trust the heavens will aid me in finding an occasion where I can demonstrate my gratitude in practice. Your majesty may be assured that my feeling of gratitude will never be effaced."

Gudovich was unable to hold discussions with Frederick because he lacked instructions. To conclude peace, and if possible, an alliance with Russia, a Prussian envoy had to be sent to Petersburg. The choice fell on the twenty-six-year-old Goltz. He was an aide-de-camp and gentleman-in-waiting who, prior to his departure for Russia, was made a colonel by the king.

As a gift to Peter he took a Prussian order, and Frederick wrote: "I flatter myself with the hope that you will accept it (the order) as a sign of friendship and the sincere relations I wish to have with you. You obliged me even before your accession to the throne and have done so countless times since you have been on the throne. I flatter myself with the hope that an occasion will present itself that allows me to express all my gratitude in practice. In acting so kindly, so exceptionally, as rarely happens in our age, you must expect the wonder of all. This is eminently justified by Your Majesty's action. Your very first instructions upon taking the throne evoked the plaudits of our entire citizenry and of the benevolent quarters of Europe. Let your rule be a long and fortunate one!"

Peter replied: "Your highness. You do, of course, jest when you so praise my reign and marvel at inconsequential matters, whereas I am compelled to be amazed at your deeds. I see in you one of the world's greatest heroes."

Frederick II, in sending Goltz to conclude the peace, provided him with these instructions: "The essential goal of your mission is cessation of the war and the complete detachment of Russia from its allies. The positive disposition of the Russian emperor gives us hope that conditions will not be severe. I am not at all aware of the specific views of the emperor. All that I do know about them revolves around two major points, namely that the affairs of Holstein are at least as close to the emperor's heart as those of Russia, and secondly, that he is involved greatly in my interests.

"You must constantly impress upon the Holstein favorites, the empress, or even better, the emperor himself, that heretofore I have refused all offers of alliance with Denmark as the emperor wished at the start of the war, for I hoped that he would be pleased.

"Let us consider the offers of peace these people can offer us. (1) They will offer to move their forces beyond the Vistula, return Pomerania to us, but wish to keep East Prussia either forever, or until the conclusion of a general peace. Do not accept the latter. (2) But, should they desire to keep Prussia forever, let them reward me from the other direction. (3) Should they wish to vacate my possessions in order that I guarantee them Holstein, sign immediately, particularly if you are able to talk them into guaranteeing Silesia. (4) Should the emperor wish that I promise to maintain neutrality in the event of war with Denmark, sign, but demand the greatest of secrecy. (5) You may say that I would urge the emperor to help the king of Sweden against his opposition and that the Russian envoy announce to the [Swedish] Senate the peaceful intentions of his government. This declaration surely will force the Swedes to peace. In this manner the emperor will become the peacemaker of the entire North and will begin his reign in brilliant fashion.

"(6) Try to learn the views of the Petersburg court. Does it wish to end the war in order to ease domestic affairs, or prepare for a Danish war, or does it wish the role of mediator between the warring powers? (7) You must use every occasion to instill in the Petersburg court mistrust of the Austrians and the Saxons. If mistrust turns to envy, all the better. You may describe the craftiness with which the Austrians endangered the Russian forces, something witnessed this year by all. You may suggest the cowardice of the Austrians and the devious political means they employed to attain their goals."

Frederick described his personal agitation about Goltz's assignment to Petersburg. "What basis did we have for assuming that the negotiations in Petersburg would take a positive turn? The courts of Vienna and Versailles guaranteed Prussia to the deceased empress. The Russians calmly ruled over it. Would the young rulers, recently enthroned, reject the conquests guaranteed by the allies? Would not the love of acquisition or the glory that this would endow the commencement of his rule restrain him?

"All these difficult questions filled the spirit with uncertainty about the future. But the outcome was far more fortunate than could have been imagined.[24] It is so difficult to guess secondary reasons or to discern the various springs that determine the will of man. It turned out that Peter had a magnanimous heart, and kind and lofty feelings that are not usually found in rulers. In satisfying all of the king's wishes, he went even beyond that which could have been expected."

Goltz arrived in Petersburg on February 21. He turned first to the English envoy, Keith, who remained loyal to the policy of the previous cabinet and who was distinguished by his advocacy of union with Prussia. He pointed out important people who favored Prussia and those who were against it. It turned out that there were far more of the latter than the former. But the emperor's personal views and the disposition of the people closest to him insured success for Keith and Goltz.

The Prussian interest also was served in that the Austrian, French, and Spanish ambassadors irritated the emperor by refusing to visit his favorite, and the one closest to him, Prince George of Holstein. Understandably, Goltz hurried to Prince George with greetings from his king, in whose service the prince was still listed.

Goltz presented himself to the emperor on February 24. He barely had time to convey his message, offer congratulations on his ascent to the throne, and assure him of the friendship of his king, when Peter showered him with the most fervent assurances of friendship and proclamations of his boundless respect for Frederick II. He wished to render him clear proof thereof and whispered in Goltz's ear that he had much to talk about with him.

After the audience Peter went to attend the liturgy. Goltz followed him to church. During the service the emperor talked constantly with him about Frederick and the Prussian army, his detailed knowledge of which amazed Goltz. There was not a regiment in which Peter did not know three or four generations of commanders and leading officers. That very evening, during a card game, Peter showed Goltz a ring on his finger with a portrait of Frederick. He also ordered that a large portrait of the king of Prussia be brought in. After supper, Peter talked with Goltz for a long time. He told him how much he had suffered in the preceding reign for his attachment to Frederick and how happy he had been when removed from the Conference, for this had been done thanks to his respect for the king.

Peter told Goltz on March 2 that he would be very pleased were the king to send proposals for peace terms. In reporting this to Frederick, Goltz urged that the proposals be sent as soon as possible; otherwise the opposing party, which was very large in number, might take advantage of Prussian slowness. Mitchell, the English envoy at the court of Berlin, let Keith in Petersburg know that the Prussians had intercepted a dispatch from Breteuil, the French ambassador in Petersburg, in which it was said that in a few months all would be as it had been under Elizabeth because Volkov was dedicated to the old system body and soul.

Writing about this to Frederick, Goltz said that Ivan Shuvalov and Melgunov were united with Volkov and that the intercepted letter would help break Volkov's neck. In his famous letter Volkov related how this attempt to break him was made. "Steuben (Captain Steuben, formerly in Petersburg with Goltz) came forward as informer against me, claiming secret meetings with Count Mercy (the Austrian ambassador). With special reference to me, the king of Prussia sent the intercepted letter, allegedly Breteuil's, in which my talents and zeal were ardently extolled. For this reason I was taken for interrogation as a villain and questioned in such manner that my accusers were hidden from me. The emperor did not question me personally. Lev Naryshkin and Alexis Melgunov consoled me with assurances that when peace was concluded my danger would pass. They let me understand that I must say nothing contrary to the wishes of the king of Prussia."

Having received news from Goltz that Peter had granted him the privilege of drafting peace terms, Frederick did not tarry in this matter.

To increase further his influence in Petersburg, he sent Count Schwerin there with the draft. The latter was well known to the emperor because he had been taken prisoner by Russian forces and had lived in Petersburg for a time.

Schwerin brought a letter with him. Frederick wrote: "Be so kind as to receive the draft of the terms of peace from me. I am sending it to please your imperial majesty. I entrust myself to my friend. Do as you wish with this draft. I will sign anything. Your advantages are also mine. I know no others. Nature has endowed me with a sensitive and grateful heart. I am sincerely moved by all that your imperial majesty has done for me. I will never be in a position to repay all that I owe you.

"Henceforth, everything that you desire, anything that I can do, I will do so that your imperial majesty will be convinced of my readiness to anticipate all your desires. I am sending Count Schwerin, although I really should send persons of higher rank to your imperial majesty. But if you knew the position in which I find myself you would see that I cannot send such men. There are none; they are all engaged. During this war I have lost 120 generals. Fourteen are prisoners of the Austrians. Our exhaustion is terrible. I would despair of my situation but I find a still faithful friend in the greatest of all European rulers. He prefers honor over political calculations."

On March 29 the emperor told Goltz to discuss peace with Privy Secretary Volkov because the chancellor was sick. A few days previously Goltz had written Frederick that he would spare no effort in securing a satisfactory conclusion of this matter, surmounting if possible the impediments which the opposite side increasingly was trying to create for him.

Volkov's account serves as clarification of these words. "The emperor told Goltz that he should give me the peace proposals sent to him by the king. He set an hour, telling me to wait for him. Herr Goltz, knowing that I resided at court, visited the Semenovsky Regiment to see Andrei Andreevich Volkov. Not finding him at home, he immediately reported that he could find me nowhere. Here my arrest and complete misfortune were decided. But, in miraculous fashion, Baron Ungarn had smoked tobacco at my place all day and so acquitted me. It all turned into a joke on Andrei Andreevich.

"For my part, knowing that war with Denmark was inevitable and that any suggestion to the contrary might cost my life, I strove for the following: (1) put off preparations for this war as long as possible; (2) retain both East Prussia and Pomerania and exploit them; and (3) to find a way, deferring to the king of Prussia if need be, to involve ourselves in the European peace-making. This is not so much to gloss over our eternal shame as to hope that when Europe is pacified our best friend, the king of Prussia, will not allow us to begin a war with Denmark.

"Therefore, using the pretext of the Danish war, I reasoned continually that while our army was still beyond our borders we could not possibly return to his Prussian majesty the lands won from him. I pushed the matter to the point that, along with Privy Councillor Wolf, I was ordered to draft counter-proposals. The draft will be found in my papers. It does not agree entirely with my wishes but anyone aware of what times were like then— the impetuosity of the former emperor, and my own situation—would be surprised, and hardly believe, that I dared so frequently to stand for the interests and the glory of the fatherland. This was all the more the case when I arrived with the draft. Prince George and Baron Goltz were present. Mr. Wolf became frightened and lied. He reneged on the fact that he was in agreement with me. He noted, perniciously, that he barely had time to look out of the window before I had everything ready.

"In contrast to him, I possessed sufficient true diligence, if not bravery, to arm myself not only against Prince George and Baron Goltz but against the former emperor as well. Finally the first two held their tongues and he, the emperor, had to assay my draft. Such a negotiator was not to Baron Goltz's liking. He then obtained a copy of my proposal so as to study it better and then wrote new proposals of his own."

Goltz tried to read this draft proposal to the emperor privately, without witnesses. Having received Peter's assent to all the articles, he sent the draft to the chancellor with this note: "I have the honor to present to his highness, Chancellor Vorontsov, the draft of the peace pact which I had the fortune to read to his imperial majesty, who favored me with his approval of all its provisions." According to this agreement, signed on April 24, all the King of Prussia's lands occupied by the Russian army in this war were to be returned. Both rulers agreed to include the king and the crown of Sweden in the peace terms. A separate paragraph read that both rulers, sincerely desiring a still closer alliance to facilitate the security of their possessions and for their mutual benefit, agreed to commence at once efforts to form an alliance.

After the conclusion of peace the preparation of a draft of alliance "in line with current considerations" was begun. The treaty was to be a defensive one. Were one of the signatories attacked, or were hostile activity initiated and continued, the other ally would be obligated to send an army of 12,000 infantry and 4000 cavalry. This force must remain until the injured party receives full compensation, or pay 800,000 rubles annually. One ally might not sign either a peace or truce with the enemy without the knowledge and consent of the other.

In the first secret article it was stated that his royal Prussian highness, being most pleased by the considerations and concessions permitted him by his imperial majesty of all Russia from the moment of his ascent to the Russian throne and at conclusion of the eternal peace as well, wishes, as a sign of his gratitude, to assist in every way that his Russian majesty receive the dukedom of Schleswig from the king of Denmark and satisfaction of his entire rightful claims. Accordingly his highness, the king of Prussia, pledges and solemnly obligates himself to reason with and urge the Danish court to satisfy his imperial majesty. His imperial majesty, in turn, promised flexibility in this matter.

Should the Danes prove unresponsive to these efforts and remain stubborn, forcing the Russian emperor to resort to arms in pursuit of his ancient hereditary possessions, his highness the king of Prussia will create no obstacles and will provide the emperor a corps from his own army. If, during the course of a Danish war Russia should be attacked by the Turks or Tatars, the king of Prussia promises to send the military forces specified in the treaty, apart from the military forces assisting in a war against Denmark, or will pay the specified sum of money.

In the second secret article Frederick pledged to aid in the election of Duke George of Holstein to the duchy of Courland. The former duke, Biron, was to regain rule of Würtemburg as a principality, Amt Bigen, and the estates of Milich and Gaskich since Biron had renounced all rights to Courland. In the third secret article the allies pledged to disallow any change in the form of the Polish government. In the event of the death of the Polish king, Frederick promised all due assistance to assure that the election of the king of Poland be satisfactory to the Russian emperor.

In the first separate article it was stipulated that the king of Prussia not help Russia with armed forces in war with Persia, Turkey, and the Tatars, and that the Russian emperor not aid Prussia with force of arms in war with France or England. In such cases aid would be given in the sum of 1.2 million rubles annually.

The second separate article stated: "His imperial majesty of Russia and his royal highness of Prussia, observing with great sympathy the heavy repression their respective co-religionists have suffered for many years in Poland and Lithuania, have joined to ensure that Greek Orthodox dissidents, and those of the reformed Lutheran religion, dwelling in Poland and Lithuania be protected in the most efficacious way. Through friendly yet determined influence on the king and the Republic of Poland the aforementioned dissidents might regain the religious and civil rights taken from them. If this purpose can not be achieved for the moment, the dissidents must suffer as at present until better and more propitious times."

Major General Prince Nicholas Repnin was sent as ambassador plenipotentiary to Prussia. He found Frederick II in camp in the village of Zeitendorf, not far from Breslau. On June 29 Repnin presented himself to the king and gave him a scarf and medal as gifts from Peter III. Repnin asked whether the king wished these to be changed for any reason but Frederick stated his satisfaction and gratitude for this courtesy. He ordered that nothing be changed.

Repnin then reported that the emperor wished renewed evidence of friendship and requested the king to act as intermediary at the congress in Berlin between Russia and Denmark. Thus he wished the king to send a minister plenipotentiary there. Frederick replied that he had foreseen the emperor's wish and had dispatched Count Finkenstein to Berlin. The emperor might instruct him directly and he, the king, had told Finkenstein to defer to the emperor in every respect. The king inquired about the emperor's departure for the army. Repnin replied that he knew nothing definite but that when he departed from Petersburg the emperor intended to join the army.

Repnin dined with the king on June 29 and 30. Both times Frederick drank to Peter's health, saying that he "cannot drink enough times to such a precious health."

Frederick did not have to be asked to be intermediary between Peter and the king of Denmark. He greatly disliked the war with Denmark because he had to participate in it and commit part of his army and because, as will be seen later, he had fears about Peter leaving Russia to campaign against Denmark. It has been remarked that Frederick at first news of Peter's accession calculated that the relations of the emperor to Denmark could have a most beneficial influence on relations between Russia and Prussia. But now, when success had exceeded all expectations, the need was to avoid a Danish war, or delay it as long as possible.

TROUBLE WITH DENMARK

In Denmark the news of Peter III's accession necessarily caused an increased military buildup. This was reported to Petersburg by Korf, the Russian envoy in Copenhagen. "The emperor's entire attention is on Holstein," reported Goltz to Frederick on February 25. "I know for certain that the Danes will attack me," the emperor told Goltz. The latter replied that he doubted it. Denmark had no desire to make an enemy of the Russian emperor. It would prefer friendly agreement. Furthermore, in keeping with the dignity of the great Russian monarch, it would be much more natural to act as peacemaker of the north instead of taking by force of arms the prize which the Danes, in all probability, would yield voluntarily in consequence of a categorical demand by Russia. "I suspect," added Goltz, "that news of the unfriendly intentions of the Danish court has been manufactured by hostile courts fearful of the understanding being readied between Russia and Prussia, so as to sow confusion."

On March 1 Korf was sent a memorandum in which he was ordered to convey to the Danish ministry that while the emperor's desire grew ever more sincere to continue and expand the long friendship and good neighborliness with the king of Denmark, it was all the more saddening to observe the opposite from the Danish side; namely, military preparations and threats. The emperor therefore felt compelled to demand a formal explanation: did his highness, the king, intend to live with him in harmony and satisfy his rightful demands regarding the duchy of Schleswig? In the event that this was not the king's intent, necessity as well as maintenance of his incontestable rights would require the emperor to adopt measures that might result in extreme calamity. But such calamities could be avoided by acting now.

To this declaration Korf received the reply that the king by no means was avoiding formal representations to the emperor; he was prepared to live not only in peace but also in agreement and friendship. Should his majesty, the emperor of Russia, deign to renew the present treaties he might delegate one of his ministers and accept or suggest a place to confer suitable to both parties, for example, Hamburg or Lübeck, and the king would do likewise.

At the end of March Goltz again impressed on Peter that it befitted his dignity more to yield some minor areas that he might seize from Denmark and instead gain renown as peacemaker of the north. The Danes would never dare attack first and their every move stemmed from fear of attack. The following memorandum was sent to Korf on March 24: "The last response of the Danish court and the heightened preparations since then on land and sea only serve us, and the whole world, as indisputable proof that Denmark has no intention whatsoever of dealing with us in a friendly manner. Instead, viewing its long and undisturbed rule over stolen lands as a right, it clearly is attempting to gain time in the hope that our army will not always remain near Denmark, which grants us means for fair satisfaction. Circumstances meanwhile might change in Denmark's favor. Therefore the Danish court, omitting mention of satisfaction due us, in its reply briefly suggests lengthy negotiations.

"We should take no other decision than to declare the fairness of our position to the world, which is aware of it, and take advantage of the following circumstances: (1) our army is primarily located in Pomerania and hence close to Holstein. Upon successful conclusion of peace with the king of Prussia there is no obstacle to attainment of new achievements in Holstein and a return home with new glory; (2) not only can we field first class forces against the Danes, we are in a position to add to the fame of our forces as well. They are accustomed to campaigning and victories at a time when the Danish forces have not waged war for many years.

"(3) Denmark enjoys some local advantages because its army will remain in its own lands and close to its forts. But our army, aside from not having to spare foreign areas, enjoys further advantages. Its rear will be protected by either neutral or very friendly states. The king of Prussia, thanks to his special friendship, has granted us one of his fortresses, Stettin, as a supply post. Should the need arise we are certain he would not refuse Küstrin also.

"(4) Perhaps Denmark attracts many who wish it well inasmuch as few wish our strengthening on the Baltic Sea and in Germany. But we note that the Danish court has no direct allies from whom actual help might be obtained. In contrast, we have the king of Prussia, a ruler indispensable for this war and one who shares our interests completely. Sweden, if not in a position to take advantage of this situation against the Danes, can harm us all the less, having many inducements to wish us success.

"Nonetheless we are disposed to exercise every means of escaping these extremes, and therefore have decided the following: (1) to accept the meeting suggested by the Danish courts; (2) to fix the place as Berlin; (3) to hold the meeting by July 1; (4) we assign you and our councillor, Saldern, to be the plenipotentiaries; (5) our proposals at the peace congress must serve as an ultimatum and their refusal will ruin the entire congress; (6) the king of Prussia will serve as intermediary. Nevertheless, while these negotiations are proceeding, it would be unforgivable for us calmly to await their outcome, especially since we expect so little fruit from them. Thus, having taken part in a war between the king of Prussia and the empress-queen [Maria Theresa of Austria], and desiring to participate in the forthcoming peace, we must prepare our army in Pomerania for a campaign."

The Danish court agreed to everything and Prussia was very happy. Goltz wrote Frederick: "I am almost positive that war will not begin this year. No matter how hastily both sides send their deputies to Berlin, they would arrive no sooner than mid-July. Before the first proposals are made and serious negotiations commenced, it will be August, and soon it will be too late to begin a campaign."

Much hope was placed on the second plenipotentiary, the Holstiner, Saldern, a man totally loyal to Prussia. In one of Frederick's rescripts to Goltz the king directed the latter to meet with councillor Saldern and tell him that the king would express his gratitude in material terms. Goltz also was to prevent Saldern's return to Holstein because he could still be useful to Frederick in Petersburg. Regarding Saldern's appointment as plenipotentiary to Berlin, Goltz wrote the king that he would very much like to keep Saldern in Petersburg but that he also would be very helpful in Berlin in making an agreement should there be any such chance.

WHEN FRIENDS FENCE: AUSTRIA AND RUSSIA

Frederick II wished to delay the Danish war because it interfered with his desire to defeat Austria, now abandoned by Russia. Immediately after Peter's accession at the presentation of the diplomatic corps to the new emperor, the Austrian ambassador, Count Mercy, who heretofore had played the leading role in Petersburg, congratulated Peter. Mercy also expressed confidence that the new emperor would continue in the glorious principles of his deceased aunt, and would support the relationship of allies hitherto enjoyed with the empress-queen and her husband, the holy Roman emperor. Peter replied briefly and dryly: "I trust we shall remain friends with their majesties."

Three days later Chancellor Vorontsov announced that the emperor of certainly wished peace, and would lend every effort to that end. Peter no longer allowed Mercy in his presence, reversing completely the latter's previous stature. People who formerly had ingratiated themselves with him now anxiously sought to avoid him. Of the higher dignitaries, not one consented to transact business with him. A memorandum was sent to Prince Dmitry Golitsyn in Vienna on February 9: "No matter how reverently we respect the obligations concerning this war assumed by the empress, our dear aunt of sacred memory, and regardless of our desire to preserve them, at the present moment, due to the unbearable exhaustion of the treasury and the soldiers, we find these obligations onerous. Therefore, to secure the welfare of our citizens and the successful commencement of our reign, and desiring to see, after such long duration, an end to bloodshed, we wish no delay in declaring this to the courts of our allies in this war.

"We recognize well that this determination on our part, although a fair one, nevertheless at first will appear rather strange to the allied courts, especially Vienna, and will evoke differing interpretations. Yet preferring the welfare of our nation to all else in this world, we cannot act otherwise. In taking this action we wish as well that our allies might be led to recognize a similar truth with respect to their own lands. In the uncertainty of war nothing is reliably foreseen or foreordained.

"Striving solely for the restoration of the peace that is so necessary for all Europe, and again to demonstrate our selfless views in this connection, we enjoin you to inform her majesty, the empress queen, with every courtesy, that commencing with the day of our accession we are discontinuing subsidies to the court of Vienna. Moreover, you may, according to circumstances, reiterate that to facilitate this generally beneficial cause we have no desire to sacrifice all gains achieved by Russia in this war, at the sacrifice of much blood. It is incumbent on you to use every opportunity to impress upon the court of Vienna that a truce is the best way to speed peace negotiations."

When Golitsyn communicated this message to Count Colloredo, the Austrian vice chancellor, and to Kaunitz, the Austrian chancellor, they answered that the court of Vienna and its allies long ago had demonstrated to the world their desire for peace. The Congress of Augsburg had not met solely because England and its allies did not desire it. The court of Vienna was unable to respond to the Russian declaration without the concurrence of its allies. For the moment Vienna would await further clarification from St. Petersburg concerning the emperor's wishes in facilitating the restoration of peace in Europe. They then asked whether it was true that Chernyshev's corps had been recalled from the Austrian army and a truce signed between the Prussian and Russian forces. Golitsyn replied that he had no information about this.

It was necessary to provide further information as to how Peter wished to facilitate the restoration of peace in Europe. These clarifications were contained in a note of April 9.

"To await a general peace like that of Westphalia [1648] means to wage war constantly without assurance that such an imposed peace will be satisfactory to all parties. A peace of this kind cannot be a lasting one. At the Peace of Westphalia it was necessary that all parties affirmed possessions already held in addition to rights and liberties. Now the problem is to satisfy the claims and desires born of the war itself. But these claims are so diverse that there are practically no means to achieve their complete resolution. It must be recognized that when this war began much effort was expended in drawing in as many powers as possible. The outcome of so many treaties and obligations, so rapidly concluded, was not discussed.

"The court of St. Petersburg was alone in always insisting that the various interests and desires be harmonized before a general congress be convened. It correctly foresaw that without such understandings the congress would embroil the allies and instead of peace would fuel the war still further. Vienna and France both felt, it seems, that the diverse claims were difficult to reconcile and that little fruit could be expected from convocation of a congress. Never replying directly to our requests and solicitations, the court of Vienna tersely referred to treaties enacted in its favor and, by being silent about the claims of others, evidently expected success through great force of arms. France, refusing the claims of others even more, was so solicitous of obtaining a separate peace, one in its own self-interest, that Vienna thought solely of avoiding something being settled against its interests. And, in truth, the court of Vienna gained freedom from such danger only at the cost of great demands made by England.

"On the other hand Sweden, exhausted by this war and without hope or chance of gain, in addition to considerable loss of prestige, seemingly neither dares continue nor end this war. Denmark, in contrast, having begun to arm heavily at a time when we remain in the negotiations, clearly indicates the satisfaction we are to receive for our just claims. Nothing would please the Danish court more than to see us continue to exhaust our forces and resources on a foreign war. We would draw the reproaches of the entire world were we, having for so many years defended ourselves

solely by the rectitude of our position, now to exchange for some proposals the source of our dignity and our house. Now, when we are doubly
obligated to look after the welfare and fame of our house, and when we
have God-given means to do so, we did not follow the Danish example
by laboring to strengthen our indisputable rights with the same readiness
as the king of Denmark evidently wishes to confirm his acquisitions. We
are disposed to seek all avenues toward an amicable agreement on Holstein affairs before deciding on anything extreme.

"Every court involved in this war seems to be only waiting to see who
will make the first and most important move toward achieving peace. The
suffering people seek someone they can thank for their deliverance and
good fortune. We are, by the grace of God, the only ones who can serve
mankind in a disinterested fashion. This position derives solely from our
love of man, compassion for suffering humanity, and from our personal
respect for the friendship and favors bestowed on us by his majesty, the
king of Prussia. Consequently, we must take the first step. We therefore
command you to present the above to the court and add, in our name, the
advice of following our example and thereby avoid the consequences that
may stem from continuation of war. In this way the court will grant us
the means quietly to observe and expand the ancient friendship between
both imperial courts."

To this report by Golitsyn, Kaunitz replied that Vienna felt itself no
less useful an ally of Russia than others. The imperial vice chancellor,
Colloredo, stated that his court, and he personally, looked forward to peace
but that it was impossible thanks to the obstinacy of enemies who did not
allow the Congress of Augsburg to convene.

On May 2 another message was sent to Golitsyn: "Having achieved
the peace longed for by our empire, we could withdraw completely from
the war. But, as we know, peace cannot be secure when neighboring
peoples are at odds. Thus we find in the deep-seated hatred of the Austrian
house for the king of Prussia, with whom we are joined by long-standing
friendship, and in the mercenary motives of this house to obtain, at all
costs, Silesia and the barony of Glatsk, the entire reason why the war's
continuation comes from Austria. Because of its persistent ambitions there
is no possibility that the empress-queen, while her powers be great and
renowned, would agree voluntarily to restoration of peace.

"We foresee that our good offices will be of no value. But their rejection would serve to confirm our virtue. Taking all these circumstances into

account, unfortunately we are convinced that we must adopt extreme measures to return the earlier peace to mankind. Namely, we must assist his majesty the king of Prussia with our forces inasmuch as the continued calamities of the war are due solely to the stubbornness of Vienna and its familiar purpose of seizing from the king of Prussia the possessions ceded to him by the most sanctified treaties."

To this message Kaunitz answered: "In the declaration of the Russian envoy, her majesty the empress-queen observes the fruit of the strong desire of his majesty, the Russian emperor, to restore peace between herself and the king of Prussia. Her majesty flatters herself with the hope that the declaration is truly dictated by this feeling. It is solely for this reason that she has deigned to reply in amicable fashion. Her majesty, who never has turned away from a just and reasonable peace with the king of Prussia, remains uninformed about the most important consideration: is this ruler disposed to peace? This the empress must know first of all. Assuming Prussian assent to peace, I have the instructions of the empress to declare her sincere inclination to make peace with him, her readiness to hasten this matter and to conclude a truce and begin negotiations."

In Petersburg Count Mercy offered extensive comments on this reply at a meeting with the chancellor: "The Austrian house, in friendship for so long with Russia, has become accustomed to respecting this power as its constant and natural friend. Therefore, even in light of the recent events in Vienna, I cannot yet imagine that the court of Petersburg would change the most essential feature of its political system, specifically the alliance with the Austrian monarch.[25] Even though it is known that the present activity of the Russian emperor vexes his old allies, the rulers of the Holy Roman empire console themselves with the hope that this step is merely temporary, and that in the end the emperor will view this matter in a manner more in accord with his interests. He then will be convinced of the need to prefer the Austrian alliance to any other. This is what moved the empress to respond so moderately.

"It would be unfair and unheard of were the Russian emperor, thinking impediments stood in the way of fulfillment of his desires, to begin to ascribe them to a power which from the beginning displayed the most inclination toward a truce, a truce with a power that has not yet deemed it desirable to make its intentions clear on that point. Should the emperor of Russia employ just and open means, and with due respect for the state which for so long was his true ally, should he incline the king of Prussia towards clarification of his intentions and views, and finally, should he be impartial in his methods, he is assured of soon attaining his goal. He will accomplish it with the honor worthy of a ruler on whom all Europe has turned its eyes in expectation of the nature of the opinion it will form of his rule and intentions."

These explanations led to nothing. Frederick hurried to take advantage of circumstances and demanded from Peter not only guarantees of Silesia and Glatsk, but of all territory he might seize from Maria Theresa before the conclusion of peace. Peter replied: "I am delighted and am ready for everything. But I shall request your majesty to reach the same terms with me and guarantee territory I might take from the Danes so that I might conclude a definitive peace with them that would honor my Holstein house. Frederick wrote: "Not only will I be glad to guarantee whatever you find necessary, I seek also the honor of aiding your imperial majesty in other endeavors. Make use of the port of Stettin and all else that I possess as if it were your own. Tell me how many Prussian troops you need. Do not be the least bit modest and simply tell me how else I can be useful to you. Though I am old and broken, I myself would march against your enemies if I knew that I was bringing benefit by sacrificing myself for such a worthy sovereign, for such a generous and rare friend. You generously offer me your guarantee and your troops. Rest assured that I fully understand the worth of such a noble act. If it would please you to give me 14,000 of your troops along with a 1000 cossacks, that would be sufficient."

Peter answered: "The pact of alliance will be ready in several days. In order that its delay not hinder you vis-a-vis your enemies, *who are also mine*, I have ordered General Chernyshev to do everything possible in order to join your army with 15,000 regular troops and 1000 cossacks in early June at the latest. He has been ordered to place himself under the command of your majesty. Chernyshev is the best general after Rumiantsev, whom I cannot recall because he is deployed against the Danes. But, even if Chernyshev understood nothing, he could not act poorly under the command of such a great general as your majesty."

Thus a congress was being prepared to convene in Berlin with the goal of averting, or at least delaying, the Danish war until spring and making it unnecessary for Prussian forces to help Peter. Meanwhile a force of 16,000 Russians had joined the Prussians for the purpose of dealing decisive blows against Austria!

Austria responded with a last resort. It offered money and an auxiliary force against Denmark. The emperor replied: "I do not need money. I hope to settle with my enemies myself. Should I need help, I will seek it in another place, certainly not in Vienna."

RELATIONS WITH FRANCE

Austria, being in an extremely difficult position, deemed it necessary to moderate the tone of its protests against the change in Russian policy. France, however, did not consider this essential.

When the Russian envoy, Peter Chernyshev, handed Duke Choiseul the declaration regarding peace between Russia and Prussia, the latter, barely able to hide his irritation, answered: "I cannot conceal the fact that this declaration surprises us exceedingly. Without any prior communication with allies, a system that seemed to be so firmly established suddenly and completely has collapsed! My sovereign, the king, acted differently three years ago, and a year ago, even though he felt the desirability of making peace for his citizens just as strongly. In every case he preferred the interests of his allies to those of his own. You must grant our court its just due because you conducted those talks."

"The circumstances are different now," answered Chernyshev and expounded on how Peter's action evidenced his concern for the welfare of his people and his philanthropy in general. "However," objected Choiseul, "Meeting obligations should be honored above all." "Our conversation," noted Chernyshev, "is beginning to touch the question of rights. In this way we may stray far and still disagree with each other." With this the conversation regarding the Russian declaration ended.

"Matters at the French court are now very critical," reported Chernyshev. "The land forces are in a poor state and there is little hope for success in the next campaign. The navy is even worse. The English are seizing many ships. Other vessels dare not put to sea. Consequently, trade is suffering. There is a large deficit in the treasury. The people have become impoverished. Dire need forces tax after tax on them."

The response of the king of France was written in the strongest phrases. "His majesty is prepared to agree to proposals for a firm and honorable peace. But in this matter he will act always with the full approval of his allies. He will accept only those proposals governed by honor and honesty (par l'honneur et par la probité). The king would feel guilty of treachery were he to participate in secret negotiations. The king would dim his glory and that of his country were he to desert his allies. The king is confident that each of his allies will abide by the same principles. The king cannot ignore the foremost injunction handed by God to rulers—faithfulness to treaties and exactitude in carrying out obligations." Louis XV ceased speaking to Chernyshev at court receptions.

In Petersburg meanwhile the court was preoccupied by a vital matter. It was demanded of the foreign diplomats that they make their first visit to Prince George of Holstein. Breteuil, Mercy, and the Spanish envoy, Marquis Almodovar, answered that they would call on the prince if he would notify them first of his arrival. The prince found this unacceptable, whereupon the chancellor, having invited them, announced in the name of the emperor that they would not be granted an imperial audience until they agreed to call on Prince George. Duke Choiseul told Chernyshev that he found it strange and surprising that two different matters were so confused in Petersburg. One was completely private and it was of no inherent significance whether important figures agreed on visits or not. These things occurred frequently at all courts. Choiseul once disagreed about visiting Prince Charles, the emperor's brother. He had disagreed and visits still had not been exchanged. This the court of Vienna considered to be an extraneous matter. Yet, at the Russian court this assumed a quite unexpected and unusual meaning.

The other matter, that of audiences, was an affair of state. It is indispensable that envoys be allowed to see the rulers to whom they are accredited. Otherwise they cannot perform their duty and their presence at courts is completely superfluous. "I request you," Choiseul ended, "to report this to his imperial majesty's court, and to present the incompatibility of the distinction that this court finds in this matter as well as the necessity to grant our minister audience with the emperor without further delay. Such strange confusion of two distinct matters may be explained only in that excuses for a rupture are being sought."

On Chernyshev's report Vorontsov wrote to the emperor: "Yesterday Baron Breteuil was expounding his even-handed notions. I expressed sufficient reasons to rebut him. This unpleasant conversation, heated on both sides, lasted about an hour. It ended with the conclusion that, insofar as his audience with your imperial majesty is concerned, it would be reported to you by me. I did not express hope that your majesty would rescind your stated intention no matter how willing you were to show signs of friendship to the king of France. Breteuil finally asked only that he be informed of your majesty's latest resolution. He stated, in addition, that if nothing positive developed, he would request his recall by the first courier."

After this conversation Chernyshev let Choiseul know that the emperor had received the Swedish, Danish, and English ministers because they had created no difficulties about calling first on Prince George. Breteuil's audience had been delayed because he did not wish to follow the example of the other ministers, although the emperor desired the friendship of the court of France. The delay in granting an audience to Breteuil in no way should cause coldness between the two courts. The emperor would regard flexibility by the French court in the matter of visits to be a renewed sign of the friendship which he intends irrevocably to maintain and further confirm.

"The last two points," wrote Chernyshev, "were accepted in a decent fashion by Duke Choiseul. He expressed satisfaction that I clearly explained to him a second time the meaning of this. I noted that this court, observing this important point, would incline readily toward a solution of the question of visits to his highness, Prince George. The incident occurred solely because of the boorish, stubborn, and ill-reasoned disposition of Breteuil. The court will smooth over his awkward conduct."

But the French court did not yield in the matter of the courtesy visits. On May 27 Chernyshev wrote: "This court accents its own irrationality in this problem. Having gone so far, thanks to pride and stubbornness it does not wish to make a shameful concession. It has been determined to recall Breteuil from Petersburg and assign him as ambassador to the court of Sweden." Choiseul told Chernyshev that a chargé d'affaires, or a resident, in other words a third-class diplomat, would be assigned to Petersburg. His duties would not require participation in ceremonials. Thereupon Chernyshev announced that he was departing France and leaving as chargé d'affaires the embassy secretary, Khotinsky.

COMMUNICATIONS WITH ENGLAND

In Petersburg it was thought that the change in policy, the close alliance with Prussia and the coolness toward Austria and France, would bring Russia and England together. From the first moments of his rule Peter turned with complete trust to Keith, the English envoy, as a man who more than all others must sympathize with his new policy. Goltz, upon arriving in Petersburg, also turned to Keith for advice and instruction. Keith rendered him the friendliest favors.

But Keith in Petersburg and Mitchell in Berlin clung to the old English policy of Pitt. Yet the new English ministry of Lord Bute [May 1762] looked on things differently. It did not wish to spend money in support of Prussia, Frederick now being totally useless to England. But like Peter, who did not inquire into the views of the new English ministry, views that were supported so strongly by the Russian envoy in London, Bute similarly was unaware that under the new emperor the existing political arrangements would collapse.

On news of Peter's accession to the throne Lord Bute said to Prince Golitsyn that the emperor alone was in a position to bestow peace on Europe. "We feel," said Bute, "that in his current poor circumstances the king of Prussia cannot comfort himself with the hope of obtaining peace without significant concessions. It has been almost six weeks now since, at my king's command, I entrusted Mitchell, our minister in Berlin, to notify the Prussian ministry that the time finally had come to think seriously about this matter and that this court cannot fight forever for his Prussian highness. According to the Prussian delegates here, their king now hopes to find greater favor at the Russian court but, of course, such hope is chimerical. It is natural for the Prussian ministers, like drowning men, to grasp at anything and find comfort in the flimsiest hopes. I cannot think that the emperor would trade his natural allies for the king of Prussia.

"This court, in striving for peace, cannot for this reason seriously desire that the Russian forces in the field against Prussia be removed. Were this done, rather than peace the war would continue. The king of Prussia can fight the empress-queen for a long time. This our court does not desire. Rather, in preserving the king from certain defeat, it endeavors to lead him to sacrifice his provinces to Maria Theresa as justice demands. I ask you to hold my comments in strictest secrecy, for I have spoken to you not as a minister of the king, but as a friend who is to be trusted fully. One frankness in exchange for another: I would like to find out from you which part of the Prussian holdings the emperor wishes to keep himself?"

"Up to this time," answered Golitsyn, "I have no information about the emperor's intentions. I can conclude from the manifesto only that he wishes to emulate his predecessors in everything. Consequently, he wishes to hold to his natural allies, specifically with the court of Vienna. Then, also in accordance with the example of his predecessors, to preserve and maintain the friendship of his British majesty. My emperor sincerely wishes peace, but an honorable peace. As you justly noted, lord, the king of Prussia cannot obtain peace other than by sacrificing a substantial part of his provinces. He cannot find comfort in the hope that the emperor, unbefitting the glory of his exalted name and the good of his empire, would exchange the interests of his chief and most useful allies in the interest of such a dangerous neighbor as the king of Prussia; that he would remove his forces from Prussia and return these territories to Frederick II, who himself understands them to be lost irretrievably.

"Such action would be inconsistent with glory, or honor, or the security of the emperor, who intends to glorify the commencement of his reign with the annexation of the kingdom of East Prussia. This would accord with the rights of conquest, the more so as this province [East Prussia] is not connected to the German empire. Considerations relating to the other conquests could be abandoned in exchange for some not so burdensome payment by the king of Prussia."

In describing this conversation, Golitsyn added: "Bute, it seems, was very pleased with my answers. I must report that they are much bored here with the alliance with Prussia and gladly would use the first decent opportunity to abandon it. Thus your majesty enjoys the position not only of petitioning the leading allies for a fair settlement, but also of holding the Prussian province as a permanent possession. The English court readily will agree to this."

On this message Chancellor Vorontsov wrote: "Golitsyn's memorandum deserves high praise and approbation. It should be answered by explaining the state of affairs here, relating his imperial majesty's assent to discuss the previous arrangement, and explaining that except for a friendly exchange no negotiations have begun with the king of Prussia, although a trusted man has been sent there by his majesty." Prince Golitsyn's report was dated January 16; the emperor read it on March 2. While Elizabeth was still alive Golitsyn had received an order to return home to become vice-chancellor. Gross was assigned in his place. But King George III ordered that Golitsyn be advised of Gross's unacceptability. As a result, Count Alexander Vorontsov was appointed as envoy with full plenary powers.

Before Golitsyn's departure Bute notified him of the news from Magdeburg, where Frederick II was in residence, and of Goltz's assignment to Petersburg. Bute expressed strong dissatisfaction that Frederick had not informed London of the instructions given to Goltz. "This means," said Bute, "that the instructions cannot be pleasing to us. It is suspected here that, first of all, the king of Prussia, will attempt in every way possible to raise the Russian empire against Vienna, to the considerable prejudice of European liberty. Secondly, he will do this in order to obtain the most beneficial terms from the Russian emperor, or to come to agreement with Russia against Denmark."

Bute told Golitsyn to keep their conversation in the greatest secrecy. But Peter dealt otherwise with Golitsyn's message. He showed it to Goltz and not only permitted it to be copied but forwarded it to Frederick. Upon receiving it Frederick wrote to Peter: "I would be the most ungrateful and undeserving of men if I did not acknowledge and eternally thank you for your generous acts. Your imperial majesty uncovers the treachery of my allies. You help me when the whole world has abandoned me and it is to you alone that I am obliged for all the good that happens to me." Frederick ordered Finkenstein to show Golitsyn's dispatch to Mitchell, the English envoy in Berlin. When the latter notified his government, Bute replied that the Russian envoy either did not understand him, that perhaps his memory served him wrongly, or that Golitsyn had been carried away by his loyalty to Austria. In any case he, Bute, never said anything of the kind.

The new Russian ambassador assigned to England, Count Alexander Vorontsov, received the following instruction from the emperor: "(1) It is incumbent upon you to employ all possible means to instill in the king of England the same good intentions toward the king of Prussia that he entertained previously. (2) You must seek occasion to demonstrate to the king, and even more to the English people, the artifice of their favorite, Lord Bute, with regard to the king of Prussia. You should suggest to them the shame of the entire nation were England, in particular, to abandon the king of Prussia and conclude a separate peace with the queen of Hungary. (3) Endeavor with all your resources to extinguish the friendship the king still holds for Denmark and use every opportunity to break their allegiance completely.

"(4) With all due diligence you must attempt to draw England into the alliance between Prussia and myself, letting be known, on one hand, the great trade benefit that it might derive therefrom, and on the other hand the disaster that would occur in the contrary case. (5) They should note especially that were Russia to bar the following goods to England, namely hemp, mast timber, copper, iron, and hempseed oil, without which England cannot do, it would be ruined completely. (6) Maintain friendly relations with the Prussian envoy very diligently. Should you hear or receive any kind of negative views about his majesty from the English ministry, you must immediately report it to him so that he might forward it to his court."

SWEDEN, POLAND

It was noted that during the first relations between Russia and Prussia in the new reign, relations that governed all political matters, the question of Sweden had arisen. From Stockholm Ostermann [the Russian ambassador] wrote Peter that most Swedish affairs greatly depended on learning his wishes. "Everyone here," reported Ostermann, "considers that war between Russia and Denmark is inevitable and talks of your majesty's wishes to conclude a triple alliance between Russia, Prussia, and Sweden." After relating the rumors, Ostermann reported a declaration made to him by Ekeblatt, the minister of foreign affairs, that Sweden, exhausted by the war, must think of an honorable agreement with the king of Prussia.

The emperor was quite happy about this agreement, which actually followed. But he paid no attention to its motivation as stated by Ekeblatt, namely, Sweden's exhaustion, and demanded that Sweden participate in his war with Denmark.

Ostermann conversed with Ekeblatt on July 4. Having heard Ostermann's proposal for joint action against Denmark, the Swedish minister replied that he would relay it to the king. Subsequently he offered his opinion in informal and non-diplomatic terms. He began with the expression of the king's firm hope that the emperor, through kinship[26] and benevolence toward Sweden, would look with a kind eye at the actual condition of the Swedish court. The very same reasons that moved this court to peace with Prussia moved it against a new war. Thus the king would be very pleased to learn of an amicable agreement between Russia and Denmark. Respect for the emperor and for the Swedish obligations regarding the guarantee (of Schleswig, by Denmark) forced Sweden to seek a course inoffensive to all. "I reassure you," ended Ekeblatt, "that this court will not bend to any flattering proposals of the Danish court contrary to the interests of the emperor."

"If your desire is truly to see an amicable settlement of our affairs with Denmark," objected Ostermann. "it seems to me that your court should exert its influence on the Danes. Should this prove ineffectual, your material support of the emperor's claims and assistance to the Russian fleet in Swedish ports and Russian forces in Pomerania will be the best means of achieving your goal." Ekeblatt replied that he could give no formal response in such a delicate matter.

But it was easy to guess from his words the meaning of the king's answer, stated to Ostermann on June 18. "The king is unable to provide the emperor further assurance other than to reiterate the earlier, confidential statement about the exhausted condition of the government. This condition prohibits any undertakings that might give even the slightest cause for disrupting amity with any country. In this connection the king was very pleased to learn of the praiseworthy, peaceful attitude of the emperor concerning his willingness to reach an understanding with the Danish court. He sincerely anticipates this and pledges to assist in every way possible.

"With respect to the emperor's desire for support of Russian forces in Pomerania in return for a fair subsidy, and entry of Russian ships into Swedish ports, the king will not fail to do everything commonly referred to as *officia humanitatis* (humanitarian assistance) should any Russian ship in need be forced to enter singly a Swedish port. Similarly, for a fair subsidy, Russian forces will be shown every possible solicitude." When Ekeblatt handed the king's response to Ostermann, the latter asked: "May we count on *officia humanitatis* not being extended to Denmark?" "It shall be difficult to refuse this to the Danish court," replied Ekeblatt.

Ostermann was recalled. Privy Councillor Count Münnich was assigned in his place.

Likewise recalled was Voeikov from Warsaw. He was assigned to the army according to his own long-standing wish, as is seen in his letter to Vorontsov. Count Keyserling, who had been in Poland, and then in Vienna, was assigned in Voeikov's place.

The king of Poland and elector of Saxony, as the weakest figure [in this configuration of affairs] had most to lament in respect to Russia's change in policy. Alarming rumors spread throughout Poland that great danger threatened the country should Prussia join Russia. Undoubtedly the two powers would reach an understanding regarding Poland. Certainly Russia would gain several Polish lands for returning East Prussia to Frederick II. Count Brühl attempted to reconcile the Czartoryskys with the [Polish] court in the hope that their nephew, Poniatowski, who was in Lithuanian service, might act on behalf of the Polish court through his influence on the new empress [i.e., Catherine], the fruit of former favors in Petersburg. This hope was soon dashed. But man cannot live without hope and in Warsaw, in March, 1762 the hope was that Peter III's policies, especially the confiscation of church estates, would create disturbances in Russia.

Warsaw fed on this hope until it came to pass. In the interim Warsaw experienced difficult moments. The close alliance between Russia and Prussia was unparalleled in history. No benefit could be expected from Frederick II. Peter III, in his attachment to Frederick, long had been hostile to the house of Saxony. This hostility waxed when Empress Elizabeth agreed to the elevation of Prince Karl of Saxony, son of Augustus III, to the duchy of Courland. Peter had intended that place for his uncle, Prince George of Holstein.

Peter was very cold to Prince Karl when the latter arrived at Elizabeth's court. When he found out from Shuvalov that the empress was angered by his coldness, he wrote his aunt that he could not act otherwise toward a prince who had tarnished himself by shameful flight at Zorndorf. Understandably, one of Peter's first thoughts upon his accession was to remove Prince Karl from his throne in Courland and to enthrone Prince George. This was easy to do. Courland was a Poland in miniature. It was subject to the influence of the first powerful man who decided to busy himself with it. The most powerful of all was the emperor of Russia. The people of Courland therefore long since had grown accustomed to viewing their dukes as governors assigned by Petersburg.

It was a simple matter in this appointment to depend on the *szlachta*,[27] for there were always groups loyal to one or the other candidate. It was easy to use a party to take the lead in such a matter. The indifferent majority was ready to recognize as duke anyone enjoying the support of Russian forces and promising promotions and grants. Peter did not inform Prince Karl of his own accession and thereby signalled that he was not considered the legitimate duke of Courland. Simolin, the Russian plenipotentiary in Mitau, under Elizabeth had labored on behalf of Prince Charles. Now he was ordered to undo his own efforts and support the party opposed to Charles.

Simolin seized upon the main reason for dissatisfaction with Charles in Protestant Courland, the fact that he was a Catholic. The Courland deputation, which arrived in Petersburg to congratulate Peter on his accession, was told how little in line with the fundamental rights of the duchy of Courland it was to have a Catholic prince as their duke, not to speak of other considerations. At first the movement against Prince Charles was made in the name of the elderly Biron. Only at the end of June did Simolin advance the candidacy of Prince George, to whom Biron granted his rights. As a consequence, three parties formed in Courland—for Prince Charles, Biron, and Prince George.

OBREZKOV IN TURKEY

The change in Russian policy found reflection in relations with Turkey as well. Obrezkov [the Russian envoy in Turkey], unaware of his court's radical change in policy, informed the new ruler on February 19 of the activities of the Prussian envoy in Constantinople and did so, as was his habit, in very uncomplimentary terms. He wrote of the envoy's particular efforts to move the Porte to add, before spring, an article of alliance to the treaty of friendship and trade. Apart from promises, the envoy attempted to convince the dignitaries of the Porte of the harm to be suffered were it not to unite its interests with those of the king of Prussia. He extolled the might and the extraordinary military capabilities of the king. Later, seeing that such praise was in vain, and that the loss of Kolberg no longer could be concealed, according to Obrezkov he substituted his supercilious language for one that was almost servile, and began to declare to the Porte that without its real and rapid assistance Prussia's many enemies would force the king into reverses. He would be compelled to yield to Russia, which awaited him with open arms. This could not be in the interests of the Porte.

Observing that the Porte displayed neither solicitude nor fear, the Prussian envoy urged that the Porte at least should make moves that would require the courts of Petersburg and Vienna to shift some of their forces to the south.

Observing these solicitations, the Porte decided to query the Russian, Austrian, and French ambassadors about the state of European affairs. A senior secretary came to Obrezkov and, after various comments, asked him his opinion of the Prussian envoy's representations and the course the Porte should follow. Obrezkov answered that the Prussian importunities were scarcely surprising. The king of Prussia, mistaken in his designs to conquer a substantial part of Europe and in danger of complete collapse, now sought partners to share his pressing burdens. He was like a monkey that had tossed chestnuts into a fire and once they caught fire sought a cat's paw to pull them out.

The Porte's decision was not difficult to guess. One had merely to consider that a wise grand vizier hardly would plunge Turkey into the vortex of war solely to please the king of Prussia, a friend only since yesterday. This was especially so inasmuch as religion forbade the Turks to become involved in the discords of Christian nations.

The secretary agreed fully with Obrezkov that the Porte never would conclude an alliance with Prussia, but added, almost through his teeth, that "the Porte may be able to do one thing, namely offer its good offices to advance peace between Russia and Prussia." "This, again, is the guile of the Prussian envoy," said Obrezkov. "He wishes, by other means, to accomplish the same end, coolness between Russia and the Porte. A nation offering its good offices is offended when they are not accepted. Russia cannot accept the Porte's good offices because it cannot insult the other nations who have offered the same." In an effort further to convince the secretary, Obrezkov made him a gift of a gold watch worth 72 rubles. But in Petersburg something completely different was desired.[28]

On April 28 Gudovich, the emperor's favorite, visited the chancellor. With him he brought the emperor's verbal instructions directing Obrezkov to convey to the Porte that the emperor would not interfere should Turkey undertake hostilities against Austria. This instruction was pressed upon Peter by Goltz. He visited the chancellor on May 11 to inquire whether it had been sent to Obrezkov because he, Goltz, had informed his king of it.

Vorontsov replied that the chancellery was preparing its monthly courier and the decree would be sent with it. Petersburg was fully aware of the Porte's peaceable disposition. It had conveyed to its neighbors specific assurances of friendship. This meant that were the instructions carried out it would cause an unfortunate public impression without the least benefit. Would it not be better for Russia to refrain from pressing the Porte until the Prussian diplomat Reksen had time to seduce the Porte into a war against Austria? Let the Turkish ministry convey to the Russian resident its intentions about a diversion against Austria in Prussia's favor. In this eventuality the Russian resident would declare his ruler's unwillingness to participate in the proposed hostilities. Furthermore, Russia and Vienna shared special, perpetual treaty obligations against the Porte— both courts had pledged mutual aid against the Turks.

Goltz agreed with the chancellor that Reksen first must present the proposal. The Russian resident should not interfere, but support him. Goltz then asked Vorontsov to send instructions to this effect. Vorontsov replied that since the matter was of high importance and secrecy, it was necessary to prevent it from being compromised. To this Goltz also agreed and promised to write Reksen personally.

The fact that Goltz agreed with the chancellor's remarks is explained by Volkov, who worked in behalf of Vorontsov's proposals from the other end. Obviously, the chancellor and Volkov were agreed in this case. According to Volkov, "The emperor, under constant pressure from Prince George and Baron Goltz, ordered the chancellor to send an instruction to Obrezkov in Constantinople directing him to try to raise the Turks against the court of Vienna. He was to announce that our obligations to Austria had been abrogated. Short as the order was, the decree given to the chancellery was more complete. As soon as I was brought the protocol from the college to sign, I not only returned a written opinion to the college against it but dared to make a presentation to the former emperor in person. I prevailed to such a degree that Obrezkov was directed to volunteer nothing. Should the Turks ask whether we would help Austria, he was to reply that after such a burdensome war we would not, of course, enter into a new one."

Meanwhile Obrezkov wrote the emperor on May 20: "I have taken the liberty, in abject submission and all faithfulness, to suggest to your imperial majesty that the king of Prussia be persuaded to recall his envoy, Reksen, and abandon Prussian representation at the Porte entirely. My daring is prompted solely by submissive zeal in your service and sincere fervor in your highest interests. Prudence suggests that a continuing Prussian presence at the Porte may lead to various inconveniences to your interest, indisputable proof of which already is beginning to appear." According to Obrezkov's report, Frederick II wrote the Porte that its delay in allying with him compelled his reconcilation with Russia. At the same time he entertained the sincere, true and unshakeable determination to preserve the Porte's friendship and to act according to its suggestions in all things.

Having received instructions to hold exploratory discussions with the Porte about the diversion against Austria, Obrezkov wrote that not only was the Porte unprepared for such an undertaking, it was unlikely that it ever had thought about it seriously. Obrezkov also notified Petersburg that on May 20 the ministers of the Porte had met to discuss an alliance with Prussia. It was decided affirmatively to stipulate that the alliance would not include the present war; it would apply to the future only. When the intimate union of Prussia and Russia and the deployment of an auxiliary Russian force to help Frederick II was discovered, the Porte set aside thoughts of an alliance. On this issue it adopted a wait and see attitude.

REVERSAL OF FOREIGN POLICY

So it was that a sudden, radical and decisive change came about in Russian policy. We have observed the impression this change evoked in various countries of Europe, depending on its relation to their interests. Now let us look at the impression it made inside Russia.

After Peter the Great, and the smashing of Swedish power, Russians grew accustomed to thinking themselves safe from the West. There was nothing to fear from a weak Sweden or from a weak Poland. The alliance with Austria provided security against Turkey; the chief opponent of Russia was distant France, with which there could be no direct war. France could inflict harm solely through intrigues and bribes. The struggle with France was limited to the diplomatic sphere. But at the end of the first half of the eighteenth century such safety from the West had evaporated. Prussia, hitherto playing a secondary role, suddenly moved to the forefront. Its famous king, the most skillful captain of his day, spared no means in strengthening his state through conquest of foreign territories. Sweden, Poland and Turkey entered into the realm of Frederick II's undertakings, and his interests inevitably clashed everywhere with those of Russia.

Russia had taken an active part in the alliance designed to curb the vigor of the king of Prussia. War had demonstrated his powers all the more. War also proved the need for the allies to pursue their purpose without tiring, and Russia had persevered despite all foreign and domestic impediments. At the very moment when these great efforts were bearing fruit and Frederick II was cornered, everything had changed. This was not the triumph of an opposition which utilized the change of rulers to realize their views. There were no Russians who sympathized with Frederick II or who did not recognize the necessity of restraining him for the good of their native land.

No doubt the Russian people were burdened by the lengthy war and wished for peace, but an honorable one. An honorable peace was already in their hands, not long to be achieved. At hand was reward for all the blood and sacrifices. The new emperor would have aroused the full sympathy of the Russian people had he acted as armed intermediary in European peacemaking, had he recognized with the English the necessity that Frederick II satisfy the claims of his enemies while also tempering these claims. Frederick himself recognized the need for concessions on his part. This is evident in his instructions to Goltz. He was ready to concede East Prussia to Russia, expressing his desire to be compensated to the west. It is very likely that he had western Polish Prussia in mind. He would retain the title of king of Prussia, which makes understandable the fear among the Poles that an agreement between Russia and Prussia would be at Poland's expense.

Frederick wished to have the same position as that of Charles XII of Sweden toward the end of his career in relation to Peter the Great. He conceded to Russia its conquests in order that it help him gain the equivalent in other areas. Peter I, irritated by the hositility of his allies, had the right to do what he did, but Peter III was not in the same position in relation to his allies in the Seven Years War. His was only one right—should there be strong obstacles to peace, to refuse his share of the rewards offered by Prussia. For even though magnanimity in politics usually brings no fruit, a people hungering for an honorable peace and not an extra patch of foreign soil would be satisifed.

What Peter III did deeply offended the Russian people. It defied the general consensus and mocked the blood shed in battle, the heavy sacrifices of the people in a popular, necessary, and just cause. Peace with Prussia was honorable to no one. What was most offensive was that Russian interests clearly had been sacrificed to foreign, unfriendly ones. No less offensive was that Russia was coming under foreign influence and foreign rule, something that had not occurred even during the sad times of twenty years earlier. Then the men at the top, men of non-Russian extraction such as Ostermann, Münnich, and Biron, were at least Russian citizens who did not allow the ambassadors of foreign countries to dictate as the Prussian gentleman-in-waiting, Goltz, was doing now.

People had lived for the last twenty years in the comforting recognition of the independence and grandeur of a Russia that had powerful, decisive influence in European affairs. To what shame they had come now! A foreign envoy conducted Russian policy, something that had not happened since the Tatar baskaks.[29] Then it was less offensive, for involuntary servitude was less shameful than a voluntary one. And peace had been bought at such a heavy price! One war was ended in order to launch a new one. Why? Only because the ruler of Russia could not be satisfied by simply ruling Russia.

DISSATISFACTION

To the credit of those Russians then in high positions, it must be said that they could not reconcile themselves to the new scheme of things. One can exclude a very few nonentities such as Frederick II's dove, Andrei Gudovich. Chancellor Count Michael Vorontsov had the most difficult position because, with the change in foreign policy, all eyes were upon him. Answers were sought from him. Why did he not act in opposition by giving his own suggestions, why did he sign his name to acts that aroused general indignation? Vorontsov felt all of this; he heard these frightening questions. But he did not possess the firmness of character or other outstanding capabilities needed in a struggle. His financial situation was unsettling. And, finally, his health did not allow him constantly to keep current with affairs and to oppose foreign influences.

Even so, Vorontsov fought as much as he could. In a note presented to the emperor on January 23 concerning Russia's foreign relations Vorontsov said: "The Russian imperial court waged war against the king of Prussia for two reasons. The first was to curb the excessive power attained by this ruler, power that was causing fear in all neighboring courts. It had to be moderated. Russia's role in Europe and the exercise of imperial imperatives were impeded wherever possible by the king of Prussia. This was all the more reason to keep him from new conquests and increase of his lands at the expense of his neighbors. The second reason derived from the mutual obligations undertaken with the court of Vienna."

At the end of the note, mentioning that the congress in Augsburg now could hardly be expected to bring about peace, Vorontsov continued: "To your imperial majesty is granted the glory by Almighty Providence to be in a position of concluding this great contest for the general good of all. Russia feels the burden of war but less so than others. It has not suffered devastation within its borders and does not know what a foreign invasion would wreak. The measures that your imperial majesty may choose to hasten peace are of your choice. But it is my duty to inform the allied courts of the principles by which your majesty will govern your empire in the future. They all have stated many times that they sincerely desire peace. And, in fact, they cannot but desire it when they have exhausted their last resources to wage war. But they desire a peace that is lasting and satisfactory.

"Peace is no less necessary for England and Prussia. The former, despite its many successes, is exhausted by sacrificing enormous sums.

One blow could shake its credit and entire wealth irrevocably. The king of Prussia finds the largest part of his lands almost completely ravaged. The difficulty is in coordinating so many differing interests. But necessity will force everyone to lower their demands and be satisfied with small mercies instead of chasing dreams and exhausting themselves utterly."

The chancellor's proposals were unacceptable. Russia's participation in the Seven Years War was pointed out as necessary to contain the king of Prussia. The suggestion about acting as armed mediator and convincing all parties to moderate their claims was raised. But the decision was made to force everyone to withdraw their claims and satisfy those of the king of Prussia alone. The conference created by Elizabeth which began and then so consistently supported the struggle against Frederick II stood in the way of achieving this end. Its members even now would not repudiate their opinions. On January 29 the conference was abolished. Part of its responsibilities were assigned to the Senate, part to the College of Foreign Affairs.

Vorontsov felt obliged to underscore the timeliness of this measure, and couched his memorandum in the most flattering terms. "It is just and fitting reverently to praise your imperial majesty's royal intention, that of a great ruler, to conduct all his affairs personally and govern through his enlightenment. In this light there is no true need to continue the conference or to establish a new council. I am far from suggesting anything contrary to your majesty's royal determination to conduct all your affairs personally. Considering it also my first and responsible duty to assist in your generous concern for the welfare and glory of the empire, I am obliged to note that (1) the general affairs of Europe are in such a critical state that either a completely new system must be accepted or many changes made. In creating a new system it is needful not to overlook what is positive while avoiding what is harmful, but neither the Senate nor the College of Foreign Affairs are capable of handling all this properly. (2) In transacting business between the Senate and the colleges many people will learn of confidential matters and they will be delayed. It is quite possible as well that unclarity and disagreements will allow different opinions in different places and this dissonance will be reflected in the form of disharmony in documents reaching your imperial majesty."

These considerations led the chancellor to recognize the need either to retain the conference or to establish a similar committee with new members or former members. Vorontsov went so far as to defend the old conference. "Permit me to dare assure you that the conference, through its assiduous labors and zealous fulfilment of your monarchical will, quickly will be favored with the highest approbation and trust. Even now, honorably and with clear conscience before your imperial majesty, I can attest that its conduct of affairs always has been governed by a sincere and fervent concern for the national good and by patriotic loyalty to your majesty. No censure ever has reached to this court about it, for it endeavored to gain the respect of all courts." This patriotic declaration of the patriotic loyalty of the conference undermined the preamble of the report. The conference was not re-established. A committee of a quite indeterminate nature was not named until May 20. Meanwhile, a new order of affairs was being installed under the direction of the Prussian envoy, Goltz.

It has been mentioned that financial distress exacerbated the chancellor's sad plight. In March he was compelled to petition the emperor for relief: "I am now more than 200,000 rubles in debt. I have no other recourse than most humbly to request your imperial majesty, in your magnanimity and special favor to me to allow the treasury to assume my house and all furnishings. I would receive 250,000 rubles from the treasury or the Copper Bank (only 62,500 rubles in terms of the true cost of the new currency). If there is objection to taking my house for that sum, allow me to borrow 300,000 rubles from the Copper Bank without interest. I understand quite well, kind sovereign, that your majesty's treasury suffers large expenses due to the current situation. But now, when in your auspicious rule Almighty God grants precious peace to Europe, all extraordinary expenditures will end. The return of the army likewise will bring the return of wasted millions. Therefore with full confidence I rely on your majesty's generosity and kind consent to hear ken to my most obedient request."

Vorontsov's difficult financial straits forced him to remain in office. At the same time, he felt demoted as chancellor to become the administrator of the Chancellery of Foreign Affairs, preparing documents at the behest of Goltz or Prince George of Holstein. Sometimes the bitterness of his situation grew unbearable and, in one of those moments, he wrote Peter: "My unfortunate plight, due to my lengthy illness and weakness, deprives me of the satisfaction of seeing your imperial majesty frequently and receiving your monarchical commands and, likewise, as is due my position, of reporting to your imperial majesty concerning various business matters.

"This unfortunate circumstance saddens me greatly for in my loyalty and zeal, as well as in my faithfulness to the person of your majesty and service to you, I cannot perform my duty as I should. Thus I must relay my communications to you via third persons, thereby subjecting my acts to certain unpleasant interpretations and drawing anger, as in fact has happened. Evidently it was reported to your imperial majesty through Volkov that I labeled your undertaking against Denmark a chimera. Yet what I said was that a lengthy campaign of our army in Germany, without sufficient stores in place, without ready cash, without a stronger navy, and without the assistance of the king of Prussia or another ruler, would be completely fruitless and would lead to certain losses and infamy. This I can say to this very day in all honesty and loyalty to your majesty.

"Your imperial majesty has instructed me to act in accordance with your thoughts in discussing your inclinations toward his majesty, the king of Prussia. My principal rule has been, is, and in the future will be to execute the will of my sovereigns in everything. This rule I have not violated in the least. Your imperial majesty may rest fully assured that I have not had, nor do I have, leanings toward any nation. Insofar as the peace treaty with his majesty, the king of Prussia, is concerned, to this day I have received no report of its content and I am unaware either of your inclinations or intentions, or the conditions on which it is based and to be concluded. With extreme sorrow I learned of your allegation that I was voted to France. This gives me deadly grief.

"Should your majesty doubt my loyalty to you and the fatherland, I am unworthy of remaining one hour in my rank. Prostrating myself at your feet as I do, I humbly beseech you to free me of my sorrow and unjust censure. Should there be, which I cannot imagine, some doubt or objection about my service, I humbly request you to dismiss me and grant me freedom to spend the remaining fragment of my suffering life in peace and quiet. I trust I would not be deprived of your majesty's favor which upholding my reputation at home and beyond the fatherland, I would revere as the pinnacle of my prosperity, preferring it to any material rewards and treasures.

"It is not within me to flatter or be hypocritical. It is my wish to endeavor to serve your imperial majesty in honor and glory, faith and truth. These sentiments I shall hold to the end of my life. Should jealous or evil-intentioned persons sometimes tell you things about me, I humbly beg you to inform me immediately so that I might justify myself. As to the instructions I received last night to confer with Keith, the English ambassador, about deployment of the English fleet this summer for your disposition, I shall talk to him at our first meeting. But, your majesty does not enjoy a treaty of alliance with the English court. England, now at war against France and Spain, is in no condition to send any ships. Nor without any advantages for itself would it be inclined to do so. Furthermore, as far as I know, England has declared that it will not take part in the strife between your imperial majesty and the king of Denmark. Consequently this request may be subject to unfriendly rejection. I request further instructions regarding this matter."

Subordinate to the chancellor was the vice chancellor, Prince Alexander Golitsyn, who had returned from London at the end of Elizabeth's rule. If the chancellor was unaware of the major points of foreign policy, the vice chancellor knew even less about them. During the final period of Elizabeth's rule the chancellor was assisted by Ivan Shuvalov, who attended meetings with foreign ambassadors. Under Peter III Shuvalov had lost all influence because his policy initiatives differed so markedly with those then in ascendence.

He was assigned to the then humble activity of supervising educational institutions. Here he was forced to depend on Volkov for advice as how best to emphasize to the emperor the importance of the needs of the establishments entrusted to him. Furthermore, he had to point out the significance of these institutions. "You know better than I," he wrote to Volkov, "that government benefits when its constituent parts receive smooth and purposeful supervision. To your good offices I entrust two such parts which, in an educated age, constitute the honor and glory of nations, namely the sciences and the arts. The university and the academy (of fine arts) are under my supervision. I need rules, I need instructions."

Ivan Shuvalov found it necessary personally and for his good name to be disinterested and seek no honors. In one of his letters he tells how he rejected the office of vice-chancellor and the lands which Peter III had offered him, citing Gudovich as a witness. He tells how he stood on his knees and begged the emperor to spare him all signs of favor. But he could not be pleased at losing his influence, influence to which he felt entitled because of his principled stance. He could not be happy when the system which he served so ardently was overthrown while misfortune threatened Russia at home and humiliation abroad.

Shuvalov made his dissatisfaction known and then was treated as one out of favor. Consequently he felt it necessary to avoid the court and the emperor personally. The Prussians Goltz and Schwerin named Shuvalov as the head of a conspiracy. "The most important and dangerous man here," wrote Schwerin to Frederick II, "is Ivan Ivanovich Shuvalov, favorite of the deceased empress. This man who lives by intrigue, although inwardly despised by the emperor, nonetheless has managed his affairs so well via his friend General Melgunov, a favorite of the emperor, that the sovereign has entrusted to him the Corps of Cadets and principal supervision of the court. Both of these duties require the presence in the capital of this harmful and dangerous individual.

"This gentleman is unable to dissimulate and to conceal the unworthy and shameful designs nurtured in his heart. Fury and indignation are written on his face and I would be willing to wager anything that the scoundrel has fearsome plans in his head.

"The second of these harmful men is General Melgunov. Were he clever likely he would be even more dangerous than the former. The emperor trusts him completely. Meanwhile this man, along with Ivan Ivanovich and one other, Volkov, are his chief enemies and await only the first opportunity to deprive him of his throne.

"I have talked at length about this with the emperor and even have mentioned the names of the dangerous men. But his majesty replied that he knows of their disloyalty. He feels that he has given them so much work that they have no leisure to think of conspiracy and thus are harmless. It is very sad that the sovereign so indulges these men, who live solely with the thought of his demise. By removing these villains he could sit on his throne in complete peace. But, as if deliberately, he is willing to give them the most favorable opportunity, which they, of course, will seize as soon as possible. The emperor has decided to take personal command of the force assigned against the Danes."

Thus, according to Goltz and Schwerin, Ivan Shuvalov, the head of a conspiracy, was waiting only for Peter's departure from Russia in order to depose him. Clearly, if Peter decided to go abroad, he could not leave Shuvalov in Petersburg. Peter himself told Shuvalov: "The king of Prussia writes me that not one man who is suspect should be left in Petersburg during my absence." Shuvalov might have thought that this did not refer to him. But later, through Melgunov, Peter let it be known to Shuvalov that he was to follow him with the army as a volunteer.

Ivan Shuvalov could not act as head of a conspiracy because he was incapable of it by his very nature. But it is important to note that Goltz and Schwerin speak of the strong dissatisfaction he could not conceal and of the fury and indignation written on his face. It is even more significant that Goltz and Schwerin also considered Melgunov and Volkov when he wrote of the hatred of the Prussians and Prince George for him. "Prince George," says Volkov, "is as embittered at me as Goltz is, and so inspired by the Khorvats and the Glebovs that he went so far, when drunk and speaking openly, to accuse me of hating the Germans. This happened on June 9. He threatened to prove to me, as two times two is four, that I was the one who had drafted a plan for the expulsion of all Germans from Russia. All day the entire court witnessed my sorrow over this strange occurrence."

The Prussians say nothing of Glebov, probably because he had no influence on foreign affairs. The two chief functionaries, Volkov and Glebov, were at odds and tried to harm each other. Considering that Glebov still retained his former significance after the change of government, it cannot be said that he was content with Peter. But it was difficult for anyone to be content with the anarchy and lack of a guiding presence thanks to which, seizing an opportune moment, one could push through a decision only to see it undone at the next. The men who at first wanted to support the government of Peter III and to make it popular, observed very quickly that they could no nothing. In despair, they saw the future of their country in the hands of incompetent foreigners and ministers of a foreign master who only yesterday had been Russia's sworn enemy.

DISSATISFACTION IN THE CHURCH, THE ARMY, AND THE GUARDS

The dissatisfaction of powerful groups such as the church and the army joined with that of individuals. The harsh and abrupt decision concerning church property aroused the strong indignation of the clergy. On May 25 Goltz reported to his master: "The clergy has petitioned the emperor in Russian and Latin[30], complaining of coercion and unusual steps taken against it as a result of the decree confiscating church properties. The church could not imagine such actions even from a barbarous government. Now it must suffer them from an Orthodox government. It is all the sadder that the clergy is coerced solely because they are servants of God. This plea, signed by the archbishops and much of the clergy, was expressed in extraordinarily strong terms. It is not so much a request as it is a protest against the sovereign. Reports received last night, and three days ago, from the military governors of outlying districts speak of clerical efforts to set the people against the monarch. They say that the spirit of revolt and dissatisfaction has become so general that they do not know what measures to take. Hence they ask for instructions from the government."

It is known that violent uprisings occurred not only in the outlying districts. It is also known that the causes differed from those mentioned and therefore we can reject the second part of Goltz's message. It is difficult not to accept the first half.

When Peter was grand duke he expressed his dislike of the Russian clergy in childish ways by sticking out his tongue at priests and deacons during services. Now this matter had become more serious. On March 26 the emperor delivered a decree to the Synod. "To our displeasure we have noted for a long time that complaintants to the Synod against their supervisors or diocesan officials in the end generally have been referred back to the very persons against whom the claims were filed. The settlement of these cases causes a lengthy bureaucratic process. Consequently, either the Synod does not perform its essential functions or, still worse, favors only the diocesan officials. In this respect therefore the Synod appears to be more the guardian of the higher clergy than the strict steward of truth and guardian of the poor and innocent.

"The attached petitions of the priest Bordiakovsky and the deacon Sharshanovsky of Chernigov diocese are new and indisputable proofs of this for, despite imperial instructions dating back to 1754 about the necessity of deciding their case, these orders have not been carried out to this day. The case simply is returned to the same diocese for examination. We observe the reasons for this. It seems that equals fear to judge each other in order to avoid giving a very negative impression of themselves.

"Therefore we instruct the Synod to eliminate these temptations through strong supervision of justice. A decision is to be made in these two petitions and the same should be done in all similar cases. Let it be known by my imperial word that the smallest infringement of truth shall be treated as the most heinous of crimes against the state. This decree is to be printed for circulation throughout Russia and is to be attached to the Synod's usual instructions as well.

"There is an official at the Synod whose responsibility is to make certain that no errors occur in the conduct of daily business. The official should have been made fully aware of this function and either removed if he did not fulfull his duties or supported by his colleagues in his efforts against 'violations of truth'. There is no need for abusive decrees."

The monastic clergy was irritated by the sudden appropriation of monastic patrimonies and the lay clergy by the order to conscript priests' and deacons' sons into military service[31]. And now these discontented people received means to communicate their irritation to others. While reminding us of several decisions of the new government that were received favorably, a Russian contemporary commented: "The decisions that followed, however, evoked strong grumblings and indignation among the citizenry, most of all because Peter III was determined to alter completely our religion, for which he showed particular disdain. He called in the leading archbishop, Dmitry Sechenov of Novgorod, and ordered that only the icons of the Saviour and the Mother of God remain in the churches, that other icons be forbidden, and that priests shave their beards and dress like foreign pastors.

"It is impossible to describe how these instructions amazed Archbishop Dmitry. This wise elder had no idea how even to begin to fulfill such an unexpected command and clearly perceived that the sovereign intended to exchange Orthodoxy for Lutheranism. He was obliged to inform the leading clergy of the sovereign's will but, although this measure was delayed, it created strong discontent later and contributed heavily to the overthrow." Private chapels were closed. A foreign observer sympathetic to Peter noted the imprudence of the order to remove the icons. He added that Dmitry Sechenov was banished for his protest against this measure but soon returned because of fear of popular discontent.

The discontent of the army may be added to that of the clergy. One of the first acts of the new government was disbanding Elizabeth's bodyguards. The elimination of these "guards within the guards" understandably might have been received favorably were it not for the fact that upon the dissolution of the old Russian palace guards they were replaced immediately by guards of foreign origin, the Holsteiners. These clearly enjoyed the emperor's favor and this aroused the strongest indignation among the Russian guards. Prince George of Holstein held the most important position in the force. He enjoyed no merits and wasted no time in arousing hatred through his character and deeds. Later Goltz himself was forced to confess to Frederick II that Prince George had contributed heavily towards creating fierce hatred of Germans and hastened the fall of his master.

Once more, as in Biron's time, rumors circulated that the guards soon would be dissolved and re-assigned to regular army regiments. Peter, while still grand duke, often said that the guards, living in their barracks with their families, held his residence as if under siege, and were dangerous to the government. Peter's term for the guards was Janissaries. Thanks to these underlying grounds for dissatisfaction, nothing won approval and everything aroused grumbling. The guards complained about the change in uniforms and the lengthy and frequent drills according to the Prussian model.

A contemporary Russian witness speaks of the discontent in the armed forces and the reasons behind it. "Peter multiplied the number of dissatisfied people because, from the very hour of the empress's death, he ceased to hide the excessive attachment he always had entertained for the king of Prussia. The king's portrait adorned his ring and another, larger one, hung by his bed. He immediately ordered a dress coat in the Prussian style. Not only did he begin to wear it constantly, he wanted to dress his guards in the same fashion. Beyond that, he always wore a Prussian order, thereby ranking it above all Russian ones.

"Still unsatisfied, he wanted to change the uniforms of all regiments. Instead of the former solid green style, multi-colored tightly-fitting uniforms of Prussian cut were substituted. Finally, he ordered that the regiments no longer be named after cities but by the last name of their colonels and commanders. To crown everything, having introduced the strictest possible military discipline, he prescribed daily exercises regardless of weather. By all these measures not only did he burden the army excessively but, having irritated everyone, personally attracted the greatest vexation, especially from the guards."

The grandees, the old men holding positions of honor in the guards, had to bend to the new ways were they to avoid the emperor's displeasure and mockery. The well-known Bolotov, while visiting Petersburg at this time, describes the impression made upon him by a passing guards detachment.

"A detachment of guards was marching by, equipped, powdered, and dressed in new uniforms. But nothing surprised me as much as the man marching before the first platoon. He was a short, fat, aged man, with a sword, in a uniform covered with gold stripes, a star on his chest, and a light blue ribbon barely discernible under the tunic. Who is this man, I asked. What? Did you not recognize him? That is Prince Nikita

Trubetskoy. How can that be? I thought he was infirm, suffering from leg ailments that kept him from the court and Senate for weeks at a time. Furthermore, there was practically no way to find him at home either. Oh, they answered me, that was before. Now, God knows, times have changed; the sick and the healthy, and the oldsters themselves lift their feet and march with the young. They trample and churn the mud oh so well, just like soldiers."

The elder Razumovsky, Alexis Grigorievich, was spared a similar fate by being dismissed from all duties. But the younger one, Hetman Kirill, was forced to keep a young officer at home to give him lessons in the new Prussian drills. This still did not save him from the reprimands and the scoffing of Peter III. It was said that the emperor particularly enjoyed laughing at Razumovsky, who was naturally inept in military drills.

The ladies of the court also afforded the emperor many mirthful moments. He forced them to change from the old Russian bow to the French curtsy. Many ladies, especially the elderly ones, simply could not accustom themselves to the curtsy and their comic attempts gave Peter great glee. He watched and then mimicked them. "It was very easy to make me laugh," said one contemporary lady, later to become famous. "The sovereign sometimes purposely would make me laugh by grimacing in many ways. He was not like a sovereign."

GENERAL DISCONTENT AND PRUSSIAN FEARS

Strong dissatisfaction spread through Petersburg. Even in distant places it was impossible not to notice that there was some disarray in the government. At the commencement of the reign the sovereign ordered the College of Manufactures to be transferred from Moscow to Petersburg. But later came another decree: "Although it has been ordered to move His Imperial Majesty's College of Manufactures here from Moscow and retain an office there, nevertheless we feel that doubtlessly all of the factories are in Moscow or nearby and very few are here. Therefore, if transferred, the College of Manufactures would be performing its functions by correspondence, as it were. We instruct the College to be returned immediately to Moscow and an office to be left here, as before." An imperial decree of January 9 ordered the abolition of city police chiefs. The police was assigned to provincial offices and to the military governors. An imperial decree dated March 22 restored the office of police chiefs.

If the disarray could be noted in distant places, only in Petersburg could one observe the reasons for it. The childlike nature of Peter's character led him quickly to adopt everything he found in the circle he frequented or from among those to whom he became attached. In the company of Holstein officers to whom he had become extremely partial, Peter imitated barracks behavior and made crude revelry his favorite way of passing time. During Elizabeth's rule there was no mention of tobacco at court because she could not either. At first Peter himself could not stand it. But the moment he saw the Holsteiners, whom he considered to be exemplary and brave, smoking, he too started to smoke. When Staehlin, his former tutor, first saw him with pipe and beer, he was amazed. Peter said to him: "Why are you surprised, stupid! Have you ever seen even one really brave officer who did not smoke?" Wine followed the beer.

In the words of Bolotov, a contemporary witness, "general indignation waxed all the more when rumors spread, reaching the lowest classes, that no sooner had the sovereign mounted the throne than he publicly indulged all his intemperances and acted in a manner totally unbecoming to such a great monarch. Not only did he spend almost all of his time with Countess Vorontsova, his open mistress, but even as the empress still lay in her coffin at court he spent whole nights with his favorites, flatterers, and former friends in revelry and drinking. Sometimes he invited people who were quite unworthy of the emperor's conversation and company. Among these were Italian actresses and singers together with their interpreters. Worst of all, he talked about everything, even about highly confidential matters and government business. His voice was very loud, shrill, and unpleasant, and there was something about it that made it stand out distinctly. He could be heard from a distance and picked out from all others."

Bolotov was an aide to the chief of police, General Nicholas Korff. He accompanied him at court and observed the happenings at dinners and suppers. "Through the open doors," he noted, "we could always hear what the sovereign said to others. Sometimes we could see him and all the activity. This was satisfying only at first. Later it reached the point where we wished that we did not have to hear such conversations. Only rarely did we see the emperor sober and in full possession of his mind and reason. Most frequently he tossed off several bottles of English beer, which he liked exceedingly, before dinner. This was the reason he spoke such nonsense. Listening, our hearts bled in shame at the foreign envoys who, seeing and hearing, doubtlessly laughed inwardly. Truly, sometimes my soul was so stricken by all this that I wanted to flee such spectacles without looking back. It hurt much to see and hear it all.

"But I was never as stricken by these disgusting spectacles as by the sovereign's visits to dine at a favorite's house, whither all in favor in his suite must accompany him. Among them was my general, and many others, including their aides and orderlies. The whole herd would follow, and the host was hard put to feed and entertain everybody. The only things brought from court were tobacco and pipes. The tsar loved smoking and liked others to smoke. Naturally, everyone tried to imitate him. The tsar ordered that no matter where he went a basket of Dutch clay pipes and many pouches of knaster and other tobaccos must be brought along. The moment we arrived somewhere dozens of pipes would be lit and in one instant the whole room would be filled with thick smoke. This pleased the sovereign and, walking about the room, he would only joke, praise, and laugh.

"This would have been well enough had nothing further happened shameful to all Russians. As soon as everyone was seated at the tables the glasses and goblets would ring so diligently that, when arising from the table, sometimes all were just like children. They would begin to make noise, yell, laugh, and babble all kinds of nonsense. Once, and I can see it now, they reached a point where, having left the balcony and entered the garden, they all began to play like children on the sandy ground. Some hopped on one leg, others pushed their friends with their knees. You may judge what it was like for us to observe such a spectacle from the windows, seeing all the leading government figures, decorated with stars and orders, jumping around and pushing each other to the ground. Laughter, screaming, noise, and clapping resounded everywhere, and the goblets kept clinking away."

The hearts of Russians bled with shame before the foreign diplomats. In their reports to their courts these envoys left unanimous witness to the indecency of Peter III's revelries that aroused such disgust. We shall cite the words of the same witness regarding this unease. "Grumblings against the sovereign and indignation at his actions and deeds, which grew worse as time went on, increased by the hour among the notables and had spread throughout the nation. The truce vexed everyone, and all lamented the expected loss of Prussia. The sovereign's devotion to the king of Prussia, his hate and contempt for the laws, his extreme coldness to his wife, the empress, and his blind love for Vorontsova, also aroused great indignation.

"But most of all this feeling focused against his disdain for all Russians and the preferences granted to foreigners, especially Holsteiners, who publicly and fearlessly ventured to discuss, reckon and interfere in the sovereign's affairs. All of us were aware of the deep muttering of the people and of the discontent with the tsar throughout the country, which grew with each passing hour. We received these unpleasant rumors daily, particularly when it became known that peace soon would be made with Prussia and that huge and grandiose fireworks were planned to celebrate it. Not infrequently in leisure moments we gathered to discuss the situation. We began to fear that there might be a riot and mutiny soon, especially by the very distressed guards."

We have observed that the envoys of Frederick II, Goltz and Schwerin, soon noticed the serious discontent and informed their king. They named Ivan Shuvalov, Melgunov, and Volkov as the men most dangerous to Peter.[32] They were convinced, and so assured the king, that these men would use Peter's departure with the army in the campaign against Denmark to stage an uprising. For this reason they attempted to convince the emperor not to go, assuring him that his presence in Russia was indispensable for the good of the empire. Peter replied that he was amazed at their words, which proved to him only that they disliked him. They then turned to Frederick II and, on April 8, Schwerin wrote the king: "No one in the whole world except your majesty can dissuade the emperor from this dangerous journey. A letter from your majesty in which you advise him to remain in Russia will force him to change his mind. Because he trusts your majesty completely he probably will heed your suggestion."

Goltz wrote the king on May 2 on the same matter, proposing Peter's coronation before the campaign. But on May 4 Frederick had written Peter: "I must admit that I would very much like your majesty to be enthroned because this ceremony makes a powerful impression on a people accustomed to seeing the coronation of their sovereign. I must tell you, frankly, that I do not trust the Russians. Any other people would thank the heavens for having a sovereign with such outstanding and admirable qualities as your majesty (éminentes et admirables qualités). But these Russians! Do they not feel their happiness? Could not the venality of one worthless man lead to creation of a plot or to an uprising in favor of the princes of Braunschweig? Recall, your imperial majesty, what happened during Peter I's first absence, when his own sister organized a plot against him.

"Assume that some anxious villain, in your absence, will begin to intrigue at getting this Ivan[33] on the throne. He will form a conspiracy with the aid of foreign money to get Ivan out of the dungeon and to incite the army and other scoundrels to join him. Will you not then have to leave the war against the Danes, even though it was going very successfully, and return hurriedly in order to put out the fire in your own house? This thought, when it came to me, aroused alarm and my conscience would torture me all my life were I not report it to your imperial majesty.

"I am here, deep within Germany. I do not know your court at all, nor those whom your majesty can wholly trust, or those who may be suspect. Your ample reason therefore will have to decide who is loyal and who is not. I think only that should your majesty assume command of the army, safety demands that first you be enthroned and then, in your suite, take all suspicious personages abroad with you. In this way your majesty will be secure.

"For greater safety, all foreign diplomats should be made to follow you as well. Thereby you will destroy every seed of intrigue and revolt. So that all these gentlemen not burden you, you can always send them to Rostock or Wismar or to some other place in the army's rear so that they cannot relay our plans to the Danes. I have no doubt that you will leave loyal stewards in Russia on whom you can depend, Holsteiners or Livonians who will watch everything and report the slightest movement."

Peter replied: "Your majesty writes that, in your opinion, I must be crowned before leaving on campaign, and for the sake of the people. But I must tell you that since the war almost has begun I see no possibility of coronation beforehand since the coronation, according to tradition and for the sake of the people, must be a splendid ceremony. I cannot have a proper coronation for there is no way of quickly arranging here for everything that is needed. As far as Ivan is concerned, I keep him under strong guard. If the Russians actually wished me ill, they could have done something long ago, seeing that I take no precautions. In walking the streets on foot I yield to God's protection, as Goltz can attest. I can assure you that once you know how to treat them, you can feel calm on their account.

"Your majesty! What will these very same Russians think of me when they see that I sit at home when a war is in progress in my native land.

Russians always wished one thing—to live under the rule of a sovereign, not of a woman. I have heard from my own regiment twenty times: 'May God grant that you be our sovereign soon so we won't be under a woman's rule.' But, most important, I would never forgive myself for the base cowardice. I would die from sorrow at the thought that I, the first prince of my house, would be inactive when a war was being waged to regain possessions unfairly taken from my predecessors. Even your majesty would lose considerable respect for me were I to do this."

So it was that Peter's departure for the army was decided despite Frederick's advice. The commander in chief of the army, Count Buturlin, had been recalled to Petersburg while Elizabeth was still alive. He was on his way to explain his activity to the empress, who agreed with the conference about his mistakes. Nevertheless, that he could expect a kind reception is seen from his letter to Ivan Shuvalov: "In my sorrow I retain the sole consolation of receiving a letter from your office, as I did today, with eternal gratitude. The letter was dated September 17. It is all the more heartening in that I remain among the faithful servants of her imperial majesty. Were it up to the conference, long ago I would not have been among the living. In the beginning I was honored and courted without end. Now they bury me alive. Holy God! Never anywhere have my pauses been without cause. [Please] Intercede with her majesty on the behalf of her trustworthy servant. Unhappily now I have been asked also to give up Angiurinov to Count Rumiantsev. He is all that remains to me and all privy matters are entrusted to him. I am left as the sole clerk and scribe. I would not have expected an insult as severe as this from his lordship, Volkov."

THE RUSSIAN ARMY ABROAD

Buturlin did not find Elizabeth among the living. While traveling he received a memorandum from the new emperor requesting his generosity and good will. Count Fermor was dismissed on February 19 and retired from service. Command of the army abroad was turned over to Count Peter Saltykov. While Elizabeth still lived orders concerning Buturlin demonstrated clearly that the former commander in chief would be retired. The Seven Years War (five years for Russia) brought forth new men of ability. Among them, first place belonged to the conqueror of Kolberg, Count Peter Rumiantsev. It is understandable that Peter, having planned a Danish war, also would choose among the emerging military men and assign him to lead the campaign.

Rumiantsev spent the month of February in Petersburg, having been summoned there by the emperor. Winning the friendship of Volkov, the most active official in government, he left at the beginning of March to join his corps in Pomerania to prepare for the campaign. On May 21 he received instructions to consider war with Denmark not only inescapable but already declared, and to hasten to consolidate his forces in Mecklenburg before the Danes arrived. These instructions were forwarded in great secrecy but a friend showed a copy to Goltz. He was very displeased, for the Prussians hoped that the matter would be resolved or put off by a peace conference in Berlin.

"It would be superfluous to point out to your majesty," wrote Goltz to the king, "the cowardliness of the compiler of this decree regarding the congress and the inconsistency apparent in every word. The orders to establish stores in Rostock and Wismar and particularly to lead the army into Mecklenburg are, in my opinion, strange in the highest degree. This must not be ascribed to his imperial majesty, for the decision took place in council. Volkov, who dared to give it such final form, is at fault. The emperor concealed this order from me. Your majesty, perceive how unpleasant this is for me. Notwithstanding all the favors and trust of the emperor, the opposition party can force him to hide the most important facts from me, those which your majesty must learn before anybody else."

In the meantime Prince George of Holstein persistently tried to convince Goltz that he persuade Peter not to join the army. "It is well known to you," Goltz said to him, "how his imperial majesty replied to the king's similar suggestions. He answered that he knows the domestic state of his nation better than the king does, that he is sure of the loyalty of his subjects, and that his glory demands that he join the army. After this reply naturally I cannot request my sovereign, the king, to repeat these very same suggestions to the emperor. Why was there such haste to publish the fact of the emperor's departure? Why were the foreign envoys told to follow him? At the moment, I do not see how the emperor, in view of these disclosures, can avoid the loss of his dignity. Europe will view the cause of any change in intention to be fear of possible unrest in Russia due to the sovereign's absence."

The prince continued to speak of the poor state of the army assigned to the campaign, of the lack of money, food, and supplies. "For two months now," replied Goltz, "I have been talking to you and the emperor personally, saying that it is necessary to take measures to avoid these problems if war seemed inevitable, that it was pointless to threaten to crush the Danes if there were no confidence that everything was ready. Constantly I was told that all preparations were complete when I knew quite well that this was not so. Seeing, finally, that my representations served no cause, and could only incited the anger of his imperial majesty, I kept my place. Now, knowing the poor state of affairs, one must be resigned to an unsuccessful war which could have been avoided by negotiation."

Until receipt of his instructions on May 21, Rumiantsev was in a state of great agitation. He was troubled by the thought that there would be no war and that he would be unable to win distinction in a brilliant campaign. On receipt of the instructions he wrote Volkov from Kolberg on June 8: "It is true that my confusion was not inconsiderable inasmuch as I had no response from you, my most obliging friend. I was desperate, feeling there would be no work for me. How, having received your letter and in hope of your kind favor and priceless good will, I am all the more happy. You know that every craftsman is happy to obtain work. God grant only that everything proceeds according to my wishes and efforts. If so, I have no doubt that I shall fulfill the royal will of my great sovereign. I have submitted my report on the colonels and staff officers. True, I have procrastinated a bit, but the choices open to me were numerous. I have kept in mind that everything must be managed solely for the good of the service. I promoted no one not of the nobility or of the officer class. The moment appeared most appropriate for a purging inasmuch as infamous acts have destroyed all honor and respect for the officer."

But after this letter of a happy craftsman who had obtained work, Rumiantsev felt compelled to send totally different reports to the emperor. He wrote that the shortage of provisions was bringing him to despair. Meanwhile the Prussians, instead of helping, hindered him with demands that the Pomeranian areas be returned. But Rumiantsev's last reports found Peter without a throne.

THE PRISONER OF SCHLÜSSELBURG

June was an "uncertain and most critical time. A revolt or insurrection was feared, especially among the guards, who were extremely aggrieved." In whose name might an insurrection take place? Frederick II pointed out to Peter a rival, a man with the title of All Russian emperor before Peter, who now languished in the Schlüsselburg fortress. Peter replied to Frederick that he was keeping Ivan under strict guard. One week after his accession, on January 1, Peter ordered that the guards captain, Ovtsyn, be replaced by Prince Churmanteev. This was done "to guard a certain important prisoner in the Schlüsselburg fortress." The order read: "Should someone unexpectedly try to take the prisoner away from you, you must, in these circumstances, resist as much as possible and not give up the prisoner alive."

The instruction to Churmanteev, signed by Count Alexander Shuvalov, said: "If the prisoner be disorderly in some way or not listen to you, or if he talks obscenely, put him in chains until he calms down. If he pays no attention, have him beaten with a stick and lash, according to your judgment." Following this, on January 11 Churmanteev received a secret instruction: "This prisoner is not to be transferred anywhere or given to anyone without our orders. If permission to transfer the prisoner to a different place is given, it will be accompanied by our lieutenant general, Prince Golitsyn, or Lieutenant General Baron von Ungern with an imperial decree signed in our own hand. Should anyone other than these men appear, even bearing an imperial decree signed by us and demand the prisoner, he is not to be believed. Arrest him and write a report to our field marshal, Count Shuvalov." The same day a most secret order was sent to Berednikov, the commandant of Schlüsselburg, to admit Golitsyn or Ungern. Should they order Churmanteev and his detachment to leave the fortress with the prisoner, this was not to be prevented.

These instructions point directly to the emperor's wish to remove Ivan from Schlüsselburg briefly and support the view that the prisoner actually was brought to Petersburg where Peter saw him. This meeting must have occurred on March 22 because on that day Churmanteev received an order: "You may allow access to the prisoner by Lieutenant General Baron Ungern and, with him, Captain Ovtsyn, and everyone that Baron Ungern shall let pass." The emperor was to have been among them. On March 24 another order was sent to Churmanteev: "After the visits to the prisoner three days ago, it may be easy for him to have new ideas that will make him tell new lies. Therefore, I order you and officer Vlasiev, who is with you, to observe more strictly all of the prisoner's talk. Whatever new you hear or observe is to be reported to me immediately in all details and circumstances. Peter. P.S. Your reports are to be addressed directly to me."

Ungern again visited Ivan on April 1. Control of everything concerning the prisoner of Schlüsselburg was transferred on April 3 from Count Alexander Shuvalov to Naryshkin, Melgunov, and Volkov in consequence of the decree that gave responsibility for all affairs of the Secret Office matters to these three men. Simultaneously, new officers were assigned to the prisoner, Major Zhikharev and Captains Uvarov and Batiushkov.

Peter wrote Frederick that he was keeping Ivan under strong guard and that there was nothing to fear. He could be assured further that the unfortunate Ivan was not a dangerous rival because of his mental state. What heretofore had been known to a very few who kept the deep secret now spread to a wider circle, thanks to Peter's meeting in the presence of witnesses. Keith, the English ambassador, could report to his court completely accurate news of Ivan. The emperor, wrote Keith, had seen Ivan III and found him fully developed physically but with disturbed mental faculties. His speech was incoherent and strange. He said, by the way, that he was not the person he was thought to be, that Tsar Ivan long ago had been taken to heaven, but that he wished to retain the claims of the man whose name he bore.

A coup in the name of the grandson of Tsar Ivan V against the grandson of Peter the Great could originate only among obscure men without contacts in higher circles. For others there was one solution: to replace the father with the son and not break the hereditary line. On one hand this solution was a simple one because the son, Grand Duke Paul Petrovich, was a child and there would be no clash of wills or conflict in filial relationships. On the other hand, his infancy would deprive the movement of a leader, of unity, strength, and shape, and deprive it of concrete accomplishments. A new leader must be found among Russian subjects. But how could this be done? Many individuals and parties were involved.

CATHERINE'S DIFFICULT POSITION

Everyone's attention necessarily and naturally turned to Empress Catherine. She was well known and celebrated for behavior that contrasted sharply to her husband's. She was known and admired for her brilliant abilities, her charming and gentle treatment of people, her attention to every worthy person, and her respect for the Russian people and all that they held dear. Her influence on her husband could only be beneficial. But there was no such influence. The closest person turned out to be the most distant. The wife was cast out, as was her counsel. Catherine was the subject of open insults. She suffered along with the Russian people and a strong union was formed between them.[34]

Frederick II, having received very unsatisfactory news from Petersburg, thought at first that Catherine would be influential. Only on March 7 did Finckenstein, the Prussian minister of foreign affairs, write to Goltz that, according to the most trustworthy sources, Catherine lacked influence and contact with her would be harmful. Furthermore, she was not nearly as favorably disposed toward Prussia as the emperor was.

On December 31, 1761 Breteuil, the French ambassador, described Catherine's sad predicament to his court. "On the day set for extending congratulations on accession to the throne, deep sorrow was written on the empress's face. It is clear she will have no importance and I know that she seeks solace in philosophy. But this is foreign to her character. The emperor has doubled his attentions to Countess Vorontsova. It must be admitted that he has strange tastes. She is not smart. In appearance it is difficult to imagine a woman more ugly than she. She looks like a bar maid. The empress is in a most cruel position. She is treated with contempt. She is not indifferent to the emperor's treatment of her or to Vorontsova's arrogance.

"It is difficult to imagine that Catherine (and I know her courage and passionate temperament) will not undertake some extreme measure sooner or later. I know friends who try to calm her, but should she ask something they will sacrifice everything for her.

"The empress is winning general affection. No one performed obligations to the deceased empress more assiduously than she, duties prescribed by the Greek faith. The clergy and the people were very moved by this and are grateful to her. She observes the holidays and fasts punctually, things the emperor treats frivolously and the Russian people are not indifferent to. Finally, she neglects nothing in cultivating the love of all or the favor of individual personages.

"It is not in her nature to forget the emperor's threat to commit her to a monastery, as Peter the Great did his first wife. These factors, together with the daily humiliations, must terribly agitate a woman of such strong constitution and must erupt at the first opportune moment. The empress indulges freely in sorrow and gloomy thoughts. People who see her say that she is unrecognizable, that she withers and will soon go to the grave."

This last bit of news was written at the beginning of April. At the start of June, Breteuil reported: "The empress is displaying fortitude; she is loved and respected by all to the same degree that Peter is hated and despised."

This chronicle of events illustrates well Catherine's grievous position during the six months between December 25, 1761 and June 28, 1762. It shows us the transitions from gloomy thoughts to despair, which affected her health, and then from despair to firmness when hope of deliverance was reinforced and her adherents needed encouragement. Catherine says that from the day of Elizabeth's death her followers impressed on her the necessity of removing Peter and assuming actual rule herself. She began to favor their outlook from the day Peter humiliated her intolerably in public.

During the festivities celebrating peace with Prussia, the emperor proposed three toasts: to the health of the imperial family, to the health of the king of Prussia, and for the preservation of the joyous peace, the conclusion of which was being celebrated. When Catherine drank to the health of the imperial family, Peter commanded Gudovich, who was standing behind his chair, to ask the empress why she had not risen. Catherine replied that the imperial family consisted of only three persons, her husband, son, and herself and therefore she did not understand why she had to rise. When Gudovich communicated this reply, Peter again ordered him to go to Catherine and say with a curse word that she should know that two of his uncles, the Holstein princes, also belonged to the imperial family. But, fearing that Gudovich might soften the phrase, the emperor himself yelled the curse at Catherine. The majority of those dining heard it. At first the empress began to cry bitterly at such an insult but then, wishing to recover, she turned to the gentleman-in-waiting standing behind her chair, Alexander Stroganov, and asked him to begin an amusing conversation for the sake of diversion. Stroganov fulfilled her request.

But the matter did not end with humiliation alone. That same evening the emperor ordered his adjutant, Prince Bariatinsky, to arrest Catherine. Frightened by this order, Bariatinsky did not rush to carry it out. Meeting Prince George of Holstein, he told him of the emperor's instructions. The latter ran to Peter and convinced him to rescind the order. The order was recalled but no one could be sure that it would not be repeated, for orders were given at any pretext or to the benefit or cost of a particular figure. Catherine began to listen to the proposals of her adherents. Who were these followers?

It has been seen that Schwerin and Goltz believed Ivan Shuvalov, Melgunov, and Volkov to be the most dangerous figures waiting for the first opportune moment to remove Peter from the throne. But Frederick was to discover how wrong his diplomats were in their observations.

"The persons who were viewed as conspirators," he wrote, "were least of all responsible for the conspiracy. The real culprits worked quietly and carefully, hidden from the public."

Yet there was a time when Ivan Shuvalov had offered his services to Catherine. In one of her notes about events of her era, Catherine related that prior to Empress Elizabeth's death Ivan Shuvalov had approached Nikita Panin saying that "after refusing Peter and his wife and then sending them out of Russia, some are disposed to rule in the name of their son, Paul, who was then in his seventh year. Others want to send away only the father and leave the mother and son. All unanimously feel that Peter is incapable. Panin replied that all such ideas were merely means to internecine destruction, that it was impossible to change in one hour without revolt and calamity everything confirmed by oath for twenty years." Catherine continued: "Panin let me know about everything immediately, saying, by the way, that should the ailing empress confront the choice of keeping mother and son and exiling the father, there was considerable possibility that she would agree. But, thank God, her favorites did not proceed with this. Instead, they turned to thoughts of personal safety and began to try to win Peter's favor by courtly guile. In this they were partially successful."

This note, which was written after the event, perhaps much later, demands a certain explanation. The expression "thank God" is very understandable. Had the favorites proceeded to remove Peter from the throne, Paul would have been named emperor and Catherine would not have ruled. Furthermore, Peter's incapacity was not yet so evident and his removal could have led to what Panin suggested in his reply. "The favorites did not proceed" because Shuvalov received Panin's definite refusal to participate in the plan of the grand duchess [Catherine] and her followers.

Perhaps this refusal was insincere. Panin felt a refusal necessary to protect himself. He could have been suspicious of an offer coming from people unfriendly to him. That Panin's answer meant that he remained inactive is disproved by his conversation with Catherine about this proposal in which he impressed upon her the possibility of Elizabeth agreeing to the removal of Peter. Catherine does not tell us her answer to Panin. Perhaps it was decided to await a new proposal from "the favorites." But the latter, having received a curt refusal, thought it neither necessary nor safe to repeat their proposition. Perhaps it no longer interested them and, rejected by Catherine, they turned to Peter. In a few months theirs was the sad satisfaction of observing the suffering that Catherine experienced for rejecting their venture. Perhaps now they awaited a proposal from her. But the affair was begun and ended without them.

PANIN, RAZUMOVSKY, THE GUARDS

Prior to Elizabeth's death Shuvalov had turned to Panin with a proposal to change the order of succession. This suggests Panin's significance. His activity as envoy to Sweden during Elizabeth's reign has been mentioned frequently. Rumors circulated that he had been dispatched to Sweden as a result of court intrigue, that he had been sent by the Shuvalovs, who wished to remove a rival to Ivan Shuvalov. If this was true, it is understandably here that one finds the roots of his animosity towards the Shuvalovs and especially toward Ivan Shuvalov.

But even without this, there were other powerful reasons for hostility. Close as he was to Chancellor Bestuzhev, being, it may be said, his pupil, Panin had, in his fairly long stay in Stockholm, fervently carried out Bestuzhev's policy of fighting the dominant French influence there. Panin had matured and strengthened in this struggle. Hatred of France and the need to struggle against it became his political creed. Suddenly he was bidden to change his nature, in fact to be reborn, and to act in concert with the French envoy. That it was most difficult for the Russian envoy in Stockholm to do this is well known. He had to forsake his friends and bow to the French envoy who, now with increased means, did not wish and could not yield to the Russian envoy a position equal to his own. The more independently the Russian envoy acted, the stronger his spirit, the more burdensome his position became.

Panin could not bear this and he protested. We have seen the reprimand his protest earned. Humiliated by this reproof and depressed by his unbearable position, Panin ascribed all his misfortunes to the Shuvalovs. He accused them of rapprochement with France. Soon his protector, Bestuzhev, was overthrown. This he also ascribed to the Shuvalovs, and to Vorontsov, whom even earlier he had considered his enemy.

Now Vorontsov took charge of foreign affairs with the help of or, rather, under the influence of Ivan Shuvalov. Panin no longer could remain in diplomatic service and was recalled from Sweden.

Yet we have observed that Elizabeth did not like to take away positions from men outstanding for their capability and education. Thus the former envoy to Sweden received the important post of tutor to Grand

Duke Paul. Panin's new importance derived from the great trust of Elizabeth that this responsibility implied. This post brought him into contact with Catherine, who could not but sympathize with him as a figure close to Bestuzhev. It was this importance that moved Shuvalov to consult him on the question of elevating Grand Duke Paul to the throne upon banishment of his father from Russia.

Nothing came of this move. Peter III acceded to the throne and confirmed the misgivings of those who expected nothing good from his reign. It was more difficult for Panin than for others. True, there was a considerable cooling towards France. But the question was not of relations with France when a Prussian envoy, Goltz, guided Russian foreign policy. When policy affairs did not involve Goltz, it was only in those matters where Goltz's desires coincided with Russian interests, for example, in Danish affairs. Apart from reasons for dissatisfaction common to all Russians, Panin had special reasons. He could not maintain his influence for, given his sensibilities and habits, he could not join Peter's retinue and take part in his amusements. With his phlegmatic nature that pined for physical calm, Panin, more than anyone, could not bear the barracks style introduced by Peter. For this, the latter sharply voiced his dissatisfaction with Panin.

In Goltz's memorandum of March 30 to Frederick II, there is an interesting item regarding Panin: "His imperial majesty gladly agrees with your majesty's wish to include Sweden in the peace treaty. He told me that he will send Panin, the grand duke's tutor, there. This man is very capable. Therefore there can be no doubt of the success of the negotiations." Panin now faced going to Sweden and working, in accordance with Prussian demands, for the restoration of the absolution against which, he had fought strenuously, while previously in Sweden. But nothing could be done about it. He must go to Sweden for, in Peter's Russia, as the heir's tutor, he would lose his influence.

It was loudly claimed in Russia that Peter intended to divorce his wife, confine her in a monastery, and repudiate his son. Judging from Peter's character and the consequences of his behavior, anything could happen. He had ordered Catherine's arrest once already; Prince George's intervention would not help a second time. Related interests naturally drew Panin and Catherine together. She knew that she could depend on his assent to the change. She could be confident that during the change she would find him a man prepared to serve her with good counsel and capable of helping her in difficult circumstances. But there could be nothing more. Panin, with his character and turn of mind, could not participate actively in a movement intent on change. Even less could he stand at its head.

Panin was not among those close to Peter. Yet, even among men enjoying the special good will of the emperor, Catherine knew several persons whom she could count on. In one way or another they had given their loyalty to her. These were the grand master of Ordnance, General Villebois, Procurator General Glebov, Prince Michael Volkonsky, the nephew of former Chancellor Bestuzhev known to us in diplomatic and military matters, and the chief of police, Nicholas Korff. Some of these figures were motivated by patriotism. Others, aware that because of the general discontent, things inevitably would end badly for Peter, hastened in advance to the banner of the winning side.

But of all noble personages Catherine depended most of all on the loyalty of Hetman Count Kirill Razumovsky, who was living in Petersburg and, evidently, enjoyed the emperor's favor. Closeness to Peter could not inhibit his loyalty for, above all other inducements, none of those close to the sovereign could count on the next minute. Rumor had it that Peter wished to reward his favorite, Gudovich, with the hetmanate of Little Russia. Along with Hetman Razumovsky, his mentor Teplov was ready to serve Catherine. He was immoral, brave, intelligent, adroit, and wrote and spoke well. Teplov's zeal for change grew all the more since, by order of the emperor, he was sitting in the fortress for intemperate utterances. In an official notice concerning Teplov's relationship to the government at this time, we have an interesting decree of Peter III on March 23: "We most graciously have granted our state councillor and chamberlain at our Holstein court, Grigory Teplov, the rank of actual state councillor for his zealous service to us. We order him to remain retired as previously."

PRINCESS DASHKOVA AND THE GROWING CONSPIRACY

No matter how many men wished a change and no matter what their strength, no move could be made without the help of the guards. The guards were discontent. But it was necessary to shape and direct this discontent, and to prepare it for venting at the first opportune moment. Catherine found two instruments to this end. One was the eighteen-year-old Princess Catherine Romanovna Dashkova, born Vorontsova, sister of the favorite. After losing her mother in childhood, Countess Catherine Vorontsova was raised in the home of her uncle, Chancellor Michael Vorontsov.

A lively and talented girl, she learned foreign languages, especially French, and enjoyed and used them, particularly since there was no one in her circle who appreciated her sensibilities or mind and who attracted her.

With no one to match her liveliness, she abandoned herself to reading with the full passion of her nature. She read Bayle, Montesquieu, Boileau and Voltaire, which led to early maturity. This learning and passion for reading brought her together with another learned woman in Russia, a similarly fervent reader of Bayle, Montesquieu, and Voltaire—Grand Duchess Catherine. "Many of my uncle's friends," says Dashkova, "described me to the grand duchess as a young lady who devoted all her time to study. The respect she entertained for me evidently stemmed from this warm account. At the same time, the grand duchess aroused in me an enthusiasm and loyalty which led me into a sphere of activity about which I then thought little but which influenced the rest of my life. I do not hesitate in saying that at this time in the entire empire there were only two women, the grand duchess and myself, who read seriously. And, as her exquisite manner of treating people exerted an irresistible effect on those she cultivated, it is easy to understand how strongly she influenced a young creature like myself, barely fifteen years old, who was so receptive."

It is likewise easy to grasp that to the degree the grand duchess charmed the young Dashkova, the grand duke repelled a woman who had read Montesquieu and Voltaire. He spoke in vain to his favorite's sister, using a phrase dictated to him by someone: "Remember that it is far better to deal with crude people who are honest, such as your sister and myself, than with clever ones who suck out the juice of an orange and throw away the peel."

Princess Dashkova could not bear Peter's company. "The favorite pleasure of the grand duke," she said, "was smoking tobacco with the Holsteiners. They were mostly corporals and sergeants in the Prussian service. They were swine, the sons of German shoemakers. Evenings ended with balls and dinner in a hall bedecked with pine branches, German names matching the taste of the decorations, and talk this company found popular. They mixed in so many German words in conversation that it was necessary to know German in order not to be made fun of. Sometimes the grand duke held his celebrations in a small country house not far from Oranienbaum.[35] For entertainment there was punch, tea, tobacco, and the spirited game of "campis." What an amazing contrast to the spirit, taste, good sense, and decorum that prevailed at the receptions of the grand duchess!"

At the fearful moment when everyone was convinced that Elizabeth had but few days to live, Princess Dashkova visited Catherine at night with a question: "Can some precautions be taken against the threatening danger and to avert the calamity that is ready to overtake you? For God's sake, trust me, I will prove that I am worthy of your trust. Have you made a plan? Is your safety assured? Please give me instructions and tell me what to do." "I have made no plans," answered Catherine. "I won't do anything and I think that there is only one thing to do—meet events bravely, whatever they may be. I entrust myself to the Almighty and put all my hope in His protection."

The new emperor soon added to Dashkova's anxiety. Once he began to talk to her quietly, in broken phrases, it was easy to understand what was meant. It dealt with removing "her", as Peter referred to Catherine, and replacing her with Romanovna, as he usually called Elizabeth Vorontsova. "Be a little more understanding of us," he said to Dashkova, "the time will come when you will lament that you treated your sister with such disdain. Your interests demand that you learn your sister's thoughts and seek her favor."

Dashkova's husband had friends among the guards officers, Captains Passek and Bredikhin of the Preobrazhensky Regiment and Major Roslavlev and his brother, a captain, both in the Izmailovsky Regiment. These young officers agreed with Princess Dashkova about the need for a change in government, and the ardent young lady began to view herself as head of a conspiracy that would decide the fate of the empire. Besides the Roslavlevs, she met a third officer from the Izmailovsky Regiment, Lasunsky. She had been told that he had influence with Hetman Razumovsky. Dashkova wanted to enroll this wealthy man, popular among the guards because of his generosity, not knowing that he was involved to a greater extent than she suspected.

She was able to have direct contact with Nikita Panin because he was her uncle. She often approached him about the necessity for a change on the throne. Panin agreed with her at times, adding that it would not be bad to establish a government modeled on the Swedish monarchy. But Dashkova admits that she could not count on winning right away the trust of such a wise and prudent politician as Panin. Panin's favorite nephew, later famed as Prince Nikolai Repnin, was much more open with her. Once, after a banquet in the new winter palace, Repnin visited Dashkova at night and said in despair: "All is finished, dear cousin. Your sister received the order of Catherine and I am in the likely danger of being sent as ambassador, or more correctly, lackey to the king of Prussia." We have observed that Repnin's fears were justified. He was assigned to the court of Frederick II.

Dashkova admits that after Repnin's troubled visit she thought seriously about the enterprise. All the talk about accomplishing this undertaking that she had heard so far from her accomplices seemed to be unrealizable fantasies or plots lacking a definite principle, firmness or means of execution. Everyone agreed only that the emperor's departure for the army abroad might serve as a signal for action. Seeing that much remained to be done and the decisive moment was approaching, she turned to Panin for something definite. The scene was interesting because it is difficult to imagine a greater contrast than that between the cautious and lethargic Panin and his fiery eighteen-year-old niece.

The young woman began with the admission that there was a plot to stage a revolution. Panin listened to her carefully and began to insist on the need in such an event on holding to established institutions, on the necessity of the Senate's participation. Dashkova replied that this would be desirable, but difficult to do. Then Panin began to insist that Catherine's rights to the throne not be advanced and Dashkova had to yield. Rather, she should hold only the regency until her son came of age. Most of all, Panin expressed anxiety about the consequences of an overthrow, about the possibility of civil war. "As soon as we begin to act," replied Dashkova, "there won't be one man in a hundred to agree that the disastrous abuses aren't cause enough for any measures other than change in the person on the throne."

Finally, Dashkova announced the names of the accomplices: the two Roslavlevs, Lasunsky, Passek, Bredikhin, Baskakov, Khitrovo, Prince Bariatinsky, and the Orlovs. Dashkova had never seen some of these conspirators. Panin grew disturbed at how far she had gone without the empress's approval. Dashkova answered that she could not tell Catherine her plans because developments were still in doubt. Informing her might place the empress in a difficult position and subject her to needless danger. From her talk with Panin, Dashkova noticed that he lacked neither the courage nor the desire to join them, and that his reservations stemmed from not knowing how they were to act.

It is clear from Dashkova's account the kind of a plot this was, one that she considered herself to head. She knew of the strong general discontent, and saw the reasons at first hand. She grew irritated and thus understood well the irritation of others. She told some young officers of the need for change in favor of the empress who was, by general conviction, capable of providing a better future. The young officers agreed completely and named other young officers who also were in agreement. These men said it was imperative to launch the plot as soon as the emperor left to join the army. Dashkova spoke to Panin and he agreed that there was no other way to save Russia. But how was this to be done and what consequences would follow? Dashkova constantly used the word *conspiracy* but shows clearly that there was no conspiracy, merely talk. Dashkova very much wanted to draw Hetman Razumovsky into the circle of accomplices. She talked to Lasunsky and impressed on Panin the need for friendship with Teplov and through him influence on Razumovsky. But she learned nothing of the results of her efforts. Repnin had departed for Prussia.

According to Dashkova, it was known that the archbishop of Novgorod, Dmitry Sechenov, shared her views even though hampered by his high office, although he was not even among the accomplices. The uncle of Dashkova's husband, Prince Michael Volkonsky, reported general discontent in the army. The soldiers were angry because they were now being forced to fight against an old ally, Maria Theresa, and for the king of Prussia, whom they long had viewed as a sworn enemy. It was obvious to Dashkova that Volkonsky was quite prepared to help them. There is no basis for rejecting Dashkova's own statements about her activity. What is evident is that she wished a change in Catherine's favor and, at opportune moments, talked of her desire with others. However, her actions were limited to this. Her evidence is quite important, for she wished very much to magnify her role and place herself at the head of the conspiracy. Yet her own words suggest that her role was very small.

Foreign accounts of the events of June, 1762 exaggerated the role of Dashkova, just as they exaggerated the significance of Odart, whose activity they tied closely to Dashkova. But they did not demonstrate the precise role of the foreigner who knew no Russian. Odart was Piedmontese by birth. Vorontsov assigned him to the College of Commerce. Here he had difficulty, for he knew no Russian. Dashkova suggested that the empress employ him as secretary and so he appears in accounts by foreign observers. But Dashkova says that Catherine did not employ Odart as a secretary because, first, her foreign correspondence was very limited, and chiefly because, trying to win the sympathy of Russians, she did not wish a non-Russian secretary. Odart was made steward of a small estate that belonged to the empress personally. Dashkova maintains that Odart was not among those she trusted, that she rarely saw him, and did not see him at all for the last three weeks before the overthrow.

We have no basis for disbelieving Dashkova. But, although foreign accounts of Russia and Russian events usually are filled with errors, exaggerations, and confusion of every variety, we have no right to assume that Odart had no part in the June events or that his role was manufactured by him and repeated by foreigners on the basis of his boasting. In all probability, the clever Odart was used for Catherine's contacts with her loyal supporters just as, in 1758, the Italian jeweler, Bernardi, served Catherine in a similar capacity. Dashkova did not know that the empress was bypassing her in communicating with her followers.

Dashkova was unaware of Catherine's direct contacts with the man who more than anyone else advanced her cause in the army, Grigory Orlov. An artillery officer, Orlov was a graduate of the Cadet Corps, had participated in the Seven Years War, and stood out sharply from the crowd of his friends in personality, looks, and sociability. His vibrant, youthful nature (Orlov was twenty-seven-years old at this time) demanded forceful activity and Orlov sought its satisfaction everywhere, both in amusements for his friends and in the Masonic lodge and, finally, to raising a revolt in defense of his adored empress, whom danger threatened, a danger no less for Russia as a whole. Apart from Orlov and his brothers, according to Catherine's own witness, the twenty-two-year-old officer Khitrovo and the seventeen-year-old non-commissioned officer Potemkin "directed everything prudently, courageously, and actively" in the horse guards.

In Catherine's words, towards the end of June there were up to forty officers and close to 10,000 enlisted men among the accomplices in the guards. It turned out that there was not a single traitor among them. The accomplices were divided into four groups and their leaders met to make decisions. The real secret was kept by the three Orlov brothers. The execution of the plot was delayed until Peter's departure for the army. But it was decided that, should the plot be uncovered, the guards would be called out and Catherine proclaimed the ruling empress.

CATHERINE TAKES THE THRONE

As in 1741 when the overthrow was hastened by ordering the guards against the Swedes in Finland, the unwillingness of the guards to campaign against the Danes hastened Catherine's proclamation. The soldiers worried and the conspirators, to speed matters, began trumpeting that the empress's life was in danger. The emperor left for Oranienbaum with his favorite company while the empress remained at Peterhof. Peter was to arrive there June 29 for his name day. On June 27 the discontent among the guards grew stronger. The soldiers clamored that they be led to Oranienbaum against the Holsteiners. A soldier came to Captain Passek, one of the heads of the four detachments, and announced that the empress was probably dead. Passek told him that was nonsense. The soldier was not satisfied and went to another officer with the same talk. This officer did not belong to the conspirators and, learning from the soldier that he had seen Passek and the latter had let him go, arrested the soldier and went to report the case to Major Voeikov. Voeikov arrested Passek and sent a report to the emperor at Oranienbaum.

The news of Passek's arrest convulsed the entire Preobrazhensky Regiment[36] and disturbed the conspirators in the other regiments. It was decided to send Alexis Orlov to the empress at Peterhof[37] and take her to Petersburg. Grigory Orlov, with his brother, was to prepare everything for her arrival. Catherine observed that Hetman Razumovsky, Prince Volkonsky, and Panin knew of this decision.

She mentioned not a word about Princess Dashkova's participation. Rather, she said: "Princess Dashkova, the younger sister of Elizabeth Vorontsova, wished to attribute to herself the honor of this revolution. Not to mention her lineage, her nineteen years age of allowed no one to trust her. She said that everything passed to me through her. But for six months before she learned anything I had been in touch with all the leaders of the undertaking. True, she is quite intelligent, but her mind is spoiled by a monstrous vanity and peevish character. The leaders of the movement hated her, but she was friendly with empty people who told her what they knew, namely trivialities."

This evidence is actually quite fair and, as we have seen, is confirmed by Dashkova's own story. To be complete, it should be added that in all of this Dashkova displayed unusual zeal and self-sacrifice. Catherine felt duty-bound to distinguish and honor her. Catherine kept her peace in this matter, forgetting the contrast evoked between her words and deeds. The famous empress sometimes allowed herself such oversights when irritated by or prejudiced against someone displeasing to her. The moment when Catherine made this revelation about Dashkova was not one of the peaceful moments of her life. Dashkova's pretensions, and the resulting clashes with people to whom Catherine was strongly inclined, upset her. But, let us hear Dashkova's story of the events of June 27.

Panin was with her when Grigory Orlov arrived with news of Passek's arrest. Dashkova was upset but Panin, with his customary composure, conjectured that Passek had been arrested for some service irregularity. Dashkova asked Orlov to learn the reason for the arrest in greater detail. If he had been arrested for a crime against the state, Orlov was to return to her with the details. His brother was to be sent to Panin with the same information. After Orlov left, Dashkova sent Panin away under the pretense that she wished to compose herself. Then, donning a man's cloak, she left on foot for the Roslavlevs. Having gone just a short distance, she noticed a horseman riding rapidly toward her house. It seemed that someone whispered to her that this was Alexis Orlov, for she knew none of the brothers except Grigory. She cried out his name. The rider reined in, rode up to her, and when Dashkova identified herself, said: "I was coming to inform you that Passek has been arrested for a crime against the state. Four guards are standing by the door, two at the windows. My brother has gone to inform Panin and I have just been to see Roslavlev."

Dashkova then told him to order Roslavlev and Lasunsky to go posthaste to their Izmailovsky Regiment to receive the empress upon her entry into Petersburg. He, or one of his brothers, must race to Peterhof and beseech Catherine on Dashkova's behalf to take a carriage and come immediately to Petersburg where the Izmailovsky Regiment was ready to receive and pronounce her sovereign. Dashkova adds that the carriage-in-four in which Catherine was to ride from Peterhof was dispatched thanks to her letter to Catherine's chambermaid, Shkurina. Dashkova ordered the carriage to avoid difficulties that might arise in Peterhof from people who were disinclined to help her. Panin laughed at this precaution as superfluous.

Having talked to Alexis Orlov on the road, Dashkova returned home in terrible agitation and went to bed so as not to arouse the suspicions of her maid. Suddenly there was a strong knock on the door which caused her to tremble. She jumped out of bed and ordered that whoever it was be admitted. A young man, unfamiliar to her, walked in and said that he was

Fedor Orlov. "I have come to ask," he said, "whether it is not too early for my brother to go to the empress and bother her with a premature call to Petersburg." At these words Dashkova lost her temper. "You have lost the best time," she screamed. "How can you think of the convenience of the empress now? It is better to bring her to Petersburg in a faint than subject her to seclusion in a monastery or have her led onto the scaffold along with the rest of us." The young Orlov left, assuring Dashkova that his brother would go to Peterhof right away.

It may be said that if we accept all this as uncontrived, why can't we allow the following hypothesis. The leaders of the undertaking, disliking Dashkova and mistrusting the sister of the emperor's favorite, laughed inwardly at Dashkova's orders, for they and Catherine long ago had decided everything. Grigory Orlov visited her because he was looking for Panin. The meeting with Alexis Orlov, who was returning from the Roslavlevs, was accidental. Finally, the youngest Orlov came during the night merely to find out whether the other Romanovna had devised something for the benefit of her close relations. And, if she were loyal to the empress, did she, uncalled and unasked, intend to get involved in the affair? But let us leave supposition aside and turn to indisputable evidence. In the list of awards distributed following the events of June 28 is found: "To the hetman, Prince Volkonsky, and Panin 5000 in pension," and directly after this, "12,000 to Dashkova." Moreover, Catherine's note of August 5 has been preserved: "Grant Princess Catherine Dashkova 24,000 rubles for her excellent services to me and the fatherland."

Catherine occupied the Monplaisir pavilion in Peterhof. At six o'clock in the morning on June 28 she was awakened by Alexis Orlov who walked into her room and said in an utterly calm voice: "It is time to get up. Everything is ready for your proclamation." "How? What?" asked Catherine. "Passek has been arrested," answered Orlov. Catherine asked no further. She dressed quickly and got into the carriage in which Orlov had come.

Orlov was sitting on the driver's seat and another young officer, Vasily Bibikov, was by the door. Five versts from Petersburg they met Grigory Orlov and the younger Prince Bariatinsky, who gave his carriage to the empress, for her horses were tired. She drove right to the barracks of the Izmailovsky Regiment. Here the alarm was sounded and soldiers came running out to the empress, kissing her hands, feet, dress, and calling her their deliverer. Two soldiers brought a priest with a cross and the oath of allegiance was taken. The empress then was asked to get back in the carriage. The priest preceded them as they drove to the Semenovsky Regiment. The Semenovsky men came out shouting "hurrah!" Accompanied by the Izmailovsky and Semenovsky men, Catherine drove to the cathedral of Our Lady of Kazan where she was met by Archbishop Dmitry. A prayer of thanksgiving began and the rule of Empress Catherine and the heir, Grand Duke Paul, was proclaimed. From the cathedral of Our Lady of Kazan, Catherine went to the newly-built Winter Palace.

Meanwhile a rider from the Horse Guards rode to the third company of the Preobrazhensky Regiment after seven crying for them to go see the empress at the new Winter Palace. The roll of drums and the call to quarters were heard in the Izmailovsky Regiment and there was movement all around the city. Soldiers ran out to the parade ground. So did the officers, some of whom seemed completely unperturbed, as if knowing the cause of alarm. The officers remaining silent the soldiers, without orders, ran to the regimental grounds, loading their guns.

On the way they met Staff Captain Nilov who attempted to stop them. They did not listen to him and entered the regimental grounds. Here they found Major Tekutiev. He was pacing back and forth, deep in thought, not saying a word. When asked for orders he made no answer. The soldiers halted for a few minutes and saw a company of grenadiers moving along Liteinaia Street. Major Voeikov wanted to stop them and approached on horseback, cursing and with his sword drawn. The grenadiers paid him no attention. Voeikov began to strike at their muskets and caps with his sword. They cried out and went after him with their bayonets. Voeikov fled at full gallop. Fearing they might catch him on the Simeonovsky bridge, he turned right and rode into the waters of the Fontanka up to the horse's chest. Only here did the grenadiers leave him alone.

Seeing this scuffle, the third company marched, whereupon the remaining companies of the Preobrazhensky Regiment followed over other bridges to the Winter Palace. Here they took posts inside the palace. The Semenovsky and the Izmailovsky regiments, having arrived earlier, surrounded the palace and posted guards at all entrances and exits. A bishop left the palace with a cross to administer the oath to the Preobrazhensky Regiment.

In Catherine's words, the men of the Preobraezhensky shouted to her: "Forgive us for being the last to come. Our officers held us up. We have brought four of them to show our resolution. We wish the same as our brothers." The cavalry was in an unusual mood of happiness. The empress recalled the fearsome hate these guards felt for their leader, Prince George. Therefore she sent an infantry detachment to his house with the request that, to avoid trouble, the prince not leave his home. But it was too late. Some cavalry had been there, beaten the prince, and sacked his house.

In the new Winter Palace Catherine found the Senate and the Synod in session. Teplov quickly wrote a manifesto and drafted the oath. The manifesto read: "The danger that threatens the entire Russian state has become clear to all true sons of our Russian fatherland. Our Greek Orthodox faith was the first to feel the tremor, and then the violation of its traditions. In this way our Greek church experienced the ultimate threat, the danger of replacing Russia's Orthodoxy with another faith. Russian glory moreover, raised on high by victory at arms and much bloodshed, has been betrayed by the treaty of peace signed with the [German] scoundrel. Furthermore, the domestic order that is the salvation of our fatherland has been insulted utterly. Therefore, convinced of the danger all this represents to our entire loyal citizenry, we have been forced to act, accepting the help of God and His justice. We have observed with particular attention that the desire for this action among our loyal subjects springs of clear conscience and full good faith. We have acceded to the Russian throne and our all loyal subjects have taken solemn oath to us."

The manifesto truly was compiled in haste (á la hâte). There was very much to do. The empress emerged from the new Winter Palace and, on foot, received the troops stationed around it. More than 14,000 soldiers and guards were present. Earth-shaking shouts of the soldiers and the people greeted the empress. These forces and the Petersburg residents could be counted on. Now orders needed to be issued to the fleet, and coastal forces, and the forces stationed abroad.

To arrange for these orders, the empress went to the old Winter Palace with the senators and Teplov, who served as secretary to this extraordinary council. Admiral Talyzin was ordered to Kronstadt as plenipotentiary. A memorandum was sent to Vice Admiral Poliansky. He was to announce Catherine's accession to the admiralty and fleet, administer the oath, and do nothing of a military nature until further notice. Instructions went to Lieutenant General Peter Panin in Königsberg to replace Rumiantsev as head of the Pomeranian corps because Rumiantsev was suspected of devotion to Peter III.

Panin's instructions read: "We have, as of this date, successfully mounted the sovereign Russian throne. Observing your zeal and dedication to us, we now name you full general and instruct you to take complete command of the corps now under the command of General Rumiantsev. Upon receiving this, you are to return immediately with the corps to Russia. We intend to honor the new peace with Prussia; therefore take every precaution to avoid any cause of irritation. General Rumiantsev has been sent special instructions about transfer of command to you and his return to Russia."

Having reason to think that the military forces abroad might be needed in Russia and wishing thereby also to preserve peace with the king of Prussia, Catherine entertained no wish to join with him in war against Austria. Instructions to this end were sent to Chernyshev. "Our intention was and is to use all means possible to obtain a general European peace. Even so, the peace and welfare of our throne demand that you and your corps return to Russia immediately. Should the king of Prussia attempt to impede this, you and the corps are to unite with the nearest units of the army of the Holy Roman empress. As to the peace concluded recently with his majesty the king of Prussia, we decree in our imperial name that you solemnly convey to him that this peace will be honored sacredly and uninterruptedly so long as his majesty offers no signs of breaking it, especially now in view of the circumstances."

Finally, a memorandum was sent to Governor General Brown of Riga. "Since we have acceded successfully to the Russian throne by the wishes of the sons of the fatherland, it is incumbent upon you, in our faith in you, to take all measures necessary that the people's wishes, with God's blessing, be assisted through your good offices. In the opposite situation you are to employ all means and force to overcome all wrongful resistance. Do not consider anyone's standing and do not accept any instructions other than those signed by me."

Paper declarations would not suffice. The success of these instructions in the main depended on the decisions of Peter III. The defense of his rights, offered him justification for waging a struggle. He could join the army abroad quickly and find support in Frederick II who, "especially in these circumstances, could provide cause for disrupting peace," as was stated in the memorandum to Chernyshev. For this reason it was decided to pre-empt Peter III. Catherine, at the head of her loyal troops, wished to march to Peterhof. The Senate received a hand-written instruction:

"Honorable senators! I am now leaving with the army to confirm and insure the throne. I leave in complete faith in you as my supreme government to safeguard the fatherland, the people, and my son. Counts Skavronsky, Sheremetev, General Korff and Lieutenant Colonel Ushakov are to be present with the troops and they, as well as Privy Councillor Nepliuev, are to live at court with my son."

At about ten o'clock in the evening Catherine, on horseback and dressed in the uniform of the Preobrazhensky Regiment, in a cap decorated with oak-leaf clusters and with her long, beautiful hair let out, left Petersburg with her forces. Princess Dashkova, also on horseback and in Preobrazhensky uniform, rode at her side. These uniforms were of the old style introduced by Peter the Great and thus reflected the national spirit. The moment that Catherine was proclaimed the guards, as if on order, had thrown off the new uniforms introduced by Peter III, which they called foreign, and tore them up or sold them practically for nothing. Before the departure from Petersburg the chancellor, Vorontsov, visited Catherine with reproaches for her actions. Instead of replying, related Catherine, he was led to church to take the oath. Dashkova tells this differently. In her words Vorontsov, seeing his remonstrances ignored, moved away, refusing to take the oath. "Be assured, your majesty," he said, "that I shall never, by word or deed, bring harm to your rule. For proof of the sincerity of my words, order one of your most dedicated officers to keep my home under surveillance. But never, while the emperor is alive, shall I break my oath to him."

We have a letter from Vorontsov to Catherine on that same day, June 28. "Kindest sovereign! The untried fates of the Almighty have deigned to elevate you to the imperial throne. As my first duty I, in falling to your imperial majesty's feet, most humbly request you to remove me from my present post and magnanimously to free me from all responsibilities in order that I might end my remaining days in peace and quiet. Do not think, most kind sovereign, that I do not wish to end my life in service to your majesty for any other reason. I call God as my witness that I am in no condition, due to the exhausted state of my health and the daily ills that plague me, to carry out my duties as I would like. A similar request was made last year to the empress of blessed memory, and to the emperor upon his accession to the throne. But I have not had the fortune of being granted this request. This I await from the gracious hands of your imperial majesty together with your good will. I throw myself at your feet. With servile reverence I am, your imperial majesty, your servant, Michael Vorontsov."

It cannot be surmised from this letter that its author refused to take the oath. Besides, such action would have made a request for retirement superfluous. Without the oath there could be no service. In any event, Vorontsov remained as chancellor. Prince Nikita Trubetskoy and Count Alexander Shuvalov arrived from Peterhof. They also were taken to swear the oath. Catherine adds that they came to Petersburg to kill her. But Catherine knew these men so well, and their inability to take a life, that she could have stated something like this only in a state of great irritation.

Vorontsov, Trubetskoy, and Alexander Shuvalov came to Petersburg to obtain news but, according to some sources, this was a pretense to slip out of Peterhof away from Peter. We have seen that the emperor was staying in Oranienbaum. With him were Chancellor Vorontsov and his brother Roman, Field Marshal Count Münnich, Count Alexander Shuvalov, Prince Nikita Trubetskoy, Vice Chancellor Prince Alexander Golitsyn, the Prussian envoy Goltz, the three Naryshkins, Melgunov, Marshal Izmailov, Lieutenant Generals Prince Ivan Golitsyn and Gudovich, Privy Secretary Volkov, Privy Cabinet Councillor Olsufiev, the old tutor Staehlin, and several others. Of the ladies there were Countess Elizabeth Vorontsova, Countess Anna Vorontsova (wife of the chancellor) with her daughter Countess Strogonova. Countess Razumovskaia (the hetman's wife), Princess Trubetskaia (wife of Prince Nikita), Countess Shuvalova (wife of Count Alexander), the daughter of the prince of Holstein-Beck, Countess Brius, Naryshkina, and others.

THE LAST EFFORTS OF PETER III

On the morning of June 28, at the very moment that Catherine was being proclaimed empress of all Russia in the cathedral of Our Lady of Kazan, Peter, in Oranienbaum, was having the usual parade of the Holsteiners. After this, at ten o'clock, he left with his retinue in six carriages for Peterhof. Gudovich preceded him but suddenly returned, upset. He quietly told Peter that the empress had not been in Peterhof since early morning and no one knew where she had gone. The emperor lost his temper at this bit of news. He jumped from the carriage and went with Gudovich on foot through the garden to the Monplaisir pavilion. He entered but Catherine was nowhere to be found. Only her ball gown lay there ready for tomorrow's holiday.

When Peter, after many fruitless searches, was leaving Monplaisir, the rest of the group arrived. "Didn't I tell you that she was capable of anything!" yelled Peter. Incoherent talk and women's wails mixed with his curses. Then, in despair, he turned to look for Catherine in the garden. During these searches a peasant brought him a note from Bresson, whom Peter had elevated from valet to director of tapestry manufacture. The note carried news of the coup in Petersburg. This was the point at which Vorontsov, Trubetskoy, and Shuvalov left for Petersburg to get detailed information. At three o'clock a Holstein cannoneer arrived to relate that since morning there had been disturbances in the Preobrazhensky Regiment.

Because, according to rumor, the leader of the undertaking was Hetman Razumovsky, the elder Razumovsky, Alexis, who lived nearby at his estate, Gostilitsy, was sent for. The old man came but this did not help matters at all. Another measure was wiser: as a safeguard Lieutenant Devier was dispatched to Kronstadt to guarantee Peter this important base. While Teplov was drafting decrees and instructions for Catherine in the old Winter Palace, Volkov, in Peterhof, also was writing manifestos and decrees. The three soldiers sent to Petersburg to distribute these manifestos encountered Catherine on her way out of the city. They gave her all of the papers, saying they were very happy to join their brethren. Peter kept changing his mind. First he wanted to defend himself at Peterhof and sent to Oranienbaum for the Holstein force. This force arrived at 8:00 p.m. Later, Münnich's ideas won him over. The Holsteiners could not resist Catherine's large force. They were sent back to Oranienbaum and it was decided to sail to Kronstadt.

At ten o'clock in the evening Peter, with all the people at Peterhof, men and women, left for Kronstadt on a yacht and a galley. But, Talyzin, in the name of Catherine II, was already in charge there and Devier, sent by Peter, was under arrest. After twelve o'clock the galley and yacht approached Kronstadt. They were ordered to leave. The call that the emperor had arrived drew the reply that there was no longer an emperor in Russia, but an empress, Catherine II, and if they did not leave immediately they would be fired on with cannon.

Gudovich, goaded by Münnich, told Peter to pay no attention to the threats. All that was needed was for the three of them to jump ashore and in a minute the fortress and fleet would recognize his rule. But the frightened Peter hid below the deck. The women were weeping and wailing. The boats returned. Then Münnich proposed another plan: to go with oarsmen to Revel and thence by naval ship to Pomerania. "You will take command of the [Russian] forces there," said Münnich, "lead them to Russia, and I guarantee your majesty that in six weeks Russia and Petersburg will again be at your feet." But others found this plan too daring and counseled return to Oranienbaum and negotiations with the empress. This suggestion was adopted.

Having driven ten versts from Petersburg, Catherine stopped in Krasny Kabachok to rest the troops, who had been on their feet all day. Together with Princess Dashkova, Catherine rested several hours in a small room with one dirty bed for both. Their nerves were too strained to allow any sleep. But lack of sleep was not a problem. The empress and Dashkova were in high spirits and their hearts full of happy expectations.

Nikita Panin caught up with the group at Krasny Kabachok and after two o'clock in the morning wrote the Senate: "I have the honor to inform the Senate that her imperial majesty continues her march successfully. I have reached her and her regiments at Krasny Kabachok where they are resting. There is an indescribable and unabating fervor here for the undertaking, of this I assure you." Similarly, a report from the Senate was sent at two o'clock. "The crown prince is in good health and is in her imperial majesty's house. All is well in the city and orders are being carried out precisely."

The instructions forbade the passage of men and messages in or out of Petersburg. Thus, the secretary of the Chancellery of Posts[38] handed a note to the Senate given to him by the chief of the post stations. The chief had received it from Peterhof via a mailman. This note contained an order to the post stations signed by Ovtsyn, the procurator general. "Upon receiving this order, pick out fifty of the best horses, send them to the stables at Peterhof. Should Kostomarov, the aide-de-camp, demand a team of horses, give them to him." Kostomarov was arrested and when questioned related that Melgunov and Izmailov, citing an imperial decree of the former emperor, had sent him from Oranienbaum to Petersburg. There he was to tell the regimental commanders to bring their regiments to Oranienbaum.

At five in the morning Catherine again mounted and left Krasny Kabachok. There was another short stop at the Sergiev monastery. Here Vice Chancellor Prince Alexander Golitsyn met the empress with a letter from Peter. The emperor offered to share rule with her. Catherine made no answer. Then Major General Izmailov arrived and announced that the emperor intended to abdicate. "After his completely voluntary abdication I will bring him to you and thereby save the fatherland from civil strife," said Izmailov. The empress entrusted him to arrange the matter.

Following this arrangement Peter signed the abdication drafted by Teplov: "In my brief period of sovereign rule over Russia I have found the difficulty and burden actually to exceed my powers. Whether as sovereign or otherwise, I am unable to rule the Russian state. I have sensed domestic change leading toward collapse of domestic unity, and disrepute. Therefore, upon reflection, without prejudice and voluntarily, I proclaim to Russia and to the entire world that for the duration of my life I renounce all claims to rule over the Russian state. I do not wish to rule over Russia as sovereign or in any other way, or to seek such rule through the help of others. In this I give my word sincerely before God and the whole world. This abdication was written and signed by me in my own hand."

At five o'clock on the morning of June 29 a detachment of hussars under Lieutenant Alexis Orlov occupied Peterhof. One after another the regiments arrived and took posts around the palace. At eleven o'clock the empress arrived on horseback dressed in the uniform of the guards. She was accompanied by Princess Dashkova, who was attired similarly. Cannon salutes and soldiers' enthusiastic shouts rang out. After twelve o'clock Grigory Orlov and Izmailov escorted the former emperor and Gudovich to Peterhof, where they were placed in the palace's garden wing. Toward evening Peter was driven to Ropsha, the country palace twenty-seven versts from Peterhof. At nine o'clock the empress departed Peterhof and the following day, the 30th, she triumphantly entered Petersburg.

Subsequently, Frederick II, conversing with Count Segur who was going to Petersburg as the French envoy, observed: "In all fairness, Catherine is neither to be honored nor condemned for this revolution. She was young, weak, alone, foreign, at the edge of divorce and imprisonment. The Orlovs did everything. Princess Dashkova was merely a boastful fly in the carriage. Catherine was unable to rule anything. She leaped into the arms of those who wished to save her. Their conspiracy was senseless and fashioned poorly. Peter III's lack of courage, and refusal of the advice of the brave Münnich, ruined him. He allowed himself to be removed from the throne like a child who is sent to bed."

Despite the obvious acuity of this last phrase, we cannot accept the justice of this judgement. Frederick failed to explain what he meant by a properly planned conspiracy. What is evident is that the general malaise made it easier for energetic people to accomplish their ends. The movement was among the guards, but it became immediately apparent that Catherine similarly counted on the Senate and the Synod. Peter's resources were exhausted when the resistance of a few officers who wished to hold the regiments was broken. We cannot say that Peter III distinguished himself for his courage. Even had he accepted Münnich's suggestion, what basis was there for assuming that his reception in Reval and by the army abroad would have differed from that which he received in Kronstadt?

In any event, the rejoicing at Catherine's accession grew all the more because it was bloodless. Only the wine merchants suffered. "The day (June 30) was very beautiful and hot," related Derzhavin. "The pubs, cellars, and taverns were opened for the soldiers. A glorious feast commenced. Soldiers and their wives, seized by frenzied ecstasy and joy, hauled wine, vodka, beer, mead, champagne, and other expensive wines by the pitcher full and poured everything together indiscriminately into tubs and kegs, whichever was handy. At midnight the next day the Izmailovsky Regiment, drunk and gripped by pride and the giddiness of Catherine's selection of it among the other regiments to lead to the Winter Palace, assembled without knowledge of its commanders and approached the Summer Palace demanding that the empress appear and give assurance that she was well. The soldiers said rumor had it that she had been spirited away by the guileful king of Prussia whose very name all Russians hated. They were reassured by the duty officers, the courtier Ivan Shuvalov and Lieutenant Colonel Count Razumovsky, and by the Orlovs, that the empress was resting and that, thank God, she was in good health. But the men did not believe them and insisted that she appear. The empress was forced to rise, dress in the guards' uniform, and lead them back to the regiment.

"The following morning a manifesto appeared praising their fervor but also reminding them of military discipline and telling them not to believe inflammatory rumors spread by evil people wishing to upset both them and the general tranquilty. In the event of similar occurrences, their insubordination and similar impertinences would be punished according to the law. This very day the number of guard pickets was increased. Many, with loaded cannon and lighted linstocks, were posted everywhere, at squares and crossroads. These were the security arrangements in Petersburg, especially surrounding the palace which Catherine was to enter in eight days."

On August 11, 1764 the merchant Diakonov petitioned the Senate asking that he be reimbursed some 4044 rubles. This was the cost of the spirits pilfered from him during the successful accession of her imperial

majesty by soldiers and others who entered his house and took the drink
from the cellars. The Senate ordered that this petition, like that of the merchant Meder complaining of exactly the same pilferage, be sent to the chamber office for investigation. At the end of the year the Treasury College[39]
again suggested a report to her imperial majesty about pilferage of spirits
from taverns during her accession to the throne by soldiers and others. This
was refused inasmuch as a similar one existed dating to July 9, 1763. Its
approval must be awaited. But in June 1765 the Senate decided to submit
a report concerning the pilferage of June 28, 1762 in the sum of 24,331
rubles. It stated that the sums were correct and that the Senate recommended reimbursing the taverns by crediting the amount against liquor
license fees they owed, and granting a tax credit to the wine merchants.

II

EMPRESS CATHERINE II IN 1762

REWARDS AND RETURNS

The anxieties surrounding the seizure of power now receded. Now began
the more difficult anxieties of preserving it. People who helped win this
power must be rewarded. It was not an easy task, for everyone valued his
service dearly and looked around jealously to see if anyone had received
more for a lesser service. Only joyous faces were seen and enthusiastic
shouts heard. But underneath all this there was a whole sea of passions.
The price must be paid and satisfactory rewards distributed to retain followers while avoiding competition, clashes, and animosities among them.
People who had not participated in the coup who were prominent in the
previous reign could not be dismissed summarily, for excepting a very
few, they were unhappy with the previous regime and were not at fault
for the things that had upset the general populace. It was necessary to show
that none of the important and useful personages had lost anything as a
result of the coup. It had to be arranged that the past appear unfavorably
in every way and that there was nothing that couldn't be managed better
now.

In the previous reign hardly anyone was disgraced because it was instituted in an orderly way, without an overthrow. The new reign must display its superiority by not allowing anyone to be disgraced, even though it was the result of a coup. It was undesirable to suggest that important people were hostile to the new regime. The universal acceptance of the new reign, and the general sympathy for it, must be preserved. Rivalries naturally arose now among those considered insiders and among outsiders who acquired the rights of privileged insiders. Through unremitting care for the public good the people must be shown that Russia was truly rid of the terrible disorder that resulted from the absence of reasoned government. In foreign affairs, the peace demanded by the nation must be arranged. At the same time the stature and glory of the empire, which the previous reign was blamed for losing, must be restored.

All prominent participants in the events of June 28 were rewarded handsomely with promotions. The soldiers received court ranks too. Their rewards also included populated estates; some received 800, others 600, still others 300 serfs. Some received monetary rewards of 24,000, 20,000 and 10,000 rubles as well. Hetman Razumovsky, Nikita Panin, and Prince Michael Volkonsky received lifetime annual pensions of 5000 rubles. Princess Dashkova became a cavalier of the Order of St. Catherine and was given a sum of money. Grigory Orlov was made gentleman-in-waiting, Alexis Orlov a major in the Preobrazhensky Regiment. Both received the Alexander ribbon. Their brother Fedor was made a captain in the Semenovsky Regiment; all three received 800 serfs. Teplov received 20,000 rubles. Rich rewards were given to two brothers, the Yaroslavl merchants who were famous as founders of the Russian theater, Fedor and Grigory Volkov. This pointed to their participation in the events of June 28. They received patents of nobility and 700 serfs.

Catherine hurried to return two victims of the previous regime, the former chancellor, Bestuzhev, and the former procurator general, Prince Jacob Shakhovskoy. In her first days of rule the empress consulted primarily with Nikita Panin and the old senator and fledgling of Peter the Great, Ivan Nepliuev. It was important to her to have two more men distinguished for their abilities—Bestuzhev in foreign and Shakhovskoy in domestic affairs. On July 1 Prince Jacob, visiting Moscow from the country for a short time, was preparing to return when his stepson Lopukhin, a guards officer, arrived and with a troubled countenance announced that he had met two road carriages in the street. Kolyshkin, an officer of the guards who was sitting in the first, saw him, ordered them to stop, ran up to his carriage and said delightedly: "I congratulate you with our new empress, Catherine, whom God has elevated to the throne. I am now riding non-stop with her imperial majesty's instructions to Count Alexis Bestuzhev that he come immediately to Petersburg."

After this news Shakhovskoy postponed his trip to the country. The next day he received a copy of the Senate's manifesto concerning Catherine's accession and news that Prince Menshikov, who had carried the manifesto to Moscow, also brought orders for Shakhovskoy to proceed immediately to Petersburg. The large bell on the bell-tower called Ivan the Great already was ringing. The cathedral of the Assumption and the entire square were filled with people of all stations "who with joyful enthusiasm thanked the Almighty for this change toward improvement of the welfare of the fatherland."

Again finding himself in Petersburg as a result of this change, Shakhovskoy, in his first appearance at court, heard the most flattering remarks from the empress about his prior service. The wish that he again become a senator was voiced. "The daily favors occasioned me by her imperial majesty, and especially her long conversations with me regarding domestic affairs about which she needed to know, plus the trust shown, invigorated and made me indefatigable," recalled Shakhovskoy.

In the middle of July old Calchas [prophet of doom in the *Iliad*], who long before had foretold the recent events and planned for them, arrived from Goretov. Bestuzhev came directly to the palace and was received by Catherine as an old friend. The old man seemed quite senile. No one doubted that he would play a major role in the reign although no one could imagine his office since no changes were foreseen. Vorontsov remained chancellor and Panin, as before, was considered the empress's confidant. Catherine could not but return Bestuzhev and consider him a useful counselor. The old man had to be content with giving counsel on important matters, and he was asked always in the most flattering terms.

Catherine always addressed him as "Little father Alexis Petrovich!" But she did not wish to return the chancellorship to him. She well knew Bestuzhev's stubbornness in conducting his favorite, once-established system, and support of once-established relations. Especially now, given the tangled politics of Europe requiring Russia to develop new foreign relations, a chancellor of this kind was not needed. Furthermore, a chancellor of Bestuzhev's type was unneeded given the energetic Catherine's intention of leading personally. In Bestuzhev she actually sought a kind of private secretary.

Vorontsov, despite Catherine's disposition against him, was very convenient to have at hand at the beginning of the transition period. It was intended that Panin replace him. Although he too was a proud man, partial to his own system, he was more flexible thanks to his character, his deliberation and his caution. Basically he was fresher, more ready for innovation and more flexible mentally than Bestuzhev, who occasionally seemed to be a stranger from another world.

It is very probable that Bestuzhev dreamed of returning to the chancellery. Rumors reached him that he was thought too elderly for this demanding post. But there was another important obstacle to full recovery of his earlier influence. Had he been disgraced under Peter III he would have joined those held innocent of the injurious acts of Peter's rule who needed no exoneration. But Bestuzhev fell during the reign of Elizabeth, who had left a warm memory among the Russian people. Her memory was treasured even more following the six-month reign of her nephew. Bestuzhev felt a strong need for exoneration. A letter to his nephew, Prince Michael Volkonsky, is interesting in this connection. "The justice I request I find so necessary that, even though I have received many other kindnesses from her imperial majesty, I would consider it the height of happiness and joy to win it during the short life left to me. Otherwise, to my great shame and sorrow, my former arrest will leave me defamed as a criminal. This could lead me before my time to the grave. Even without this I hear already many things thanks to her imperial majesty's trust in me—that I am becoming childish, that my memory is gone, that I can't do anything. This is due to jealousy.

"Consider, your eminence. I am thought incapable of service because of my age or weak memory. But could anyone half my age of 70, persecuted and victimized for two and a half years and deprived of even the scantiest information about European affairs, master European politics as quickly as I did on my return? Always with God's help, and with my customary zeal, I certainly could still serve well. This would be the case were my present situation to improve and I were delivered from abuse. But I am not envious and, according to the proverb, I give the books to him who knows them best. I wish nothing for myself, neither glory, great fortune nor riches, for I have one foot almost in the grave. I wish only to leave an honorable name.

Yet it was precisely Bestuzhev's desire for exoneration that compli-
cated matters. To justify Bestuzhev meant to accuse Elizabeth. Nevertheless, Bestuzhev's wish came true. On August 31 a memorandum appeared
in which Catherine said: "Count Bestuzhev demonstrated clearly the
perfidy and forgery employed by men of ill will to bring this unfortunate
fate upon him. He awakened our sincere compassion and our happiness,
for in delivering him we act in concert with that fair justice with which
we commenced our rule. In this matter he further confirmed to us all that
the greater the charges the more care is required in their investigation.
Otherwise, censure can befall a blameless person.

"Our most gracious aunt, Empress Elizabeth, as is known to the world
and to us, was perspicacious, enlightened, and kind. In addition, she was
a just monarch. But, apart from God, the reader of all human nature, no
mortal can penetrate another man's mind. Thus, undoubtedly, in opposition to her desire and will, the matter of Count Bestuzhev unfortunately
for him, took a bad turn. In defense of her name and the virtuous men with
whom she ruled generously and humanely, from the sincere love and
respect we feel for her, and in the name of our Christian and monarchic
duty, we have determined that Count Bestuzhev be recognized by all as
more than ever worthy of our deceased aunt, his former sovereign, and
of our own special patronage. This we enact by our manifesto and return
to him with previous seniority, the ranks of general and field marshal,
actual privy councillor, senator, and cavalier in both Russian orders, as
well as a pension of 20,000 rubles per year."

Somehow propriety was preserved regarding the memory of Elizabeth. But in reading the manifesto what were the feelings of her survi-
vors, such as Trubetskoy, Buturlin, and Alexander Shuvalov, members
of the investigative commission in the Bestuzhev affair? Or of Vorontsov,
considered the foremost enemy of the latter; or of Ivan Shuvalov, who was
considered the man responsible for the most important events of the
second half of Elizabeth's reign? These men now felt it convenient not
to be too sensitive about this issue.

Bestuzhev had demanded and received a solemn vindication. But two
others also had been disgraced in his affair, two men once close to Catherine—Adadurov and Elagin. They received no high acquittal of charges
but simply were recalled and generously rewarded. Adadurov, formerly
a state councillor, was made privy councillor and president of the College
of Manufactures. Colonel Elagin achieved the rank of actual state councillor so that he might attend cabinet sessions. In a letter to Poniatowski

Catherine mentioned the men whom he knew: "Teplov rendered great service, Adadurov is delirious, and Elagin is here."

THE FATE OF THE FAVORITES

Of the figures close, or considered to be close to the former emperor, Gudovich, Volkov and Melgunov were arrested briefly, evidently to prevent them from any activity on behalf of Peter III. Initially there was the same fear of Goltz. It was even thought to intercept his correspondence, blaming the soldiers. This idea flashed briefly and disappeared. Gudovich retired to his village in Chernigov. Volkov, a talented man who could be very useful, was not allowed to retire. He was named vice governor of Orenburg. He was treated in exactly the same way that Elizabeth treated Nepliuev at her accession. But we shall find that Volkov would not remain as long on the Central Asian frontiers as Nepliuev. His letters of justification may have made an impression, especially when nothing was found in the accusations against him. Melgunov also was banished temporarily to the southern frontier.

Melgunov's name was closely linked to that of Ivan Shuvalov. It was easy for the latter to justify the forced financial levies imposed to aid Peter III in his plan for accompanying the army abroad. He did not hesitate to recognize the new regime. But neither Catherine nor the figures close to her liked him. Under Elizabeth his influence had been too large and too important in the destiny of everyone, beginning with Catherine. He was too prominent, his character too strong, and his presence too pervasive. And therefore he was inconvenient. He was known abroad and corresponded with personages whose opinions were valued highly in Europe. Catherine was told that, in a letter to Voltaire, Shuvalov disrespectfully referred to the events of June 28, ascribing them to the young woman, Dashkova. This added fuel to the fire. The most sensitive nerve had been touched, for Catherine assigned leadership of the movement to herself. The others were merely instruments. Her irritation with Shuvalov erupted in an unusually strong form. Shuvalov's position was most uncomfortable; he could hope eventually to extricate himself only by going abroad.[1]

Countess Elizabeth Vorontsova found a short sojourn abroad necessary because of her place in the previous regime. On June 29 she returned to the home of her father who, in the words of his other daughter, Princess Dashkova, was not at all happy with her return. He had never liked Elizabeth particularly and she did not accept his influence to the degree he wished. There is a note from Catherine to Elagin about Elizabeth

Vorontsova: "Perfilievich, have you told any of Lizabeth's relatives that she should not traipse into the palace? Otherwise, I fear she will flit over tomorrow for amusement." To avoid this, Elizabeth was banished to her father's estate near Moscow. After the coronation, when the court had departed from Moscow, Elizabeth settled there until her marriage to Brigadier Poliansky. Later she moved to Petersburg. Her relatives were angered because during Peter III's reign she had done nothing for them. Now they were angry at her sister Catherine (Dashkova) for the same reason.

Chancellor Vorontsov wrote in August to his nephew, Count Alexander, in London: "Concerning your sister, Princess Dashkova, I may inform you that we receive as much affection and use from her as we did from Elizabeth. We are closely related in name only. There is no sincerity, no openness, and still less help or hope that she will assist us. It seems to me that by disposition she is corrupt and conceited, and thinks mostly of vanity and her imagined wisdom. She spends her time in study and in empty things. I fear her caprices and immoderate behavior may so aggravate the sovereign empress that she might be banished from court, and that our family might suffer publicly as a result of her disgrace. True, she had quite a bit to do with the successful accession to the throne of our most gracious empress. For this we must honor and respect her greatly. But when her behavior and her virtues do not coincide with her merits, only contempt and oblivion can follow. I truly am not vexed or annoyed with her and wish her the best of luck. But her indifference to us is noticeable and basically unacceptable, especially since we do not benefit from her good fortune, and could suffer needless unpleasantries from her fall.

"Knowing this, you must exercise all due care in your correspondence with her. Insofar as her husband is concerned, he unfailingly shows us his former courtesy and affection and behaves prudently and moderately. Mr. Odart also participated in the happy change of rule and, being a very judicious man, his behavior is careful. He shows us his loyalty and gratitude. He received permission to go to Italy to bring back his family. He has been gone a month and so far has not received a reward other than 1000 rubles for his trip."

Count Alexander, having learned of the rise of one sister and the fall of the other, berated the first for not helping the second. "According to the news from Petersburg," he wrote Dashkova, "her imperial majesty grants you great favors. Therefore, I cannot justify your indifference to the fate of our sister Elizabeth, I do not even know what has become of her. For your services you should have asked one recompense, forgiveness for Elizabeth, in preference to the Catherine ribbon. Then you would not have betrayed your philosophical principles, which led me to believe in your indifference to worldly grandeur." Count Alexander addressed the empress directly to request mercy for his sister and received this answer: "You were not mistaken in believing that I have not changed toward you. I read your reports with pleasure and hope that you shall continue to act so commendably. You must stop worrying about your family's fate, regarding which I have noted your concern. I shall improve your sister's situation as soon as possible."

But this possibility was slow in coming and the impatient Count Alexander continued to needle Dashkova in his letters. He poked at her with rumors reaching him that she had taken everything belonging to her sister, Elizabeth, and had not given her even the essentials before she was sent to the country. Count Alexander wrote that it was not only family kinship but also gratitude that required him to defend Elizabeth. Dashkova wanted to catch him on this point and, dismissing rumors that she took possession of her sister's things, wrote that she could not so treat a sister whom she sincerely loved. "You know, of course," she wrote, "that I am not obliged at all to her or to any of my relatives. I love her and look after her in a sincere way. Since I am not forced to do this out of gratitude, my feeling naturally stems from a purer source."

Count Alexander grew even more annoyed. His response repeated with delicious irony the news of the exquisite humanity Dashkova practiced in comforting her unfortunate sister, that this was a monument to her self-sacrifice and would be held up for edification by posterity. "You are sensitive," he wrote, "in wishing to diminish the virtue of gratitude because this is something you do not have to any considerable degree. To free yourself you say that you are not obliged in any way to your relatives. Allow me to remind you that you are mistaken. First of all, you are obliged to your sister for your husband's assignment to Constantinople and for many other small favors. She delayed your journey to Moscow and offered you a house just given to her. As to our father, I shall not enlarge on your duties to him. Everyone knows moreover of the concern of your aunt and uncle for your education and for providing for your future."

The empress understandably found no reason not to be magnanimous to a personage known in Europe. Münnich was not dangerous because of his age and his foreign origins, which isolated him. Besides, the old man still could be useful. Under Peter III Münnich wished to be governor of Siberia or chief director of the Ladoga canal. He received neither appointment under Peter. Catherine appointed him general director of the Baltic port of Narva, of the Kronstadt and Ladoga canals and the Volkhov rapids.

So it was that the people who assisted in the change were rewarded. Opponents either were forgiven or punished very lightly in comparison with the punishments associated with other coups. It remained for serious and indefatigable governance to display the contrast between the new and the old rule.

CATHERINE AND THE SENATE

Among Catherine's papers there is a handwritten note in French. It relates that on the fifth or sixth day of her reign the empress attended a meeting of the Senate which she ordered held in the Summer Palace to speed government business. The Senate first discussed the sore lack of money. It also reported that the price of bread in Petersburg recently had doubled.

Catherine responded that she would direct her personal funds to governmental needs inasmuch as she was a member of the state and that everything belonging to her belonged to the state. In the future she would make no distinction between her personal interests and those of the state. With tears in their eyes the senators rose to applaud and thanked the empress for these sentiments. Catherine gave instructions that funds needed for government expenses be taken from her funds. To lower the price of bread in Petersburg she temporarily prohibited grain exports. Within two months this produced low prices for all foodstuffs.

The issue of allowing Jews to enter Russia then arose. This created great difficulty for the empress. "Eight days have not yet passed," she thought, "since I came to the throne, and was elevated to it for the defense of the Orthodox faith. I deal with a people that are religious, with a clergy with nothing to live on thanks to the rash confiscation of property. As is usual following an event of such magnitude, people are uneasy. To commence rule with a decree allowing free entry of Jews would be a poor way of calming people. Yet it is impossible to say that the free entry of Jews is harmful." Senator Prince Odoevsky led Catherine out of this difficulty. He arose and said: "Would it not be pleasing to your imperial majesty to see what Empress Elizabeth personally wrote in the margins of a similar memorandum?" Catherine asked to have it brought and read: "I do not wish self-interested profit from the enemies of Christ." Having read this, Catherine turned to Procurator General Glebov and told him: "I wish to have this matter postponed."

In the journals and the protocols of the Senate we do not find detailed information which appears in Catherine's note. The Senate documents show that from the day of her accession to September 1, when Catherine left for the coronation in Moscow, she visited the Senate fifteen times. Her first appearance was registered on July 1. At this session the Senate reported to the empress that on June 27 it had received instructions from the former emperor about building nine, or at least six, ships for the forthcoming campaign of 1763. All timber, regardless of ownership, was to be requisitioned. The Senate stated that the average owner would be ruined by this. There were no funds and no men for such an extraordinary building project. Furthermore, there was no need for it. Catherine annulled this decree, just as she did others, including one of June 27 disallowing deferments of bank payments and one of May 24 about creation of bank notes. On the following day, July 2, Catherine was again at the Senate to cancel all changes in the regiments introduced by Peter III. On July 4 an order instructed the Hetman of Little Russia, Count Razumovsky, to take command of all infantry regiments near Petersburg and the garrisons of Petersburg and Vyborg. Count Buturlin was to command the cavalry regiments situated near Petersburg.

On July 6 Catherine visited the Senate after ten o'clock with a manifesto, bearing her signature, that contained a thorough description of her accession. "The fatherland aroused itself," the manifesto read, "seeing above it a ruler and sovereign who, rather than concern for the welfare of the state entrusted him, enslaved himself to his passions." Then follows an indictment of Peter's disrespectful behavior at the deceased empress's coffin. "He looked with merry eyes at her coffin and spoke ungratefully about her." Then "first of all he moved to assault the ancient Orthodox faith in a willful way, having himself abandoned the church of God and forgotten prayer. When conscientious citizens, observing his irreverence for the icons and contempt and abuse of church rituals, dared to mention this to him with prudence and humility, they barely escaped the consequences that a willful, unrestrained ruler not subject to any human court, could wreak. Later he began to think of ravaging churches, and even ordered some to be demolished. Laymen of fervent faith and sometimes of weak health who were unable to leave their homes, were forbidden by law to have God's churches in their homes.[2]

"He also disdained natural and civil law. He had one son, granted to us by God. At Peter's accession he did not wish to proclaim him heir, an act done arbitrarily for the ruination of our son and ourselves. He intended either to renounce completely the rights received from his aunt or to give the fatherland into foreign hands, forgetting the natural law that no one can grant another a greater privilege than one he holds himself. He neglected all the law of the land, disdained all judicial affairs, and wished to hear nothing of them. He squandered government funds through withdrawals harmful to the state. Following one bloody war, he wished to commence a new one that was untimely and of no benefit to Russia whatsoever. He hated the guards regiments that always had served his sainted predecessors loyally, and began to employ them in useless ceremonies. He splintered the army with so many new regulations that it no longer seemed to be an army belonging to any one ruler. It was done as if to enable soldiers to usurp their leaders. He imposed on the regiments the foreign views, sometimes even corrupt ones, and not those that would create unity through uniformity."

There are some details regarding Peter III's abdication in the manifesto: "He sent us two letters, one right after the other. The first came via our vice chancellor, Prince Golitsyn, in which he requested that we allow him to return to his homeland, Holstein. The second came via Major General Michael Izmailov. In it he voluntarily tendered his abdication and said that he no longer desired to rule in Russia. Furthermore, he asked that we permit him to go to Holstein with Elizabeth Vorontsova and Gudovich. Both letters were full of endearments even though sent several hours after he had ordered us killed. This exact fact was communicated and truly confirmed to us by the men to whom this matter was entrusted."

The manifesto ended with this promise: "Our sincere and true wish is to prove in actual deed how much we want to justify the love of our people for whom, we acknowledge, we have been placed on the throne. In the same manner we solemnly pledge our imperial word to guard all domestic institutions of our cherished government in order that each branch of government in the future shall have limitations and regulations providing for the proper order. In this way we hope to preserve and guard our autocracy and empire, which misfortune has buffeted somewhat. We hope to keep all true sons of the fatherland from injury and despair."

After reading this manifesto the empress "asked the Senate for the original of Peter III's abdication of rule of Russia. Having read it, she ordered it stamped with each senator's seal and preserved in the Senate. It was read in the Senate and so sealed."

THE DEATH OF PETER III

That very day, July 6, an event occurred which necessitated a new manifesto. News came of the violent death of the former emperor in Ropsha. Dashkova says: "I found the empress in complete despair. It was clear which difficult thoughts troubled her. Here is what she told me: 'This death brings inexpressible horror to me. The blow shatters me.' "

An announcement appeared on July 7: "On the seventh day after accepting the Russian throne we received news that Peter III, the former emperor, experienced a hemorrhoidal attack, as he had frequently in the past, and fell into a most severe colic. On this account, disdaining not our Christian duty and holy commandments which must be exercised on behalf of those near us, we immediately ordered that everything necessary for his health be sent to him to prevent ill effects and for rapid recovery. But to our great sorrow, last night we received a message informing us that, by the will of God, he had died. Therefore we gave instructions that his body be brought to the Nevsky monastery for burial there. We exhort and admonish all loyal citizens through our imperial and maternal word to pay last respects to the deceased without remembrance of adversity and to pray to God for the salvation of his soul. This unexpected destiny is the will of Providence, the ways of which are unknown to us. What lies in store for our throne and the fatherland is known only to It."

The day after publication of this manifesto, July 8, Nikita Panin arose in the Senate with these words. "I know of her imperial majesty's intention to attend the burial of Emperor Peter III at the Nevsky monastery. Because her magnanimous and forgiving heart overflows with sorrow and deepest grief at this early and accidental death of the former emperor, from the moment she received this news she has been in continual shock and tears. Although respecting the necessity of this duty, Hetman Count Razumovsky and I nonetheless have suggested that her majesty, to guard her health and out of love for her Russian fatherland, set aside this intention in concern for the welfare of her loyal citizens and to avoid many consequences. Her majesty has not given her blessing and I find it necessary to ask that the Senate as a whole, in its devotion, request this of her."

"The Senate, feeling the justice of Senator Panin's suggestion, immediately visited her majesty's private chambers and humbly requested that she not attend at the Nevsky monastery. She resisted for a long time until at last, seeing the persistence of the Senate and the humility and fervor of the request, she agreed to a change in her plans." Peter III was buried at the Alexander Nevsky monastery.

It is unknown at whose inspiration the Senate found it necessary to display a further sign of its devotion to and sympathy for the events of June 28. On July 17 Lieutenant General Betsky was called to the Senate to hear this proposal: "Her imperial majesty has been so generous in her motherly devotion to her subjects to accept the imperial throne that these magnanimous acts must remain long in the hearts of true sons of the fatherland. The Senate feels devotedly duty-bound to erect a monument to her imperial majesty's immortal fame. You have been summoned because of your knowledge in these matters. Accordingly the Senate leaves the monument to your judgment. You are instructed to transmit to the Senate your plans regarding statues, obelisks, and medals." Betsky responded that he considered his assignment to such a great undertaking a very happy event. Although he felt unequal to the task, he hoped his long experience abroad and acquaintance with numerous learned and talented men would help him complete his task to the satisfaction of the Senate.

ECONOMIC MEASURES AND DOMESTIC AFFAIRS

Surrounded by all of the activities born of the events of June 28 and July 6, the Senate continued its work. This demonstrated that the new government wished to honor its promises. The empress attended the session of the Senate on July 3 and ordered that the price of a pud of salt be reduced by a grivna.[3] She wanted the to lower the price even more as soon as possible. This reduction totaled 612,021 rubles. This sum was to be made up from other revenue. A personal decree appeared on July 12 stating that 300,000 rubles each year of the annual one million salt tax revenue be applied to this deficit annually. The rest was to be obtained from the recoinage of copper money.

This decree amplifies Catherine's statement regarding the donations of her private funds to the government. On July 23 the Senate received these instructions: "The previous reign exhausted the Treasury and increased needless expenses. As a result, progress has been minimal. The Senate must strive to: (1) recover funds lent by the Treasury (2) sell *to the nobility* felled timberlands previously used in defense lines, and vacant land. This will assist many of them to improve their estates and will help the Treasury in this period of deficits. (3) The military and civilian staffs should be reviewed. Measures necessary to improve them shall be reported to her imperial majesty. (4) It is necessary that the colleges and chancelleries be staffed by capable men. Good service should be rewarded properly. Officials having limited means should have no reason for graft. Each is entitled to a decent salary. The required funds are to be found in sources other than new taxes on the populace and reported immediately to her imperial majesty. (5) Slanderous lawsuits must be stopped and legitimate means found to render satisfaction to everyone."

Catherine repeated Elizabeth's decree of August 16, 1760 about graft in the strongest terms. She directly referred to the evil habit inherited from old Russia of viewing service as linked to the right to exact contributions[4]. The personal signed decree of July 18 states: "We have heard much concerning this for a long time. Now we have observed the extent to which in fact graft has grown in our government. When someone seeks a position, he pays. When someone defends himself against charges, money protects him. Plaintiffs strengthen their crafty intrigues with gifts. Many judges turn their bench, from which they dispense justice in our name, into trading centers. They transform the calling of judge, entrusted to them to be performed unselfishly and impartially, into an income-producing office seemingly designed to improve their finances. They do not view it as service to God, sovereign and fatherland. They accept loathsome bribery to convert slander into legitimate charges and the pillage of state revenues into state profits. Sometimes they even make the pauper rich and the rich paupers.

"These models, found in high places since they have no fear at all, are followed by even minor judges in distant places, stewards, and various investigative officials. Money is accepted for illegal activity and fees are attached citing non-existent regulations. This occurs in matters that otherwise can only meet our favor. Our heart was troubled when we heard from Lieutenant Colonel Prince Michael Dashkov, a guards cuirassier, that Jacob Renber, the registrar of the Novgorod provincial chancellery, took money from the poor for the recent administration of the oath of loyalty to us. For this we have ordered Renber sent to Siberia for life. Nor shall anyone charged with extortion, so odious to God, escape our anger, for before God we have pledged justice and mercy to the people."

In the note cited Catherine complained that prior to her reign "almost all forms of trade were granted to individuals as monopolies[5]. Accordingly, measures against monopolies could be expected early in the reign. Regulations governing trade in fact appeared on July 31. (1) The grain trade was permitted at all ports. Duties were set at half those charged at Riga, Reval, and Pernov. Renewed was Peter the Great's rule allowing grain exports only if the Russian price was cheaper. (2) These regulations applied also to salted meat and to livestock. (3) The port of Archangel received status equal to that of Petersburg except that the higher duty remained in force. All ports and customs offices were allowed to accept all goods traded at Petersburg. (4) Rhubarb was to be freely-traded. (5) Potash and tar remained under governmental supervision to preserve forests, as Peter had intended. (6) Free trade in pitch was established. (7) Flax and bristle exports were permitted. (8) Export of linen yarn was prohibited. (9) Duties were removed from silk imports and from export of beaver pelts. Shemiakin's privileged status in this trade was withdrawn. (10) The Chinese trade was exempted from duties. (11) Farming out in the seal and fish trade was forbidden. (12) Farming out tobacco was prohibited. Shortly thereafter farming out of customs to Shemiakin was halted.[6] He had held it since 1758, paying two million rubles annually into the Treasury. The franchise was revoked for improper administration and breach of contract.

The Senate, having instituted the instructions of July 3, reported that the price of salt could be reduced by another grivna. Salt could then be sold in Russia for thirty copecks per pud; in Astrakhan and Krasny Yar where salting of fish was widespread, at ten copecks, and in Archangel for fifteen copecks only to fishermen salting fish. The transport of Lake Elton salt to Nizhny Novgorod cost the treasury much money. Furthermore, it was black and not of good quality. There was a better salt, Iletsk salt. Efforts should be made to obtain it. Salt should be sold by the Treasury, but trade in it should be allowed as well. Salt traders should be given salt at thirty copecks per pud. There was no risk that they would sell it at a high price, falsify the weight, or mix it with sand because purchasers would buy from the Treasury.

The drop in the price of salt by another grivna meant a loss of 604,027 rubles annually. To meet this deficit the Senate proposed new taxes: (1) Distilled spirits sold in taverns throughout the country at thirty copecks per pail[7] and five copecks for pails of beer and mead. It was calculated that this would yield 352,565 rubles from liquor (for 1760 and 1761) and 182,559 rubles from beer and mead. The total sum would be 635,122 rubles. This tax was permissable because tavern liquor sales were voluntary and therefore not burdensome. (2) Twenty copecks per measure of grain for beer instead of five copecks. (3) Farming out of inns to the highest bidders. (4) Sale of salt at the Treasury price and its export. (5) A tax of two percent on promissory notes in litigation.

Elizabeth's measures to aid merchants who suffered severe losses in the fire of June 29, 1761, when warehouses of hemp and other goods burned, remained without action. Catherine demanded a report from the Senate. The Senate stated that on March 21 the former emperor approved grants to merchants of half of the total lost in the fire. The funds were to be advanced by the Copper Bank without interest for ten years. Payment had not been made because funds of the Copper Bank had been directed to the most pressing needs. It was unlikely that such a large sum could be drawn on the bank in the future.

As a consequence, the Senate began deliberation on the report prepared for the deceased empress but unconfirmed because of her death. This report proposed that half of the sum lost by the merchants be credited to them in import-export duties at the port of Petersburg. The term would be five years. The empress approved this plan. To avoid similar disasters she instructed the Senate to plan for stone warehouses. If the Senate could not find funds for these structures, she would advance a loan.

In describing the distressed state of the empire at her accession to the throne, Catherine said: "Practically all peasants belonging to monasteries and factories disobeyed the authorities. Peasants of the nobility began to join them in disobedience. Major Generals Alexander Viazemsky and Alexander Bibikov were sent to deal with the refractory industrial peasants. They resolved complaints against factory owners on the spot. More than once they had to resort to force of arms, even cannon. The unrest did not end until the Goroblagodatsky Works reverted to the Treasury because of the two-million-ruble debt owed by Count Peter Shuvalov. Similar unrest occurred at plants owned by the Vorontsovs, the Chernyshevs, the Yaguzhinskys, and others.

"The Senate's indiscriminate distribution of these factories and the peasants assigned to them caused this entire harm. These industrial disturbances found no end until my manifesto of 1779 dealing with the labor of industrial peasants."

One of two things must be assumed. Either the disturbances halted because of the transfer of factories from private into government hands, or as a consequence of the legislation on laborers. If the latter is accepted, all of the harm cannot be attributed to the Senate's distribution of the plants to private individuals.

On the ninth of August the empress personally accepted a memorandum at the Senate dealing with factories. It proposed that the Treasury receive ten percent of all private production of copper, wrought iron, cast iron, and all other products manufactured in private factories. Plants currently being built would be exempted for ten years. Catherine signed it as follows: "Let it so stand. Concerning the distribution of government plants and the peasants attached to them, an investigation is to be undertaken." At this session she instructed the senators (1) to determine "the measures necessary for the much-needed preservation and increase of forests[8], and (2) that Prince Jacob Shakhovskoy head a commission, as part of the project for a code of laws, to examine the civilian ranks of state service."

Earlier, on July 3, Catherine had signed a decree concerning the peasant disturbances. "The welfare of a country, in accordance with the laws of God and of man, requires that all who have acquired their estates and rights legitimately be safeguarded in them. Likewise, each is to remain within the limits of his duty and his calling. Therefore we are determined inviolably to maintain the nobility in their estates and holdings and render the peasantry obedient to them." But news of new peasant uprisings continued. In the presence of the empress, on July 19 the Senate heard the report of Major General Tevkelev on rebellious peasants in Kazan and Orenburg provinces.

Catherine issued instructions on July 9 that chapels in private homes, closed in the previous reign, be legalized. The question of monastic landholding was another, more difficult question. Catherine, while attending the Senate on July 3, gave instructions to study the clergy for the purpose of finding satisfactory means for its support. The clergy was impatient and had petitioned for the return of its estates. On the fifth of July the empress transmitted this request to the Senate for discussion and a report on its findings.

More discussion! Meanwhile Metropolitan Arseny (Matseevich) of Rostov, in a letter to Count Bestuzhev, portrayed the effects of Peter III's decrees. "I should not burden your lordship with a request at this time.

However, dire need demands it, for with the removal of the ecclesiastical estates and monastic lands, starvation threatens. Previously, all our grain was on our estates, in granaries. No grain was kept in church buildings other than that already ground and ready for use. When the decree was issued the military governor of Rostov immediately sealed all granaries on church estates. He inventoried all livestock and fowl and assumed control of them. He left the clergy, our lay workers and myself without subsistence. There will be nothing to eat after the supply in the drying room is consumed. There will be no one to celebrate the liturgy and nothing to celebrate it with. Everyone will be compelled to go out into the world with the beggars. I humbly beseech you to show mercy to the houses of God, that your efforts return the patrimonies to us. A small number of horses was left to us, but there will be nothing to feed even them. We are not sorry that our horses, with mares and foals, were taken to Petersburg by the colonel from the College of War. He was assigned specifically for this purpose. We do lament that these horses, of such fame and quality, apparently were confiscated not for the sovereign's use but because we seemed guilty of something. Our military governor in Rostov is Councillor Peter Protasiev. Isn't it possible to have him transferred?"

Shocked by Peter III's decree, the clergy exchanged letters of lamentation. Metropolitan Timofey of Moscow wrote to Arseny of Rostov: "Insofar as the misfortune that you mention is concerned, this sad metamorphosis has touched us all. It constrains our life and causes tribulation (nunc non solum vestram sanctitatem, sed omnes nos dolenda ista tetigit metamorfosis, quae vitam nostram ad gemitus et dolores ducit)." Archbishop Ambrose wrote to Arseny on July 15: "I greet you on occasion of the general happiness inspired by the accession of her imperial majesty to the throne. Thank God that we have been delivered from the yoke of ideology. Now, as you can observe from the manifesto (concerning the coronation), we request your grace to visit Moscow in September and assist with this matter." Metropolitan Timofey wrote Arseny on August 2: "I received your epistle on August 1 and noted sadly the unhappy circumstances that you mention. In our area these measures occurred in outlying areas only. Livestock was inventoried and everything taken away. Moscow did not experience such insolence. All horses were listed but to this day they have not been confiscated and remain in our hands. But, this is small comfort, for we look with sorrow on the irreparable harm the peasants visited on our lands. Timber cut, hay plundered, and in places small livestock and fowl taken before the inventories. In other places they were picked clean during inventory—ponds emptied of fish. One can only imagine the devastation done by officers during the inventory, and by the peasants as well. Even near Moscow, at my Cherkizov pond, the inventory officials dared fish more than once. However, they were replaced more than once for this also. In these disturbing circumstances, hope is our sole joy." But the metropolitan ends his letter sadly: "Hope is being destroyed by dissension among the brethren (spem mutat discordia fratrum)."

The Senate drafted a resolution on July 16 dealing with the clergy's petition for the return of confiscated estates. (1) The estates were to be returned. (2) All peasants, in addition to the tax of seven grivna per soul, were to be assessed a ruble each. The Treasury would use fifty copecks of each ruble for support of invalids; the church authorities at monasteries and other holdings to which peasants would be returned, would receive the other fifty. (3) Peasants were not to be governed by monastic lay workers[9] but by elected men and elders, selected annually by the peasants themselves.

The Senate and the Synod conferred on July 18 to discuss this report. The clergy was satisfied with the first point. Regarding point two, Afanasy of Tver said that money payment would be difficult for the peasants. The fifty copecks per ruble for upkeep of monasteries and seminaries was not enough. In his opinion, the policy of the Synod during the reign of Elizabeth should be restored; namely, the clergy should contribute 300,000 rubles yearly. Collections for bishops and monasteries should be left to them.

Gideon of Pskov and Benjamin of Petersburg joined the prelate of Tver. Palladius of Riazan supported the Senate's position, as did Dmitry Sechenov of Novgorod. This was the "dissension among brethren" lamented by Timofey of Moscow. Dmitry of Novgorod felt it imperative to create a commission of laymen and clergy to compile organizational charts for monasteries, bishoprics, and seminaries. All prelates agreed with the Senate that peasants be supervised by their own elected people.

Dmitry Sechenov's suggestion of a study commission was accepted because only its findings could determine whether fifty copecks was enough, and all arguments and complaints ended. Naturally, the commission dragged out the matter. Then arose the question of supporting the monasteries and bishoprics while a decision was pending. Should lands be returned prior to a decision?

That Catherine found the question difficult is seen in her letter of August 8 to Bestuzhev. "My dear Alexis Petrovich. I ask you to look over the enclosed papers and give me your opinion. The problem is whether to create the commission without having returned the estates, or whether to return the land and then form the commission. Please help with your advice."

Bestuzhev's counsel, perhaps influenced by the letter of the prelate of Rostov, resulted in Catherine's decree of August 12 which returned all synodal, diocesan, monastic and moveable and immoveable church property to allow appropriate support of the clergy and its management of the same. The College of Church Landed Property was instructed to withdraw and the officials assigned to manage church holdings to depart.

This was Catherine's activity in domestic affairs in the first two months of her reign. It was a difficult time for her. The transition of June 28 could not pass without ethical consequences, without a certain ethical malaise. Many years of skilled, firm and auspicious rule were needed for Catherine to establish her authority and presence in Russia and Europe, and the legitimacy of her rule. At first her acceptance was not universal, and Europe lacked confidence that Catherine would be able to hold the throne.

These circumstances led Catherine to cultivate her followers and to increase their number. She had to be cautious, make concessions, and compromise. Catherine wrote Poniatowski that she must be exceedingly careful, that people were watching her. "I shall have to do a thousand more strange things," she wrote. "If I make concessions, I will be admired; if not, I do not know what will happen."

Let us assume some conscious exaggeration in these words. Let us assume that Catherine wished to emphasize her difficulties in order to keep Poniatowski away from Petersburg. But there was truth in the exaggeration. Catherine clearly did not believe she would have to do a thousand strange things. But she did realize that the insistence of some powerful men to appoint a permanent council was one of them. This made her very uncomfortable, especially since the leading advocate of a council was Nikita Panin, whose views were well known.

The very men who, at Peter III's removal, planned to place his young son on the throne and proclaim Catherine regent until his majority, now insisted on a permanent council. Why? Did they want to guard against the influence of favorites? An irritating and insulting motive! Yet there was a feeling that Catherine would be susceptible to favorites in leading the government. Even so, a permanent council, placed above the Senate, could be guided by favorites. Under Peter II the Secret Office had failed to limit the influence of the Dolgorukys. Hence there was some other purpose; the proposed imperial council might be the vehicle to accomplish something else.

Catherine was dissatisfied. Her suspicions flared. For the moment concessions were in order, temporary compromises until such time as they could be set aside. In the manifesto returning Bestuzhev to favor written or copied in Catherine's own hand, we find the following words: "Moreover, we appoint him (Bestuzhev) first imperial councillor and the first member of the new imperial council to be created at our court." But the printed version of the manifesto managed to exclude these words.

CATHERINE'S CORONATION

To secure herself against various "strange things" it was necessary to hasten the coronation. The empress's visit to Moscow was scheduled for September 1. The coronation arrangements were entrusted to Prince Nikita Trubetskoy. In planning for the empress's chambers in the Kremlin, he wrote to the Cabinet head, Olsufiev: "In looking over the Kremlin chambers in which the most gracious empress wishes to reside, I find no place for a church. Knowing her great feeling for God and aware that she cannot be without a church close to her, I have found a way to deal with this situation. I have decided to build a covered walk from the empress's apartments to the Presentation cathedral, which is quite close by. Because the church is very cold, I will construct warm rooms there." This decision was approved by Catherine.

The care of the crown was entrusted to I.I. Betsky. Princess Dashkova tells an interesting story showing clearly how the events of June 28 dazzled everyone. On the fourth day after the overthrow, Catherine and Dashkova were together. Betsky asked permission to enter. He entered, fell to his knees and begged the empress to reveal whose influence was paramount in her accession. "I am obligated for my accession to God and the citizens who chose me," replied Catherine. "In that case," said Betsky in a desperate voice, "I no longer have the right to wear this symbol of excellence." With these words he began to remove the Alexander ribbon he was wearing. Catherine asked him what he was doing. "I am the most unfortunate person," answered Betsky, "for your majesty does not recognize in me the sole hero of your accession! Was it not I who influenced the guards? Was it not I who threw money to the people?" Catherine and Dashkova grew troubled, thinking that Betsky had lost his mind. But Catherine soon found a way to calm Betsky. "I recognize the degree to which I am obligated to you," she said. "And since I owe my crown to you, who other than you would be better entrusted to prepare it and everything else I must wear at my coronation? So, take care of this. All jewelers of the empire will be at your service." Ecstatic, Betsky showered her with compliments and thanks.

Of the twenty-five senators, twenty were to go to Moscow for the coronation—Count Bestuzhev, Count Razumovsky, Prince Trubetskoy, Buturlin, Chancellor Count Vorontsov, Count Alexander Shuvalov, Sumarokov, Peter Chernyshev, Prince Odoevsky, Prince Alexander Golitsyn, Count Peter Sheremetev, Prince Shakhovskoy, Nikita Panin, Count Skavronsky, Prince Volkonsky, Count Roman Vorontsov, Count Ivan Vorontsov, Count Michael Golitsyn, Suvorov and Brylkin. Five remained in Petersburg: Nepliuev, Nikolai Korff, Zherebtsov, Ushakov and Kostiurin.

Panin submitted a memorandum about this. "When Admiral [Alexei] Golitsyn remained here as sole senator (during the coronation of Elizabeth), the relevant decree granted him principal command of all civil and military affairs. In the present event an entire Senate department of five senators will remain. Should not the senior senator be assigned primary responsibility for the maintenance of order although it be understood that the senators shall govern jointly in the name of the Senate. The senior senator, Nepliuev, does not have a house in which he can live decently because he is poor. Furthermore, as the leading official in the city, he should be given a guard, as much for honor as for occasional needs. He must preside at holidays and receive visiting foreign dignitaries. Perhaps he should move to the wooden Winter Palace and be given a guard and 500 rubles a month for subsistence.

"Keeping in mind the new situation and departure from a populous capital where the memory of the great event is still so fresh, it is a matter of state that this situation be handled carefully and presented properly to the public. Before the party departs Nepliuev should be awarded a blue ribbon to give him greater authority and increase the people's obedience.

This public sign of trust cannot be criticized because he is older than those who do not possess it. Of those that do have it, most are younger than he. He has served for fifty years and always has been helpful in serious matters."

Panin charged Teplov to forward this note to the empress. On the twenty-seventh of August he departed for Moscow with the heir to the throne. He was, obviously, unhappy about his relations with Catherine. He was troubled by Grigory Orlov's influence and by the delay in establishing the imperial council.

Bestuzhev reacted otherwise. The crafty old man remembered the power he enjoyed during Elizabeth's reign thanks to his friendship with Alexis Razumovsky. He now ingratiated himself with Orlov, avoided insistence on anything unpleasant, and displayed unlimited loyalty. For this reason he became "little father Alexis Petrovich."

Dashkova and Teplov were unhappy too. The prediction of Dashkova's uncle, the chancellor, came true: pushing herself forward as a participant of the events of June 28, she drew Catherine's ire. Her clash with Orlov fed this irritation. Teplov complained that he no longer held Catherine's trust and that Elagin was undercutting him. Catherine may have cooled toward Teplov because of his close ties to Panin and Dashkova, but Bestuzhev might have hurt him as well. On his return Bestuzhev had examined the investigative material used in charges against him. He made his own comments which, needless to say, were not secret to Catherine. They pointed to Teplov as a traitor who had informed on Catherine and her correspondence with Hetman Razumovsky. "My secret," wrote Bestuzhev, "could be known to nobody except Teplov. Since he was angry at Elagin and Bestuzhev, only he could be the secret informer. If in the new secret council he continues to foment quarrels among everyone, Adadurov's humility, clear conscience and skill, rather than gall, will prevail."

In any case, Teplov was dissatisfied. This is observed in his letter of August 29 to Panin, who had left for Moscow. "Having grieved a bit about your departure with our kind princess (Dashkova), I visited her majesty and had the good fortune to give her your sealed letter. Her majesty, after reading it and thinking me familiar with the contents, said: I do not know where that decree is. You probably have the first draft, bring it to me! Hearing that I did not know the letter's contents nor the decree mentioned, she said it was the decree concerning Nepliuev. This was in the morning, before services. At three-thirty in the afternoon I returned and brought it, newly copied, to her. Then she showed me a resolution she had written on a report about Perfiliev, I believe, and asked whether there were errors in the language.[10] I could only show a very small one. As it is, it was written very correctly. I then reported the case of Todtleben. Her majesty expressed regret that she had forgotten about him and said this should be taken care of before her departure. When I told her that the original ruling on Todtleben was among earlier papers, her majesty told me to bring them. I left. Soon after her majesty sent me Münnich's letter with the comparisons of the ports of Baltitsky and Reval, and instructed me to send it to you when I wrote next. The contents of Münnich's letter shows that her majesty sends it for your amusement. And truly, the expressions therein are progressively funnier. Toward evening I brought the ruling on Todtleben.

"In conclusion, let us talk of princess Dashkova who, it seems to me, is deeply grieved after your departure. I am with her almost constantly. Her spirit, though uneasy, constantly gushes astonishing ideas. Private discussions with this kind, sensible lady constitute my sole comfort, for my spirits are depressed by anxiety. She fed me well. My one portion would equal four of yours. We dined together with princesses Kurakin and Repnin. Laughter greatly aided our digestion, the more so in that our dear hostess added spice [to the talk]. I am losing patience but I try to remember that if you are strong, you must not cloud your virtue in easy assumptions and that two months are not enough to say that one has enough experience at court. The imperial council should decide everything. When I am in Moscow I at least can say that I am closer to my Ukrainian household guardian deities. It is true that anyone who is to be dismissed can't hold on by force. To serve without the empress's confidence is the same as dying from ataxia. For God's sake, preserve your health and don't worry about the affairs of Petersburg. That is the one remedy for you, the princess, and for him who will love you all his life."

On September 1 Teplov wrote: "Yesterday evening her majesty gave the order to Nepliuev personally. I am including an exact copy for you to read and including the first draft so you can compare the two and observe the changes. In my opinion, the chief difference is that the registry of the decree concerning a Senate office is deleted. The new version is thereby shorter. Actually, the force and content of the old one remain. To be sure, everyone prefers his style as an author and so the editor has moved words around, from front to back and back to front, as if to show great improvement of our concept. It is much more difficult to express an idea in written form than to change words around. But, a person like myself, with no stature, must swallow everything.

"Elagin is my friend, but I think he will admit that it is not for him to teach me language. His "mozhite" [may], which you find in the decree instead of "mozhete" [may],[11] is convincing proof that my vanity is not completely inappropriate. I am enclosing the printed manifesto concerning Count Alexis Bestuzhev. The original is in a hand unfamiliar to me. Everybody is curious as to who composed it, saying it is very well written. But since I know nothing about it, it is not difficult to give an answer. My reply: I do not know and I see and hear of it now for the first time. This reply leads some to believe that you are its author." Panin was pleased to find that his suggestion about Nepliuev was carried out.

On the appointed day, September 1, Catherine left for Moscow and on the ninth stopped at Hetman Razumovsky's estate, Petrovskoe, near Moscow. Members of the Synod and the hierarchy, ladies of the court, cavaliers, generals, and other dignitaries of both sexes gathered at Petrovskoe on the eleventh to offer congratulations. Archbishop Dmitry of Novgorod, as the senior member of the Synod, spoke first. The orator spoke not of hopes for the future but glorified the deed accomplished. "The royal city of Moscow, instead of lighting lamps, looks with burning hearts of love upon its mother and ruler who has performed deeds of renown and merit to the fatherland and to the church. Come forth, defender of the fatherland, come forth, defender of piety. Enter into your city and sit upon the throne of your forefathers."

The elected hetman of the Zaporozhian cossacks and an elder attended also to convey to the empress the congratulations of the entire host. The Zaporozhian stated the necessity of authority and obedience to it. "In the wisdom of His creation," he continued, "God eternally and steadfastly made the river seek the south, the magnet the north, the clouds the east, the sun the west, and man legitimate rule. This is our entire and necessary duty, which requires us to observe it so firmly that it seems engraved on the tablets of our heart. When the Tsar of heaven led your imperial highness to the Russian throne with His right hand we, the sons and fledglings of the Cossack Host of the Lower Dnieper, like children and nestlings of your eagle's nest, could not but tremble with unspeakable excitement and extend our greeting. May the God of all spirit and of all flesh bless the spirit of life in your imperial majesty through which all Russia lives, moves and prospers, and may He grant most precious health and long life to the august vessel that is the holy ark of that spirit!"

The triumphal entry into Moscow took place on the thirteenth of September. "The streets were decorated with spruce branches, similar to garden trellises cut in the shape of different figures. Each house had galleries built in front for the public to see better. Rugs and other fabrics were hung from them, and from the windows and walls." In the cathedral of the Assumption, when the empress had kissed the icons and relics and taken her place, and the tsarevich the place of the tsarinas, Dmitry of Novgorod began the homily. "Stand in beauty O ruling city and wonder, exclaiming, whence cometh this glory to me, this mother of the native land? See in His holy church the one of piety entering as if into the heart of the Russian kingdom. Come unto us, defender of our pious faith, you who have bedecked and safeguarded the church and the fatherland with your maternal shroud. Come, cessation of our sorrows and our grief, source of our joy. The mother observed her holy church abused and impoverished and did not allow the fatherland to be plundered brazenly and brought to sorrow and grief. She did not let Russia be shamed, defamed and mocked by false rulers. How terrible it is to hear of it—whether by sword, by arms, by bloodshed? No, but byscorning her own life, fearing not death, setting hope only in God."

The coronation took place with the usual ceremonies on September 22. The metropolitan of Novgorod spoke, glorifying the events of June 28 as an act of God. "God has placed the crown onto your head. He saves the virtuous from misfortune. He saw your pure heart before him. He knew your chaste habits. He saw that in your unbreakable patience you sought no aid other than His. We know, and say unanimously, that your head sought not the crown nor your hand the scepter merely in search of fame or worldy treasure. Solely your maternal love for the fatherland, your faith in God and aspiration to humility, your pity for Russia's troubled and suffering children, induced you to assume God's task. You observed the embitterment of your people. The church, near collapse, saw it too, as it did the troubled state of Russia, and it was concerned. Only you displayed the resolution to intervene. All powerful Lord God, this creature is not of human wisdom and strength, but a product of God's unwritten fates and wise counsel. This miracle will be glorified by teachers of Your word. Historians will write of it in books, scholars will read of it with yearning. The illiterate will hear of it gladly. The last generations of man will tell of this to their children and glorify the greatness of God. And now, when the dark clouds have been dispersed and autumn has changed to bright spring, let summer begin God's pleasure.

"We congratulate you too, dear heir, for the precious throne and the coronation by God of your kind mother. What your mother has accepted today, someday you shall have as well. Consider that her crown is also yours. All that is required will be given you. Her throne is your throne, your council, your army, your Russian tsardom."

On commemorative medals minted for the coronation there was a bust of the empress on the front. On the reverse was engraved "Orthodoxy and the Russian fatherland saved from threatened calamity by the heroic spirit of her imperial majesty joyously raise this shield ornamented with oak clusters." It included the name of her majesty, on whom Providence has bestowed the crown. Before them is a smoke-wreathed altar with religious, military, and civil symbols. The Russian fatherland is shown pouring incense representing its prayers and heartfelt wishes for a long life and happy rule to its dear monarch and deliverer. Engraved at the top is "For the salvation of the fatherland and the faith" and at the bottom "Crowned in Moscow, September 22, 1762."

The metropolitan reiterated the beneficial significance for church and state of the events of June 28. There was also a foreign Orthodox prelate who visited Moscow for the ceremony. In his oration he too glorified Catherine's accession as salutary for the Russian church. He pointed out obligations to the empress unmentioned by the metropolitan of Novgorod. Then, on September 21, the last day of the festivities, the famed Bishop Georgy of Mogilev and Belorussia read an oration.

At the outset Georgy did not hesitate in confirming that he and the entire Belorussian people were subjects of the Russian empress. "Among the subject peoples of your imperial majesty, the Belorussian people, through me, a subject of your imperial majesty, bring humble congratulations for the joyous celebration of the coronation. I know how far holy Palestine is from Israel, pressed by Egypt. The difference applies as well to co-religionists who do not dwell within Russian boundaries but under Polish rule. The lamp of faith, burning since the days of Vladimir, shines here. It flickered dangerously but has been relighted. In many places the influence of the West has subverted this. Here [in Russia] the churches ring freely in the glorification of His Name. The chants may cease, then resume once more.

"In our land many of God's churches have been taken away, others closed and devastated. The only sounds are those of owls and crows. Here, the more pious a man, the more honest he is. For a moment piety was without honor, but now it has regained its place. In our land to be pious is to be shamed. For the sake of piety, we suffer restrictions, wounds, jails, the destruction of our homes, and frequently the loss of life. Even though we be in the bonds of Egypt and removed from the blessings of your majesty's citizens, we do not wish to be remiss in expressing our joy. We laugh, and pacify ourselves through our tears. In our souls' sorrow we still celebrate, even under the worst persecution.

"Why is this so? Because the hope of our salvation gladdens us. Hope is not of the grass, or in a flower, as it is said, but in the actual fruit. You, devout sovereign, have set right the lamp of faith that was shaken in Russia. You have preserved the beauty of the churches and the psalters. You have led your pious and loyal citizens to dignity. These fruits of your one summer's harvest yield us firm hope that you will harvest the same for us. Or, perhaps, you will be unable to reap for us, or will not wish to? What you achieved in infirmity, so you can do in the seat of power; what you did not do without a throne, now you can do, placed on the throne by God. Your deed was accomplished in fear, when your life was in danger. Now your deed may be done by threatening death to your enemies. When you pledged your life as sacrifice for the faith and the fatherland, which you deigned to do, you won your purpose. This you may deign to do now that God has granted your life and so serve the faith and fatherland, and be protectress of your fellow believers. We beg you, your imperial majesty, do not shame us. In our hope and expectation save us by your hand and place us under your might!"

Count Bestuzhev had no desire that prelates be the sole glorifiers of Catherine's deed of June 28. Four days prior to the coronation the empress received from him the resolution he had proposed to the Senate. Citing the example of Peter the Great who, having achieved peace with Sweden, was named "the Great" and "Father of the Fatherland," Bestuzhev wrote: "There is no more favorable and fairer occasion than now to make a fitting gesture of thanks to our successful ruler, Catherine, who has delivered Russia from almost certain devastation, loss of our repute, and a predictable yoke and dissolution. I feel it my duty, as the eldest among my respected colleagues in the Senate, to propose that with the Holy Synod and other dignitaries we agree, upon completion of the coronation, to present in triumph, in the name of the Russian people, the title of Mother of the Fatherland to her majesty for her unstinting efforts and solicitude for the welfare of her loyal subjects." Catherine wrote on the resolution: "I feel that it is still too early to offer this proposal. It will be taken for vainglory. Yet I thank you for your zeal."

Catherine was completely satisfied with the reception given her by the Muscovites. On September 25, the third day after the coronation, she wrote Count Keyserling, her envoy in Warsaw: "It is impossible to describe to you the joy felt by the innumerable people here at seeing me. All I have to do is walk out or appear at a window and the cries commence anew."

A PROBLEM FROM THE PAST

Meanwhile, the name Ivanushka (Ivan Antonovich) was heard among some officers.[12] Peter III had met with the hermit of Schüsselburg but the latter's lot did not improve as a result. On the second day of her reign, June 29, Catherine arranged for a meeting with Ivan. Major General Silin received an order from Peterhof on that day. "Quickly, upon receipt of this note, the same day if possible, or the following day at the latest, you are to bring the nameless prisoner of Schlüsselburg to Keksholm personally. In the fortress of Schlüsselburg, have the best chambers cleaned and put in order in the best manner possible. These are to be kept in this state until further orders."

Silin reported on July 4 from the village of Mordia, some thirty versts from Schlüsselburg, that he and the prisoner were in the village. A storm had beset them on the lake and they were waiting for new boats to arrive from Schlüsselburg. They would take them to Keksholm. At the meeting with Ivan, Catherine was convince of the absurdity of the notion, held by those who had never seen Ivan, that Catherine could strengthen her right to rule by marrying the great-grandson of Tsar Ivan Alexeevich.[13] Ivan was returned to the quarters in Schlüsselburg that had been readied for Peter III.

The prisoner was entrusted to two officers, Vlasiev and Chekin. Berednikov, the commandant of Schlüsselburg, was told not to interfere. Vlasiev and Chekin were to report directly to Panin, who instructed them: "Your conversations with the prisoner should be calculated to lead him toward the spiritual life, that is, toward monasticism. He then will have to change his name and shall be called Gervasy instead of Grigory. Should someone come with a detachment, or alone, even the commandant, wishing to take the prisoner, give him to no one and treat this as a trick. You must have either a signed decree or an order from myself (Panin). If there is too much force against you, the prisoner is to be killed. He is not to be handed over alive to anybody." To the pleas of Vlasiev and Chekin, Ivan replied: "I do not wish to become a monk; it is only that I fear the Holy Spirit. Furthermore, I am not a material being." Then he said that he could be tonsured, and pray and bow to icons. But he did not wish to be called Gervasy, preferring Theodosius instead.

All of this was held in the greatest secrecy. Very few knew of Ivan's inability to rule and his name appeared on the lips only of the disgruntled. Pobedinsky, captain of the Moscow dragoon regiment, visited Count Grigory Orlov with news of the existence of a party, numbering Ivan Shuvalov as one of its members, that wished to place Ivan VI on the throne. Pobedinsky had heard this from Lieutenant Peter Chikhachev, Chikhachev from Ivan Guriev, captain of the Izmailovsky Regiment. Orlov told Pobedinsky and his friends to pursue this without fear in order to learn details.

As a result of this investigation, several officers were questioned, after which they testified. Second Lieutenant Vepreisky of the Semenovsky Regiment testified that Sergeant Lev Tolstoy, seven days before the coronation, had told him that he had heard from Lieutenant Simeon Guriev that there seemed to be a new party in the making to which Tolstoy was invited by Guriev. Tolstoy told Vepreisky that Likharev had been sent to free Prince Ivan, that Simeon Guriev was invited by Alexander Guriev, that Ivan Shuvalov and Prince Ivan Golitsyn knew about it and that, perhaps, the Izmailov Guards were mixed up in this as well.

On the day of the coronation Vepreisky had related this to Dmitry Izmailov and offered to go the next day to tell Grigory Orlov. But Izmailov said there was nothing to tell, that it was all lies, and that if the accused refused to talk, their accusers would be tortured. Captain Ivan Guriev of the Izmailovsky Regiment testified as follows. He told Peter Chikhachev that Ivan Shuvalov, and four dignitaries with him, along with some seventy others, agreed that Ivan should be sovereign. But this could not be done easily because the soldiers liked the empress. With time, there could be much bloodshed. Prince Trubetskoy was named together with Shuvalov.

Captain Domogatsky of the Izmailovsky Regiment testified that his brother-in-law, Stepan Bibikov, told him that he heard Peter Khrushchov curse the empress. In parting with Bibikov, Khrushchov said: "What are you afraid of? We have close to 1000 people in our group!" Michael Shipov, talking with Simeon Guriev, complained that he was unhappy; others had been promoted, he had not. Guriev pacified him: "I hear that a group is forming against the empress," he said. "You will be in good company—Ivan Shuvalov, Alexander Guriev, Prince Ivan Golitsyn."

Shipov noted that Panin was involved too. Guriev replied: "It is true that Panin is in as well. But there is still another group to which Korff belongs. He is preparing to restore Ivan. Our party is much better. We are for crowning the crown prince. Now Panin and Shuvalov are debating as to who should rule." Simeon Guriev testified that he had talked about several opposing parties and that the soldiers of some regiments listened. He said he had invited the sergeants of these regiments to join and told them that Likharev had been sent to fetch Ivan and proceed with this matter. All this he had heard from Peter Khrushchov but had made up the story about Likharev because he was angry. He had been on guard duty at Peterhof on June 28, had been promised rewards, but had received nothing. Peter Khrushchov, confronted by Guriev, testified that he actually had said all these things. Of Trubetskoy and Shuvalov he had heard only in passing while on the road with his battalion. He could not say exactly from whom he had heard this.

Catherine directed that the investigation be conducted without torture. The testimony cited demonstrated insult to the imperial dignity and intent to create general unrest. The Senate, sitting in full session with the presidents of the colleges, sentenced Peter Khrushchov and Simeon Guriev to decapitation and Ivan and Peter Guriev to hard labor. Their estates were forfeited to their children and heirs. The empress commuted the death sentences to exile for life in Kamchatka and the hard labor convictions to exile for life in Yakutsk.

The manifesto regarding this affair said: "We state before God and the entire world, without praising ourselves, that we accepted the Russian throne from God not for our personal benefit, but for the enlargement of its repute and establishment of justice and better order in our dear fatherland. We have proceeded in this praiseworthy intention in action, not in word. Daily we display solicitude for the general welfare. Notwithstanding our kind intentions, some restless people were found to insult the office granted us by God and to engage in subversion. They wished to replace the solicitude for the welfare of the people which we constantly tend with a mother's concern."

This was an insignificant affair. Dmitry Izmailov was correct when he said that it "was all lies." Even so, the lies revealed the underlying issues: the restoration of Ivan and questions about why the crown prince had not been crowned. In the former, Catherine granted freedom only to Prince Anton. "We intend to free only him and allow him to return to his native land in seemly fashion. As for his children they, for reasons of state that he, in his wisdom, can understand, must remain with us until our government achieves the goals it has undertaken. Should the prince wish to accept his personal freedom and entrust us with his children and their good care for a time, to be returned to him when the occasion arises, he shall tell us. Should he not wish to leave his children for the time promised, he shall remain in his present situation until such time as his children may be released, but for the moment he may choose freedom for himself only." Prince Anton did not agree to release without his children.

The Khrushchov-Guriev affair was unimportant but it could not but make a strong impression on Catherine. This was the first effort against her. Notwithstanding her efforts to portray her policies in contrast to the previous reign, despite her many labors to demonstrate daily her care for the general welfare, the first disappointments suffered by various individuals produced talk of restoring Ivan and, even worse, questions why the crown prince had not been crowned. Disenchanted individuals dared to inflame the soldiers and accuse prominent officials of being accomplices. This unhealthy atmosphere was one consequence of the events of June 28. There was the feeling that if some had been lucky then, why couldn't others find rewards now? Even the coronation could not dispell this mood.

Thus it was that in October 1763 Catherine's self-control was unable to conceal her unhappy spirits. She confided to Lord Buckingham, the English ambassador, that for some reason she was growing more and more absent-minded when in company. He described Catherine's condition in this way: "In her talents, enlightenment, and industry, the empress stands above her entire circle. Hampered by her new duties, knowing her difficult position, fearing dangers she knows still surround her, she is still unable to act independently and free herself of many people whose characters and talents she must despise. At this moment she bends every effort to win the trust and affection of her subjects. If she gains the time to do this, she will wield the power she has won for the honor and the good of her empire."

This corresponds to the assessment given by the French envoy, Breteuil. "With the exception of Panin, who is more a diligent worker than a man of wide knowledge and abilities, the empress has no one to assist her in ruling and winning renown. Nevertheless, she must hear them out and in most cases follow the opinions of these inveterate Russians (vieux russes) who, taking advantage of their position, besiege her constantly in supporting their prejudices about government policy, or for personal gain. In large gatherings at court it is interesting to observe the difficulty of the empress's task of trying to be liked by everyone and the freedom and importunity everybody uses in talking to her of their affairs and opinions.

"Knowing the empress's character and seeing the unusually gentle and courteous way she replies to all this, I can imagine what it costs her. She must feel her bondage strongly in order to bear all of this. At one of the recent receptions when she was exhausted more than usual by various conversations, especially with the drunken Bestuzhev with whom she had a long and lively exchange despite her efforts to escape him, the empress approached me and asked if I had ever seen a rabbit hunt. When I replied that I had, she said: You must find a great parallel between the rabbit and me. They flush and chase me with all their might, no matter how I try to escape views that are not always honest or reasonable. However, I reply, insofar as I am able, in satisfactory fashion, and if I am unable to carry out someone's wish, I explain why...."

In another report, Breteuil writes: "The empress conveyed the glory and the power of her position to me. She repeated some thirty times [the phrase], 'Such an enormous and powerful empire as mine.' She related many of her conclusions about Russia's domestic welfare. She told me that since her arrival here the thought that she would govern personally had never left her. The empress confessed that she was not completely happy, that she must govern people who could not be satisfied. She said she tried to satisfy her subjects in every way possible, but felt that years upon years would be needed for them to grow accustomed to her. Along with the triumphs and the luster of her position, she discovered anxiety as well. This did not sit well with her.

"The throne fascinates her. Even so, something bothers and worries her. This is easy to understand when one observes carefully the behavior and sensitivities of the people enjoying her confidence in any matter. Never has any court had so many parties. The empress displays weakness and wavering, qualities never noticed in her character. The fear of losing what she had the courage to seize is frequently and clearly evident in the empress's conduct. Any reasonably important person is awarded his influence with her. It is amazing that this empress, who always acted in a manly fashion, is weak and indecisive on the smallest matters that encounter some opposition. Her proud and supercilious tone is apparent only in foreign affairs, first because there is no personal danger involved and, secondly, because her subjects admire this tone when used with other powers."

No matter how difficult Catherine's position was, her unusually lively nature, her sensitivity in all questions, her royal sociability, her desire to understand every important person, his intellect and relationship to the problem at hand, her personal relationships with living people, rather than reliance on papers and official reports, all these were precious qualities supporting her actions and maintaining her spirits at all times. The unthinkability of descending from the moral heights of her position strengthened her resolve. Difficulties always found Catherine in her place, a ruler and one worthy of the role. Consequently, difficulties were overcome.

CAPITALS, PROVINCES, PEASANTS

After the coronation the court remained in Moscow for the last three months of 1762 and the first half of 1763. The living conditions in both capitals aroused apprehension and anxiety in the government. This had happened with Petersburg in the previous reign. A commission was formed that included General-in-Chief Chernyshev, Lieutenant General Betsky and Lieutenant Colonel Prince Dashkov of the cuirassier regiment. The commission's task was to present the Senate with a method of curtailing Petersburg's sprawl and thereby avoid difficulties in communication caused by excessive expansion. City limits and suburbs must be established. The commission must draft plans for Moscow which, due to the age of its buildings, had not become well-ordered and where frequent fires caused ruin because of close wooden construction. New plants and factories in both capitals were forbidden.

At one of her first meetings with the Senate Catherine included in a memorandum an order to reduce the high price of bread in Petersburg. A temporary ban on the export of grain was imposed and Catherine spoke of the complete success of this measure. Within two months all foodstuffs were selling at low prices. Senate records show that in Moscow on November 20 the empress attended a Senate session at which she relayed a report from Petersburg by Korff, the police chief, to the effect that since

September the price of bread had risen twenty copecks. Catherine ordered the Senate to establish stores where the public could make purchases and to find ways to lower the food transport costs to Petersburg. Merchants complained of low profits even at such high prices.

Besides information about Petersburg's high prices, there was other discomforting news. On November 20 Field Marshal Münnich reported that there was so much robbery and brigandage in Petersburg that one couldn't leave home at night without an escort. The Senate forwarded this to its Petersburg office, whence it received this report: there were some disturbances which Nepliuev, the senior senator, had reported to the empress. Orders had been issued to quell them. Several suspicious persons and criminals had been caught and after November 21 public tranquillity was established. As to Field Marshal Münnich's report about not going out at night without an escort, the office knew nothing.

News of brigandage came from other places as well. Novgorod reported robbers plundering and burning the homes of landowners. Fifteen dragoons pursued them but the robbers killed two, wounded five, and got away. They continued to pillage as before. Landowners received demands for money and threats to burn them out.

On September 17 Catherine ordered the replacement of police officials by governors and military commanders. Each governor and lieutenant governor must recommend to the Senate measures they felt appropriate for ridding their provinces of brigands. Soon thereafter there was news that brigands had attacked the Yaroslavl mint. Then news came of robberies on the Schlüsselburg, Ladoga, and Narva roads. In the southwest, a gang of twenty-seven robbers invaded the Trinity-Bitiutsk monastery, whipped the treasurer and keeper, burned other monks, and extorted 1630 rubles and pillaged other things.

Peasant disturbances continued. The peasant Azabaev brought a false manifesto to the Kazan police, allegedly dated July 7, about Catherine's accession to the throne. The "most libelous statements" were inserted. For example, it stated that the empress's peasants who, in previous years, were given to bishops, monasteries, and assigned to factories, must work in these factories no longer, reverting to a tax-paying status.[14]

It was discovered that the manifesto was written by Kuzmin, a clerk from the village of Krasnaia Gorka in the Kazan district. He confessed that he had written it while under guard in the Kazan ecclesiastical detention home [spiritual consistory] where the factory peasant Kulikov, belonging to Count Shuvalov, was also held. Azabaev stated that factory peasants belonging to Shuvalov had made copies of the false manifesto and gone among their brethren, stirring them up. They had taken promises from them not to work at the plants. Everyone wishing to work was beaten, their homes plundered, and driven from their homes. In November the Senate received reports from the chief administration of factories that peasants assigned to crown and private plants were being refractory everywhere. They had left their jobs in many factories without permission. Despite repeated warning from the chancellery, they refused to work. In the opinion of the local office, these peasants would not be pacified short of the use of military force. The College of Mines was in agreement. The reports make clear that peasants at the crown factories and private concerns were equally mutinous.

Quartermaster General Prince Alexander Viazemsky was sent to pacify these peasants. His instructions were that he first return them to servile submission, see that they remain subdued, then discover their leaders. This accomplished, he was to inquire into the oppression they suffered. If the stewards being complained about were not found, the peasants were to be returned to work at their assigned factories. This was to facilitate quick resolution of disputes. The stewards were to pledge in writing that henceforth they would not demand anything unnecessary from the peasants. They were especially to avoid harassment such as that discovered at the Petrovsk factory belonging to Evdokim Demidov. If, despite pleas and warnings, the peasants would not desist, they must be pacified by force of arms. This was not to be undertaken except in extreme emergency.

Procedures for investigating complaints were set. The peasants would choose a representative, or Viazemsky would appoint one. The representative, or another trustworthy man, would present all grievances and proof. The charges were to be investigated fairly and both sides heard. Whereas peasant insolence is always harmful, humaneness does not permit peasants to be abused beyond measure, particularly if physical harassment is involved. If the stewards were truly at fault, they must be punished. But the peasants must not become so presumptuous as to believe their superiors would fear them if they did not like their dutiful work. If a steward had been very inhuman, he might be punished publicly. If someone demanded excessive work, he could be punished privately not giving cause to plain folk to overstep their submissiveness. With all this completed, Viazemsky was to examine the mines to determine whether free labor would be better. This might avert future disturbances and make the mines more stable and productive.

In the Senate Catherine announced on November 7 that crown peasants living in the richest province, Kazan, had been driven into great poverty. Without the permission of local officials they could not buy even piglets because allegedly they would eat acorns, not one of which had been planted. The empress ordered an official dispatched to investigate this disorder. Schwebs, vice president of the Senate staff, was chosen.

Still remaining were the church peasants. The commission to consider the problems of church land was formed only at the end of November. Its members were Metropolitan Dmitry of Novgorod, Archbishop Gabriel of Petersburg, Bishop Sylvester of Pereiaslavl, Senator Count Ivan Vorontsov, courtier Count Boris Kurakin, the master of the horse, Count Sergei Gagarin, the procurator of the Holy Synod, Count Alexis Kozlovsky, and State Councillor Grigory Teplov. The empress supervised it personally. It was to follow the Spiritual Regulation and the decrees of Peter the Great,[15] "for we cannot offer anything better" said Catherine in her instructions to the commission.

These instructions meant that the commission must allocate income from clerical estates (1) for upkeep of bishops' households, monasteries and churches, (2) for establishment of schools and (3) for homes for invalids. The instructions began: "The Holy Synod knows well that knowledge of the word of God is the basis of the people's welfare. All human virtue derives from this. Lamentably, we observe that our common people remain quite distant from this necessary condition. Not only do many priests fail to lead their flocks in righteousness but, frequently uneducated themselves, offer harmful examples. The Holy Synod knows as well of the large temptation in law and Orthodoxy to sacrifice church property to the demands of this world, whereas the immortal values pleasing to God are neglected or are absent entirely."

There was need for the commission to make haste. On December 12 the Senate, with the empress in attendance, learned that 8539 monastic peasants had rejected all obedience to monastic authorities.

In one of her notes Catherine wrote that some 49,000 industrial peasants and up to 150,000 monastic and patrimonial peasants were in open disobedience. In another note Catherine said that generals Prince Viazemsky and Alexander Bibikov were sent to calm the peasants. "More than once they were forced to use arms, even cannon, against them."

In the instruction to Prince Viazemsky there was this question: could peasants assigned to factories be replaced by free labor?[16] The question had to be answered negatively because of the scarcity of population when compared to area. On October 15 the Senate received a decree from the empress: since there are many unsettled places in Russia and many foreigners are asking permission to settle, her imperial majesty allows the Senate to admit, without lengthy inquiries, everyone wishing to settle in Russia, save Jews. Apart from exclusion of Jews, admission of non-Orthodox immigrants might not be popular. Addressing this concern, the decree added: "Her imperial majesty is confident that with time this measure will redound to the glory of God, the Greek Orthodox faith, and the welfare of this empire." It is worth noting that the previous day Court Councillor Andrei Shelig announced in the Senate office in Petersburg that he had submitted a report to Panin, in the empress's name, about a confidential plan to settle immigrants on empty lands in Orenburg province. Panin told him to proceed to Moscow.

The decision to accept foreign settlers meant that it was all the more important to return Russian runaways to their places and prevent them from fleeing. Seventeen Old Believer villages in Starodub and Chernigov provinces presented a petition. These villages had been built by their ancestors, it stated, who had crossed the border. They had settled in wooded areas, ploughed substantial land, and mown much hay. During Elizabeth's reign three villages were returned to the monastery of the Caves in Kiev. The preceding emperor had granted six villages with more than 4000 souls to Andrei Gudovich. If this were to continue it would halt people from crossing the borders because landowners could not be free. The inhabitants therefore petitioned that these villages be transferred to the crown. Gudovich, the "dove" of Frederick II, now was without influential friends. The Senate ordered a report prepared for the empress specifying that the villages allotted to Gudovich not be given to him because they were settled by runaways. Were they granted to him the previous landowners, to whom the runaways belonged, would have the right to demand their return or ask for compensation.

Keeping in mind the need of holding the number of dissatisfied people to the minimum, Catherine looked with unpleasant feelings through the list of debtors unable to meet their obligations to the Treasury without loss of fortune. There were some fifty noble households alone and more than one hundred when other categories were added. The empress wrote the

Senate of her dissatisfaction with people who had fallen into debt through unrestrained spending simply for the sake of luxury. She could not agree to allow them means for continued squandering or to tempt others to do so. Nevertheless, she wished to ease somewhat the burdens of those incurring debts prior to her rule by safeguarding innocent children of spendthrift fathers against poverty and sorrow. This would not be done at the Treasury's expense. A commission consisting of Peter Panin, Elagin, Eropkin, and Yakovlev was appointed to examine the situation of each debtor and recommend to the empress the best way to save him from ruin.

Information about bribery among provincial officials did not cease. In the presence of the empress the Senate session of October 23 discussed a petition from the commander of the Ostrogozhsky Regiment, Konovetsky. It charged that Lieutenant General Count Cantemir granted many favors to Colonel Teviashov, who oppressed people, and to others. In return Cantemir had received substantial crown land under the guise of resale. This land he settled with cossacks from the village regiments. Some three hundred homesteads were built. Catherine created a commission on the spot and personally appointed Major Scherbinin of the Izmailovsky Regiment as chairman.

THE QUESTIONS OF AN IMPERIAL COUNCIL

Between September and the end of the year Catherine visited Senate sessions eleven times. At the first Moscow session Senators were told to attend from 9:30 to 12:30 in the morning and not to discuss outside matters. The question of an imperial council, in connection with reorganization of the Senate, was not resolved. As before, Panin was the prime mover behind this. He wished to safeguard the reign against the influence of favorites. We have observed his attitude about Elizabeth's reign, against which he had much resentment. He had not been allowed to play the principal role and had been exiled to Stockholm. There his position had been difficult and demeaning thanks to the political realignment which he ascribed to his hated rival, Ivan Shuvalov, and his relative, Count Peter Shuvalov.

These were Panin's memories of Elizabeth's rule and it is not surprising that in his call for an imperial council he referred to this reign in the sharpest tones. "The Senate presides over all colleges, chancelleries, and offices. Everything flows to it. Yet, under rule of a monarchy, it cannot make law. It rules according to enacted laws and decrees issued at various times, some of which perhaps are not the most fortunate since frequently they were enacted in response to peculiar situations. Consequently, notwithstanding instructions that business be conducted smoothly and in the interest of the government, the Senate actually is unable to perform this function for its first rule is to observe the flow of events and act in accord with decrees and laws given it.

"If this were not so, the Senate would overstep its bounds and the flow of government business frequently would halt. Rather than prompt solutions, endless discussions and arguments over new laws would ensue. This is not to speak of the material, time and ethical factors prohibiting discussion of laws in meetings covering many matters. Each senator and every official comes to a meeting like a guest to dinner who knows neither the taste of the food nor the dishes to be served. Therefore it is evident that the primary, true, and general welfare of the state resides in the sovereign. He cannot transform decisions into reality other than by wise delegation of responsibility to a small, select group.

"If a decree were to deal in plain language with one specific matter, the procurator general would be the general supervisor to whom everything is entrusted. In the Instruction he is termed the eye of the sovereign. But the sovereign, reserving to himself the right of legislation, is unable with a single eye to follow the entirety of government business, subject as it is to the stresses of change and circumstance. Therefore the procurator general fundamentally is merely the eye in the Senate that observes the order of business and secures the proper execution of the laws. We may agree that Yaguzhinsky and Trubetskoy exercised their office in broader ways. But it should be noted that the former was, at that time, the sovereign's closest adviser while the sovereign was creating an empire and establishing a government. We know the kind of people and the means the sovereign had. It is enough to remember that the vice chancellor was placed on the executioner's block only to teach the new senators how to sit decently and discuss matters in the Senate.

"During Elizabeth's reign Prince Trubetskoy, serving the first part of his procuratorship, was in office accidentally, by favor of the court. He did not merely oversee the laws and procedures. Rather, he was in a position to do everything, which he did, and capriciously corrupted everything. Later he became the servant of favorites and chance persons. This epoch deserves special attention. Everything in it was sacrificed to the present, to the whim of men, and to various outside and unimportant matters. The circumstances of the deceased empress's accession demanded wise policies, at least to conform to the still uncompleted government reforms of her great parent. The immediate result was the abolition of the cabinet which, especially toward the end when Biron fell, had assumed a form competent to pursue the general welfare of the state.

"Her majesty, recalling that her sovereign father maintained a privy cabinet which issued only specific orders, directives and letters, commanded that such be created for her as well.Then chance and various exploited this household office to advance their whims and interests and thereby created a cleavage between the government and the sovereign which did not serve the public good. These favorites and courtesans made a nest for themselves in which they served their caprices rather than the interest of the government.

"It became the most injurious institution, not only the most harmful element for the government, but for the sovereign as well. It injured government because through imperial decrees and orders everywhere, it was the source of all the sudden events and deceptions that corrupted justice, orderly business, and the public welfare. It harmed the sovereign because the very personages who employed such cowardly means to conceal themselves from the public made every effort to shift to the sovereign blame for everything they were unable to accomplish. In a concealed and unusual government position of this kind an individual might, in pursuing his personal aims, feel immune before the law and unaccountable to the public.

"Flatterers would say to the sovereign: you have your cabinet. Issue your orders through it. But this is a harmful distinction! It is like saying that all government posts do not belong to the sovereign when all government resides in him. The sole difference is that when government officials conduct the sovereign's business the public blames all disappointments and mistakes on them, something they must strive mightily to avoid. They cannot carelessly impose such burdens on the sovereign. They are, in their honor and calling, responsible for their behavior not only to their sovereign but to the public as well.

"Truly, the government lacked the guidance of its sovereign. Meanwhile the flow of daily business continued as usual through force of various decrees. The sovereign had been removed from governing. Capricious and accidental individuals subverted the cabinet, they corrupted the formalities and order of business, flooded it with superfluous issues, and dispensed prejudiced decrees that never resolved anything. But this was not enough. They created yet another post, stranger than the first. They did not hold command of military units yet issued official orders as if they did. They poked their noses illegally into the affairs of some people with respect to property division and inheritances. Houses were taken from some, returned to others.

"Meanwhile important and chance individuals found no limits to their desires and ambitions and the business of government suffered. Complete confusion reigned. The most important matters and positions became the rewards and ranks of the favorites and the obsequious. Favor and seniority determined positions everywhere. There was no room for ability and virtue. Everyone, on his own and depending on his influence at court, served whatever government posts he thought best calculated to allow him to destroy an opponent or to unite with another against a third. Any remaining privileged positions were used to abuse the domestic order for the sake of foreign interests. Then, because of all this, if not actually due to everyone's interlocking envies, a war commenced at the very moment that shamelessness, extortion, plunder, luxury, chicanery and dissipation reached a peak in estates and hearts.

"The unexpected war demanded all the resources of the country. The scattered elements of government and rule must be reassembled. The conference was created. It was a monster unlike anything yet seen. Nothing about it was of an established nature. Consequently, it was irresponsible. A rule was extracted from the sovereign stating that decrees issued by the conference were to be honored everywhere. The sovereign was separated from all affairs and consequently remained ignorant of their effects. The soul of government was the favorite, who either agitated or choked it. His labors produced merely wind and inconsistency. Accomplishing nothing, by whim he left government and responsibility in the hands of the daring Volkov.

"Volkov, pretending to guide the chancellery in an orderly fashion that was completely absent, in essence was the prime minister. He ruled the ministers, worked on matters of his own choice and forced ministers to sign documents by citing the sovereign or favorites to mask his purposes. This is essentially the form, or better said, the fault of our government. The cobbler doesn't confuse an apprentice with a journeyman and hires the man to fit the work. In contrast, at court I have heard from people close to the sovereign a self-seeking proverb: if favor is shown, there will be enough for everybody.

"The maternal resolve of your imperial majesty to employ the power of sovereignty invested in you by God and the people to institute and strengthen proper forms and methods of government is an act of salvation. With respect to your instructions to me, I fulfill them by presenting an act to be signed by your majesty. I dare flatter myself in thinking that this proposed project, which establishes the executive arm of the supreme legislative body, from which as if from one source and one sovereign laws will flow and express the monarch's personal will, safeguards the autocracy from sometimes concealed violators.

"I must humbly note as well that, as you know, there are among us those who would abhor this new manner of government for their own obvious, special reasons. Your imperial majesty therefore cannot yet consider this undertaking as benefitting fully the good of the people. Your care and a new strictness is demanded if your imperial majesty's council is to take form immediately. Otherwise it is impossible to doubt that from the very outset these individuals will seek means to stop it or, at least, to change it to a form suitable to them. Therefore it is incomparably better to establish and make use of it rather than to allow disruption of what has been established, as has happened." The impression this proposal must have made on Catherine can be imagined. She had the weakness of unfairly referring to Elizabeth's popular reign, sharply pointing out its failings while maintaining silence about its accomplishments. But the proverb, "one cannot see a log in your eye through a twig in someone else's," is relevant. Here the log in the eye of the author was of such dimensions that it could draw only amazement and suspicion. No matter how hostile Catherine's disposition toward the Shuvalovs, the picture of Elizabeth's reign drawn by Panin could appear to her only as a pasquinade dictated by extreme personal enmity. A man who allowed himself to be so carried away could not expect to awaken respect for his counsel. This was all the more so because the sovereign to whom the proposal was directed was disposed to look at him with some suspicion.

Panin was wide of the mark because he aroused Catherine's self-esteem against him. Under Elizabeth, he said, things were in a terrible state. Unworthy people won Elizabeth's trust and did what they wished. To avoid the same thing under Catherine, an imperial council was needed.

This implied that Catherine's intelligence and ability inspired no confidence. Her favorites were at hand already. To neutralize them it was necessary quickly to create the sole vehicle of salvation—a council.

But was this truly the proper vehicle? A council had existed under Anne, which was called the Cabinet. This was the period of Biron's influence.[17] The cabinet, according to Panin, acquired "a form competent to satisfy the sovereign's every concern." The miraculous creation Panin advanced as a cure for all evils, including the seekers at court, was actually not what it appeared. This creation had been unable to safeguard Russia from Biron. Now this same ineffective structure was being proposed with great urgency. The proposal mentioned opposition to a council to which the empress should pay no attention. Before deciding any significant matter, she must not listen to varying opinions. A council would allow her to reject counsel and without thinking sign any proposal presented to her!

The council proposal presented to Catherine for signing by Panin said: "Long before assuming power in Russia, and cognizant of the essence of rule of this strong and great empire, we recognized also the reasons for neglect of government in certain circumstances. Among these were weaknesses in dispensing justice, neglect of the welfare of the country, and other defects which at times intruded into every sphere of government. This was particularly true at the accession of Empress Anne when autocratic rule itself was shaken.[18]

"Such developments detrimental to government undoubtedly occurred partly as a result of the fact that personal influence was stronger than the rule of government institutions. In part it was a result of the absence of basic institutions capable of preserving steadfast government.... Failure to establish these at an early date, in addition to abuses thereof, finally led to such a state of affairs in our beloved fatherland that, when the most vital issues were at stake, it was thought superfluous and unnecessary to convoke the highest institution. Which true and sensible son of the fatherland cannot recall without emotion the way that Peter III, the former emperor, ascended the throne? Cannot this grievous state of affairs be likened to barbaric times when there was no settled government or written law?"

The proposal envisaged the Imperial Council to consist of six members entitled imperial councillors. "Among them shall be secretaries of government departments who shall keep their business offices in their departments. They shall include (1) the state secretary of Foreign Affairs and a member of the College of Foreign Affairs, (2) the state secretary of Domestic Affairs, a senator, sitting also in all offices of his department, (3) the state secretary of War, with membership in the College of War, the Commissariat, the offices of Supply, Artillery, Engineering and the Cadet Corps and (4) the state secretary of the naval department, also a member of the Admiralty.

"All lawful business of the government and our monarchic, sovereign rule shall come under our purview and care. When the Senate is not in session, reports, memoranda, proposals, petitions, and information about all aspects of proper government shall be submitted to us. In other words, all matters relating to the sovereign's concern for and augmentation and improvement of government shall be the business of the Imperial Council. The Imperial Council is nothing other than the place where we work in behalf of the empire. To this end all matters coming before us must be divided, according to subject, among the state secretaries. They then shall examine them in their departments, revise them as appropriate, and submit them to the Council. We then shall issue our resolutions and instructions. In our sessions each state secretary shall report on developments in his department subject to imperial decision. The imperial councillors, after discussion and exchange of opinion, shall make specific recommendations. By our sovereign order we will make our final determinations."

The proposal ended by speaking of the division of the Senate into six departments.

Catherine did not sign this document immediately. She first commented on certain phrases. About the phrase in the introduction "Cannot this grievous state of affairs be likened to barbaric times" she noted: "True, we should lament that situation. But it is not true that, because of it, we were worse than the Tatars or Kalmyks. Even if we were, it still seems to me that the use of such strong words is inappropriate to refute. Personal opinion cannot justify defamation of the entire nation and our ancestors."

The proposal termed state secretaries ministers. Catherine wrote: "Cannot the word 'ministers' be rendered in Russian and given exact definition?" Catherine did not notice, or did not choose to notice, other oddities. A complaint in the introduction noted that the cause of all disorders was the greater influence of individuals as compared to government institutions. Things had gone so far that upon Anne's accession to the throne autocracy was shaken. Yet everyone knew that at that time Russia was ruled by the Supreme Privy Council. The word "minister" could not be translated into Russian and given proper definition. It was simply passed over. The same is true for the phrase "barbaric times."

The proposal was rewritten. Catherine made changes in it as well. Instead of a council of six members she wrote "up to eight." The names of the members were listed as Count Bestuzhev, Hetman Razumovsky, Chancellor Count Vorontsov, Prince Jacob Shakhovskoy, Nikita Panin, Count Zakhar Chernyshev, Prince Mikhail Volkonsky, Count Grigory Orlov. Assigned as state secretaries were Panin for domestic affairs, Vorontsov for foreign affairs, and Chernyshev for the military. Finally, on December 28 Catherine signed the official manifesto. But it was not made public and the Imperial Council was never established. We shall see that for important matters Catherine formed a commission or council consisting of members she chose as was done previously.

In this instance Catherine once more acted with the timidity, indecisiveness and attention to all opinions for which foreign envoys criticized her at this time. These were the very diplomats who observed Catherine with the same shrouded eyes used previously to regard Elizabeth's behavior, cersuring her for being slow and careless.

Catherine did not listen to Panin and sought other opinions. Some commented on secondary matters only. One person advised her to restore the old name, the Supreme Privy Council. Naturally the most interesting to Catherine were those of the grand master of ordnance, Villebois. "I do not know," wrote Villebois, "who drafted this proposal. But it seems to me that, under the guise of preserving the monarchy, he subtly leans toward rule by the aristocracy. An imperial council required and established by law, along with its influential members, in time could acquire the status of co-ruler. The empress, in her wisdom, will discard everything in it which in the future might engender harmful consequences. Her spirit and wisdom are such that she requires no special council. It is her health only which demands relief from the unbearable burden of uncompleted business reaching her. For this she needs merely to divide her private cabinet into departments with a state secretary for each. It is also necessary to divide the Senate into departments. The imperial council will allow her subjects too much proximity to the sovereign and the subjects may wish to rule together with the sovereign."

FOREIGN POLICY

We have seen the French envoy, Breteuil, characterize Catherine as weak and indecisive in domestic policy and complain of her proud and supercilious manner in foreign affairs. He explained this by saying that there was no personal danger involved in the latter and that by using this tone with foreign countries she wished to please her subjects. We shall not attempt to deny the last assertion but will observe that Russia's position, thanks to Elizabeth's activities in the Seven Years War, was very advantageous. Each nation left this war in a drained condition. Russia felt this less than others. The position Russia gained during the Seven Years War allowed its policies to decide the fate of the major warring powers. Elizabeth had brought Frederick II to the edge of disaster. Peter III had saved him. Now it was up to Catherine to renew his plight or to save him. The difficulty was in the choice.

It is understandable to expect, especially in view of the language of her proclamations, that Catherine would return to Elizabeth's policy. She would move her forces to help Austria and force Frederick II to come to terms at the beckoning of the allies. In this situation East Prussia would go to Russia. This was how the elderly Field Marshal Saltykov understood things. Immediately upon news of the events of June 28 he reoccupied the Prussian areas just abandoned. Then he received orders to vacate them once more. The empress announced that she would honor the peace with Prussia. Naturally she would not have done this were she certain that the army and the people definitely favored renewing war with Prussia. But she knew that the existing discontent stemmed not from ending an unpopular war, but from Peter III's subordination of Russian to Prussian interests and from the baleful influence of the Prussian minister in Petersburg. A further source of irritation was the humiliating manner in which an alliance was forged with Prussia solely to begin a new and totally useless war.

Consequently Catherine feared no discontent were she to uphold the peace with Prussia and in so doing avert war with Denmark and preserve Russian honor without spending Russian money and blood. The previous reign held responsibility for the loss of prestige and embarrassment connected with the peace with Prussia. Catherine stood in need of peace because of her unstable political situation and desire to devote herself to domestic affairs and improvement of the lot of the Russian people. Her aim was to win the affection of Russia and to legitimatize the events of

June 28. These purposes were expensive, which made it important to end the cost of maintaining an army abroad.

Only an extreme situation could justify war. Was there an extreme situation? Was it imperative to preserve the empire and maintain its influence in Europe? Was it necessary to restrain further the powerful neighbor who cared nothing of the means used to attain his ends? This aggressive neighbor now had been restrained. Frederick II emerged from the Seven Years War without resources to start another, without allies, fearful of offending Russia and of multiplying his enemies. He wished, in any manner possible, to win its friendship. Was it in Russia's interest to weaken Prussia completely and thereby sacrifice it to Austria and France? This would benefit the former primarily, which then would gain preponderance in the Germanies. Was not Prussia vital to the balance of power in Europe?

It might be observed that Austria, because of its many nationalities, could never be as dangerous as Prussia for Russia. But we cannot accept the view of earlier times when later times offer new experiences and new sources of life. For Catherine and her advisers the fundamental question was this: since Russia no longer had to fear Frederick II, who did not have long to live anyway, was it necessary to crush Prussia for Austria's benefit? Was it needful, simply to return Silesia to Austria, to break the peace and launch a war which, considering Frederick's gifts, might be drawn out thanks to the exhaustion of Austria and France?

Peace was a necessity in the Polish question as well, which was coming to a head. The death of King Augustus III was expected daily. In the Europe of that day Montesquieu's dictum (in *The Spirit of the Laws*) that weak neighbors were the best to have, was applauded widely. The wish to cultivate the weaknesses of neighboring powers stemmed from this source. Attributable likewise to this outlook were policies to support the existing forms of government that preserved these frailties, and treaties designed to prolong them. The agreements between Russia, Prussia, Austria, and Denmark to existing governance in Poland and Sweden had these aims. Whereas theoretical and practical advantages existed, nonetheless there were considerable difficulties. A weak state cannot remain independent, for it must be influenced by strong neighbors, whose interests then clash. A weak state is an arena for a duel of the strong, each of which thereby loses its secure borders. They struggle over the weak state, which no longer separates them but drives them toward a collision. Poland, now weak, was the arena of struggle between Russia, Prussia, Austria, Turkey, Sweden, and France. Their conflict intensified when a king of Poland was to be elected, and it was this prospect that demanded attention now.

Either a foreign prince might be selected, or a native Pole, or Piast, as his house was called at the time. Russia's interests determined that its influence alone dictate the choice of a king. The new ruler must owe his crown solely to Russia and must serve it by satisfying its demands. Of these there were three: improved conditions for the Russian Orthodox in Poland, definition of borders, and the return of refugees. True, Poland was weak; yet a powerful Russia had been unable to achieve anything in regard to these claims. This caused great irritation, for it was felt to infringe on Russia's legitimate interests and on its prestige.

It is understandable why it was so important for Catherine to satisfy these demands at the commencement of her reign. This was particularly true of the first, for it would show her to be a defender of Orthodoxy. This would be her answer to Bishop Georgy's [of Mogilev] famous appeal at her coronation. She would stand against Catholic fanaticism and as defender of freedom of conscience in the eyes of European philosophes.

The first candidate for the Polish throne was the son of Augustus III, the hereditary prince of Saxony. But he did not fit the requirements of the first condition. He could not be elevated to the throne solely with Russia's help. He was supported by France and Austria and must be beholden to them. Under Elizabeth he had been the Russian candidate also, for at that time Russia had joined Austria, France, and Saxony to restrain Prussia. But peace with Prussia now had changed the political complexion. Peace between Russia and Prussia, even without an alliance, dealt a heavy blow to Austria and France, especially to the former for it forced on it a disadvantageous peace with Prussia. Inevitably this led to a cooling of relations between Austria and Russia. These circumstances prohibited Russian support for the Austro-French candidate. In fact, he must be opposed in every way possible, a policy which produced even greater cooling between Russia, France and Austria.

But that was not all. Under Elizabeth, when the struggle with Prussia was paramount, it was logical to support the house of Saxony which was hostile to Prussia, and grant it subsidies for damages suffered at Prussia's hands. There was consistency in giving Courland to one of the sons of Augustus III. Now that it was necessary to keep the prince of Saxony from the Polish throne, it was inconsistent to leave his brother as duke of

Courland. He must be chased from Courland. This led directly to enmity with the Saxon house and with France and Austria, its patrons. Necessarily and naturally this hostility engendered rapprochement with Prussia.

Russia's withdrawal from the war allowed Frederick II gradually to move toward an advantageous settlement while retaining Silesia. But he knew well that Austria long would harbor resentment about Silesia. He had no hope of better relations with France and the political atmosphere in England was icy. He must seek favor in St. Petersburg, one price of which was participation in the affairs of Courland and Poland. Presumably Frederick would wish to remove from Courland the prince of the hostile house of Saxony. And for the kingdom of Poland he agreed to a native Pole, one chosen by Catherine. This was her old acquaintance, Stanislaw Poniatowski. It was held, even in Elizabeth's reign, that Poniatowski would seek the Polish throne with the help of Grand Duchess Catherine. Now, with the aid of the Russian empress, it was an easy matter.

Catherine told Breteuil: "I cannot be judged until several years have passed. I need at least five years to restore order. Meanwhile, I act the accomplished coquette with all of the sovereigns of Europe." Catherine desired peace and had no wish to assume the obligations of an alliance with anyone for this might lead to war. Whereas the sovereigns sought her favor and alliance, like an accomplished coquette she wished to avoid entangling obligations while not robbing them of hope and eluding definite promises. This was her wish, but it was a difficult one.

Russia had abandoned the war and was resisting alliances. In such an atmosphere it is difficult for a power to maintain its influence. For this, Catherine advanced as the arbiter of peace but the warring courts rejected her mediation. They saw no profit in it. Furthermore, Prussia was unhappy with the change in Russian policy and the threats used by Catherine to force it to peace. Austria was even less happy for, in exiting the war, Catherine was forcing it to yield Silesia and abandon its hopes.

The cabinet in Petersburg announced that regarding Poland and other countries Russia would uphold Prussia. This would not prohibit Russia from supporting Austria on the question of Turkey. Their interests would coincide on this point. In Vienna there was no wish to recognize this policy of duality. Angered at Russia for its alliance with Prussia, Vienna moved even closer to France and together with Paris acted against Russia in Constantinople.

Russia encountered a similar struggle with France at Stockholm. In the end, Russia could not maintain a position of independence. Frederick II agreed to assist Russia in Polish affairs but not without compensation. Fearing Austria and France, and finding himself in discord with England, Frederick needed an alliance with Russia, a formal defensive alliance with which he could intimidate his enemies. The Seven Years War had demonstrated how difficult it was to war against a power enjoying Russia's support. In vain did the cabinet in Petersburg seek to delay entangling obligations. Frederick II insisted and, for his help in the affairs of Poland, Russia accepted alliance with him. Let us look into the details.

THE PRUSSIAN RESPONSE

The news of the events of June 28 shocked Frederick II, by his own admission, like a bolt of lightning. Goltz's reports had aroused great concern among Frederick and his ministers, but they had not expected such an outcome so soon. Minister Finkenstein wrote to Goltz: "The one thing I wish is that this sovereign (Peter III), whom we have so many reasons to like and who, it seems, was born for Prussia's good, will stay alive and on the Russian throne." It was disheartening to lose a powerful sovereign who, in Frederick's words, served Prussia like one of its own ministers. But there was nothing to be done. One must bow to circumstances.

Chernyshev was the first to inform Frederick of Catherine's accession and of the order that he disengage from the Prussian army. The king begged him to wait three days and Chernyshev agreed. Frederick utilized these three days to launch an offensive against the Austrians. He could not count on success once Chernyshev's departure had given the Austrians heart. His calculation was correct. The Prussian attack was entirely successful and Schweidnitz was again theirs.

Thereupon news that comforted the king began to arrive. Catherine did not intend to void the peace between them. The departure of Chernyshev was felt keenly, but there was consolation in the fact that he need not detach part of his forces to help Russia in a Danish war. War could be waged successfully against Austria, now alone. Meanwhile he might observe developments in Petersburg.

Catherine signed these instructions to Prince Repnin in Berlin on June 29. "You may gather from the enclosed manifesto the manner in which we have assumed the throne by the general and unanimous wish of our loyal subjects and thereby preserved the empire from disturbance and destruction. It was thought necessary to restore the order and well-being of former days. We wish no delay in informing you of this very important event, blessed by God. We graciously request you inform the court through the ministry. Reassure it of our intention to uphold our good friendship." Appended to the instructions was a note, dated June 28, to all foreign diplomats in Petersburg. Catherine assured them that she fully intended to maintain the precious friendship with their sovereigns.

Further instructions were addressed to Repnin on July 1. "You well realize that during the last reign the corps commanded by General Count Chernyshev was placed at the disposal of the king of Prussia. This was decided without any agreement as to the length of its stay nor of the advantages thereby to be derived by Prussia. Although we do not yet know whether the corps has joined the king, you are, no matter where the corps may be, to order Count Chernyshev not only to disengage from the Prussian forces but to return to Russia immediately. We have no intention of harming the newly re-established peace and understanding with the sovereign. Until he gives cause for a breach we are disposed to honor the provisions of the treaty of April 24. In informing you of our resolution, we order you not to keep it secret. At every opportunity you are to explain it and note that, in our humanity, we wish nothing so much as to see and hasten the end of the flames of war from which mankind already has suffered so much."

On July 4 Goltz was handed a note stating that the empress found no need to convene a meeting in Berlin to settle the affairs of Holstein. The king of Prussia's mediation no longer was necessary.

In his first dispatch to his new empress, sent on July 12 from the camp at Begendorf, Repnin described how he had informed Frederick II of the events of June 28, at a moment when the king was still unaware that Saltykov's orders had not been approved in Petersburg. Throughout his talk with the king, Repnin said, "he was disturbed and very concerned that the current understanding with the empress remain in force." In the evening the king summoned Repnin to ask whether he could find out the cause for the orders to withdraw the Russian forces. Was there concern that his obligations to the former sovereign would cause him for some reason to place obstacles in the way of the empress's reign? Frederick offered assurances that, since the former emperor personally had abdicated in writing, everyone must honor such a public act. Even if he had no wish to accept this development, he was in no position to do so because his own affairs were so fragile. Finally, he immediately recognized Catherine as ruling empress. Frederick further requested Repnin to inquire of the empress whether Baron Goltz might remain as envoy to her court.

Goltz could not remain in Russia. "The empress despises me," he wrote the king on July 10, "because of my close ties to the deceased (Peter III). She assumes, quite unfairly, that I approved of the deceased's behavior toward her. Seeing me she must recall unconsciously the poor treatment of her that Peter allowed himself in my presence. I and my secretary, Dietel, have both the people and the court against us. It is enough to talk to a Russian to make him suspect in the eyes of the others." But Goltz also informed his king that the future held possibilities of alliance between the king and the successor of Peter III.

Count Keyserling, assigned as ambassador to Warsaw by Peter III, was in Petersburg at this time. A friend of Bestuzhev, he was, like Korff and Panin, a sworn enemy of France. He had cooled greatly to Austria when it entered into alliance with France and had led Russia into it. During the last part of Keyserling's stay in Vienna, the coolness had turned to enmity. He lost his earlier influence when the most important negotiation during the Seven Years War was handled by Austrian envoys in Petersburg and when friends of the fallen Bestuzhev were suspect.

Catherine, learning of Keyserling's abilities from Bestuzhev, greeted his arrival in Petersburg. She wished for his opinion on foreign affairs in general and on Poland in particular. Keyserling favored an alliance of Russia and Germany against France and, unwilling now to see representatives of the Germanies in Austria, arrived in Petersburg determined to promote a Prussian alliance. This was particularly needful with respect to Polish affairs, the handling of which was entrusted to him. He announced to Goltz: "At the moment it is not in the interest of the Russian court to conclude defensive alliances with neighboring powers. These alliances could entangle it in foreign disputes without any profit since Russia has no claims on any neighboring lands. However, I feel that the empress is not far from establishing closer ties with your sovereign than those presently existing. A treaty of alliance might be signed in which measures regarding Poland might be stated." Meanwhile the future allies continued their not particularly cordial discussion.

Repnin wrote once more that Frederick continued to distrust the peaceful intentions of the empress. When Repnin tried to allay his fears the king demanded that he place his assurances on paper for the edification of foreign diplomats. Repnin could not bring himself to this. Shortly thereafter the king was calmed by Catherine's letter (of July 24) which informed him she had given instructions about the misunderstandings created in Prussia by "excessive zeal," presumably that of Saltykov. Thereupon Frederick's talk was of incipient discord between Austria and Turkey, that developments pointed toward a rupture, about which Repnin wrote that he did not fully believe the king.

In August Repnin held a conversation with Frederick. The king began by saying that talks between England and France seemed to him to have been unsuccessful. This was strange because he was certain that both were thoroughly tired of the war. "I feel," said Repnin, "that the war is burdensome for all the belligerents." When the king agreed, Repnin continued: "Count Chernyshev already has informed the empress of the peaceful intentions of your majesty. They parallel the wishes of the empress and her highness will not refrain from mediation for the attainment of peace." "I am very pleased," answered the king, "but I cannot proceed in such an important matter without the agreement of my allies. As it stands, I do not foresee impediments on their part. I fear that the Austrian court, noting the return of your troops, will not be inclined to accept Russian mediation."

"Seeing the ambiguity in his mind," Repnin replied that the Russian army was near enough that it could "assist in reducing the obstacles to world peace." "Having once left the war," rejoined the king, "it is unpleasant to re-enter it. Furthermore, the forces might be needed at home." "Russia," replied Repnin, "seems to have no reason to fear anything. Even were there reason for alarm, the empress's army is sufficiently numerous that part could be returned to aid peace in Europe while the other part remained to defend the fatherland." The king made no answer.

At the end of July Catherine handed her advisers eight points which she had written out. (1) What should be done now when, according to the English ambassador, Keith, the situation in Europe was moving toward peace? (2) Should a delegate be sent to Augsburg for the foreign ministers' meeting and, if so, what instructions should he have? (3) Should other powers be notified of the proposal of mediation offered me by the king of Prussia via General Chernyshev? (4) In view of current circumstances, should our forces return to Russia? (5) Are there reasons, given our promise of keeping the peace with Prussia, to consider this peace useful?

If it is not, should it be changed to satisfy our needs, and if so, how can a separate article in an agreement serve us? (6) Should the renewal of the treaty with the Viennese court preserve its language or should it be changed? (7) Should the king of Prussia be informed now that devastated Saxony be cleared of his forces and returned to its former rule? (8) Are we not providing a reason for the rejection of our mediation by returning our forces to Russia, and will not negotiations at the congress be weakened as a result?

Bestuzhev offered answers in a letter of the tenth of August. "I have responded as well as I can to the eight points sent me by your imperial majesty. I have not been involved in state affairs now for some five years, my age is to be considered, as is my limited memory and weakened health due to my sufferings. This opinion is not as comprehensive as the one I drafted seventeen years ago, in 1745, when I was involved constantly in affairs of state and when memory served me better. At that time I had the honor of presenting my broad views to Her Majesty Elizabeth, your aunt of dear memory. I refer you to this document only because your imperial majesty has inquired of me whether I uphold the idea of weakening the king of Prussia. Your majesty will see that I was of that notion then, which is unchanged now as well. I submit my opinion to your imperial and enlightened reason and hold myself always ready to carry out your sovereign instructions."

On the first point Bestuzhev noted that Russia must draw the warring states to peace. Regarding the second, an effort should be made to have Russian ministers invited to the congress. This would be more difficult now due to the separate peace between Russia and Prussia. If invited, the delegates should seek for Russia's former allies a moderate compensation for the destruction and the losses suffered. This would limit in part the powers of the king of Prussia, the principal future threat to neighboring countries. Most particularly, he should not gain a position to take vengeance on Russia. The presence of Russian ministers at the congress would enhance the glory of the empress, and should elevate her to guarantor of an agreement. Nothing contrary to Russian interests should be accepted.

Concerning point three, it would be improper to convey to other nations the Prussian offer of mediation. The king mentioned this to Count Chernyshev in conversation only. Although he repeated the same to Prince Repnin, such proposals generally are submitted on paper. On the fourth: it would be better for the entire Russian force to be stationed on the territory won from Prussia. But since the order to return had been given, up to 30,000 troops should be left in Poland along the Vistula river. An additional force of up to 50,000 should be held in readiness at the border in order to stimulate the desirability of Russian mediation and respect for it. As to point five, when the treasury is exhausted, even a poor peace is welcome. The peace with Prussia brought dishonor to the Russian court, loss of glory, and was done without informing our allies; it is not a useful one. It is desirable to renegotiate it as soon as a proper justification is found.

Bestuzhev's outlook about point six was that the earlier treaty with Vienna has been weakened by the Prussian alliance. It should be renewed on the basis of Austria being a natural ally with respect to Turkey and other neighbors. On point seven, Prussia and Austria must withdraw their forces from Saxony. As to point eight, withdrawal of all Russian forces to Russia understandably would hardly incline the warring powers to seek Russian mediation.

Nepliuev asserted, in contrast, that maintaining a Russian army in Poland, on the Vistula in devastated areas, would be terribly expensive. It would arouse suspicions among neighboring nations, for how could it be explained? Finally, the Poles would become apprehensive.

Prince Volkonsky's opinion was almost exactly like that of his uncle, Bestuzhev.

Vice Chancellor Prince Golitsyn felt that any Russian ministers invited to the congress should seek to confine the unduly expanded power of Prussia. This should be done to satisfy Russia's former allies, for the future security of Prussia's neighbors, and to achieve equilibrium in Germany. This would serve Russia since the power of its only currently dangerous neighbor would be reduced. As it was, Prussian might would be augmented by the districts of Bayreuth and Anspach, which would fall to the house of Brandenburg upon the death of their margraves without heirs. Russian forces in Prussian territories should not be recalled at all until a general settlement was reached. This would deter the brave and enterprising king of Prussia. In the words of Count Mercy, Vienna gladly would resume its subsidy if Russian forces stood on the Vistula. A defensive treaty with Austria, a natural ally, should be renewed.

Voronstov also considered it reasonable to leave a Russian force in Prussia and Poland. But "it must be considered that the good of the empire demands that the peace, no matter what kind it is, should be preserved. Even fortunate military successes burden the government heavily, not to mention the chances of unfortunate incidents of all kinds. The peace with the king of Prussia cannot be viewed as an advantageous one, but there are almost no means of remaking it."

It was decided to honor the peace and to withdraw the forces from the Prussian districts. At the same time, the king of Prussia was to be compelled to seek peace with Austria and Saxony. Understandably, the former would make the latter difficult.

Instructions were dispatched to Repnin. "From your report we see, unfortunately, that, in view of the departure of our forces from his lands, the king of Prussia increasingly has displayed his aversion to peace. His action is less surprising than it is unpleasant. We can conclude, not without cause, that he thereby demonstrated his intent to pursue the war, perhaps in the hope that having withdrawn we will not soon wish to commence it anew. On the other hand, the capture of Schweidnitz allows him to move against Austria and compel the empress-queen, by force of arms, to a peace that would secure his future preponderance and that of his house in Germany. Inasmuch as our desires and policies differ completely, namely the end of war and the establishment of equilibrium in Germany so necessary to the interest of our empire, we cannot be calm until we know specifically and exactly the thoughts of his Prussian majesty. Knowing them will enable us better to decide our own measures.

"You must find an appropriate occasion to impress upon the king in conversation the idea, as if it were your own, that his noticeable inclination to continue the war cannot be pleasing to us given our peaceful disposition and accepted rules of behavior among nations. You fear that this might hinder our entry into firm friendship with him, even though both courts have certain interests in common. Should the further statements and activity of the king of Prussia disclose his obstinacy in continuing the war, you shall express our inclination and good wishes for the Viennese court. If the situation requires, say that the natural interests of both imperial courts do not permit us to abandon the empress queen entirely. Should the king of Prussia fall in battle, which can happen in war, we instruct you immediately to offer formally our mediation to his successor, promising that our mediation will bring certain peace."

Repnin raised the empress's concern by reporting that Frederick intended to take Saxony. When Repnin spoke of clearing Saxony of military forces, Frederick grew cold to him. Repnin requested the empress permit him to leave military headquarters for Berlin in order not to have his mission subjected to incivility. When Repnin represented to Frederick Austria's peaceful intentions and its willingness to negotiate a truce and peace, the king answered that he would not reject a profitable peace but would never sign one that was disadvantageous. No truce could be signed without first drafting preliminary points of agreement. Should the court of Vienna so choose, it could advance proposals. But he would make no proposals of his own and never agree to any congress.

"Winter is approaching," Repnin commented, "giving your majesty added time. There is no reason to speak of the place and manner of talks. All that is needed is the desire for peace." "I will never agree to a congress," Frederick answered. "I will make no proposals. I leave them for the court in Vienna."

"Your imperial majesty," reported Repnin, "will note that the king will not be led to peace by negotiations other than those assuring him the lands he held prior to the war and that no indemnities be demanded of him. If the Viennese court wishes advantages, it must resort to force of arms. This year's campaign has much favored him, inflating his thoughts all the more. Should he make further gains, he might even demand indemnities for losses in this war."

Catherine insisted that Frederick remove his forces from Saxony and compensate the elector, the king of Poland, for the devastation of his land. The empress's note to Repnin said: "We imagine that this will not be pleasing to the king. Nevertheless, justice demands that the offender satisfy the offended. You must remind him in proper manner on every occasion that without the satisfaction of the elector of Saxony, the king of Poland, peace cannot be established firmly."

"Whenever I barely touch on this issue or on peace negotiations," Repnin wrote, "the king breaks off the conversation and turns away with displeasure. On the news that the Austrians attempted to attack Prince Henry, he said to me: "I see how the Austrians are planning to leave Saxony. They are simply trying to get me out of there in every way possible." I remarked that the Austrians could not leave Saxony without his consent. Yet they were quite prepared for this step were he only to display a similar readiness. "I have known for a long time what to believe or disbelieve," answered the king.

Repnin's reports were certain to leave an unpleasant impression. They made evident the damage resulting from the change of Elizabeth's policy vis-à-vis Frederick II. "Upon your majesty's accession to the throne Count

Chernyshev and I reported that the king did not oppose peace. But since then circumstances have changed completely. The fear of your majesty's arms passed with the return of Russian forces to their homeland. Schweidnitz has been taken, up to 15,000 Austrians have been captured, and only some 2000 to 3000 Prussians have been taken prisoner. These gains have raised hopes here and completely changed opinions. In addition, the king's natural disposition has much to do with it."

Catherine personally wrote and sent to the foreign ministry a dispatch to Repnin. "At the proper moment, Prince Nikolai Repnin is, as if on his own initiative, to impress on the king of Prussia in conversation that his evident inclination to war might make me resist greater friendship with him even though some of our interests coincide. Should the king's conversation suggest war, the envoy shall convey the impression of my favorable disposition toward the Viennese court. Should he display peaceful proclivities, he should be encouraged by expressions at every opportunity of my devout wish for peace and moderation. Quite privately instruct Prince Repnin that should the king be killed during the prince's stay he shall offer officially our mediation to his successor, and our promise of stable peace."

Finally, Repnin was to impress upon Frederick that the continuation of the war would force Russia to assist the court of Vienna in every possible way. "I doubt whether the king can be moved to concessions," replied Repnin, "other than by force of arms. Otherwise, it is impossible."

The envoy's conclusions found support in a letter by the empress. "I would be very happy," wrote Catherine to Frederick, "to remove all hindrances to our equitable agreement. But I see no means of achieving this so long as your majesty does not withdraw from the war. I speak simply: is there no way to make peace? I could have acted otherwise than I have. I had means for advancing peace at my disposal, and I still have them. I have sacrificed substantial gains of war to my love of peace. Let us hope that others will follow this example, especially since at present any proposed gains are merely imagined. The entire difficulty consists in compensating the house of Saxony. An accommodation can be arranged for one of the princes of this house." The letter ends with a threat. "I know that the court of Vienna is inclined to peace. I could inform you of its proposals if I could expect the same from your majesty. It is unfortunate that this has not found your favor. In the end I fear that my best intentions will not bear fruit and I shall be forced to resort to steps contrary to my wishes, my inclinations, and my feelings of friendship."

Repnin discussed this with Count Finckenstein, the minister of foreign affairs, on November 26. Repnin resolutely agreed with the need to evacuate Saxony and to make compensation. Otherwise a lasting peace was impossible. "It is true that Saxony is suffering," Finckenstein replied. "But the king's hostility to Saxony derives from his certitude that it caused the war. There is written proof of this. At first Russia spoke merely of the need to evacuate Saxony. Now there is talk of compensation as well." "The secrets of their cabinets are privy among sovereigns," said Repnin, "I know nothing about them. But the whole world and I know that the king of Prussia was the first to enter Saxony, and we know the suffering it has undergone since then. Compensation for Saxony is only fair according to natural law. The offended must receive satisfaction from the offender. His majesty's aloofness about leaving Saxony and the question of peace arouse my fears that coolness between the king and her imperial majesty may result from his obstinacy. I fear that the empress may have to rely completely on the court of Vienna." "There will never be coolness from our side," replied Finckenstein. "The king firmly intends to maintain friendship with the empress." During this conversation, Repnin reported, Finckenstein was in a greatly agitated state. He spoke in a quivering voice and was trembling.

On December 21 Finckenstein informed Repnin in the name of the king and in great secrecy that the court of Vienna had conveyed an offer of peace through the mediation of Saxony. The king had responded that reasonable conditions would not find him averse to peace, and negotiators had been appointed by both sides. Whereas the count of Vienna desired privacy the king, obligated by his sincere friendship for the empress of Russia and honoring, with gratitude, her humanitarian desire for the return of peace in Europe, harbored no wish to conceal this development as a gesture to demonstrate that he wished peace. Naturally, Repnin replied, the empress would be happy to learn of this initiative toward ending human suffering. She would make every effort to remove obstacles if the king were to explain his position sincerely and precisely. Finkenstein, in the king's name, replied that the king would forward to the empress his conditions for peace without delay.

Meantime, Count Solms, the successor to Goltz, arrived at court on December 18 to attend a dinner at the chancellor's. Under the guise of conversation, he entered into detailed discussion of affairs. His king, the sovereign, began Solms, was surprised by the strong interest expressed by her majesty in the house of Saxony. The activity of the latter did not merit her intercession. Rather, it merited reproach for the joy it exhibited at the news of Khrushchov's plot against her majesty. He, Count Solms, assured him that the court in Dresden proclaimed widely in Poland that although the first attempt had been unsuccessful, another one to follow in November was certain to produce a change in the government. Were the king to abandon Saxony to oblige the empress, how could he be assured that he would not be attacked in the heart of his possessions, given the many examples of the jealousy and hatred of the courts of Dresden and Vienna. Before the war had even begun they had considered the division of his lands.

The king was prepared to conclude peace with the house of Austria were it to abandon its demands and rest content with the territorial holdings prevailing prior to the war. Great Britain, by unexpectedly signing peace with France, had disregarded Prussian interests completely and generally had begun to act very coldly. The king feared that London, to mask the injustice of its policy, might wish to circulate notions harmful to the king at this court when the king, in contrast, sought every opportunity to enhance his friendship with the empress. Her majesty, replied the chancellor, interceded for the king of Poland because of friendship, because of his constant solicitations, and because of her belief in the eternal rule of assisting quickly in national catastrophes. Not without reason, had the empress had counted on a larger flexibility and moderation by the king of Prussia with respect to her initiative, the more so in that Saxony was almost completely devastated.

Apprehension of an Austrian attack on Prussia through Saxony was no reason to delay peace, for the Russian proposal clearly stated that Saxony would be occupied immediately by its elector's forces; he would observe the strictest neutrality throughout any hostilities. The odd rejoicing about the plot allegedly displayed by the Polish court was quite surprising since there had been no news of it from the Russian envoy in Poland nor from anybody else. Finally the alleged intent to partition Prussia, the charge levelled against the courts of Dresden and Vienna, had not been demonstrated although Prussia had confiscated the Saxon archives and had published many papers from it. On this point, Solms noted that the king had clear proof of a scheme to partition his possessions.

Frederick believed that the existing circumstances prohibited Catherine from chancing a war with him because of Austria and Saxony. "In the present circumstances," he wrote to Finckenstein in December, "we must win some time and move quietly (à pas mesurés). As yet I do not know our relations with Russia. But I have important reasons to feel that they do not want to break with us. The empress is moving her forces behind her borders and I do not think that Austria has much influence in Petersburg."

RELIEF IN DENMARK

A dispatch to Korff on June 29 stated that if he was travelling to Berlin he must return to the king of Denmark and assure him of the empress's sincere desire to maintain their friendly alliance without interruption. He was to say that the empress witnessed with regret the extremes that relations with Denmark had reached as a result of the Holstein question. She recognized that the measures employed against Denmark were incompatible with the interests of her realm, whose welfare she held more important than anything else. The empress wished to confine relations to their earlier basis and to follow the general proposition that the affairs of Holstein could not disrupt the amicable relations between the Russian and Danish courts.

Korff was in Berlin when he received this note. He left immediately for Copenhagen and from there journeyed to the king's country residence, Friedenburg, where he was awaited with impatience and received with great joy. The king could not find words to express his gratitude to the empress for her assurances of friendship and expounded on his respect for the Russian people. "You are the witness," he said to Korff, "of how I always esteemed the Russian people. My respect grew as a consequence of the bravery of the Russian forces in the current war. It was sad to have to enter into a bloody war against a people whom I had not insulted." Korff wrote that "not only the court but every inhabitant of the Danish provinces through which I passed, down to the last peasant, were happy at the unexpected change in their fate. I pray the Almighty shall grant all that these poor people wished of your majesty. Exactly the opposite occurred in Berlin and the Brandenburg lands when they learned of your majesty's accession to the throne. Terror ran so high that the treasury was removed to Magdeburg by night."

The Danes counted too much on Catherine's indifference to Holstein. The king of Denmark announced that in the event of the minority of a duke of Holstein guardianship would pass to him. This step accorded with an agreement with the king of Sweden, who was a prince of the house of Holstein. Exactly this situation now existed, claimed the king of Denmark, thanks to the infancy of Grand Duke Paul. He was obliged to assume the guardianship and therefore to rule the duchy.

Catherine personally wrote to the foreign ministry on this matter. "My proclamation to all foreign powers upon my accession to the Russian throne referred to my earnest desire for peace. The move of the king of Denmark is surprising, for he has claimed the alleged right, together with me, to assume guardianship over my son in Holstein. I cannot recognize this right. In the Holy Roman empire the younger prince cannot, without the knowledge of the head of his house, enter into an agreement to the detriment of that head. The former emperor neither saw nor approved the treaty between the king of Sweden, the junior prince of the house of Holstein, and the king of Denmark, to the detriment of their brothers and the heir to Peter III. All laws of the Holy Roman empire specify that the mother enjoys right of guardianship over her son. The king of Denmark personally upheld this principle in the recent matter of the house of Weimar. All wise men agree that the right of the sovereign is strengthened by the trust of an entire people. Everyone can judge this for himself. I will not enter into negotiation with the king of Denmark until he removes his forces from Holstein."

Catherine assigned the well-known Prince George to deal with the issues relating to Denmark in rewarding him for his assistance under Peter III. Understandably, Denmark had to make concessions and Baron Bernstorff, the minister of foreign affairs, informed Korff that the king's intentions had been most innocent. "He wished merely to demonstrate that his interest was the augmentation of the German holdings of the grand duke. He had taken the opportunity to display to his highness his sincerity solely to win the future friendship of the sovereign, a friendship sorely desired in behalf of himself and his territories. Knowing now of the difference in the thinking of the empress and the king with respect to the joint guardianship and administration of Holstein, the latter cannot but desist in exercising his rights in order to demonstrate to the empress the most profound respect and amity she might imagine."

SWEDEN OBSERVES

The events of June 28 that returned Korff from Berlin to Copenhagen kept Ostermann in Stockholm. A message was sent to him on June 29 with news of Catherine's accession. He was instructed to assure the king of the new empress' certain purpose of cultivating sincere friendship with the Swedish court. In responding the king wrote that, because of their kinship, he must lament the fate Peter III had drawn upon himself. In view of the vital reasons requiring the empress to express her maternal solicitude for the welfare of the Russian empire and his own close kinship with her, he had learned with greatest pleasure of her possession of the throne and of her determination to continue amicable relations with Sweden. Through every avenue available to him the king would not fail to promote this friendship. Adolph-Friedrich underscored this policy forthwith by abstaining from the king of Denmark's claims to guardianship of Holstein.

Chancellor Vorontsov relayed to the empress a memorandum about new instructions to Count Ostermann. "When the last reign commenced, Count Ostermann received instructions to support the king and queen and their party at every opportunity. Considering that this unlimited instruction might involve subversion of the established form of government in Sweden, might not it be amended?" Catherine replied in her own hand: "With respect to the form of government, the party in opposition should be supported."

In September Ostermann managed to obtain and forward to Petersburg the report of Posse, the Swedish ambassador to Russia, on the state of the Russian empire. Posse began with the matter closest to him, the relations between Russia and Sweden. He wrote of the desirability of preserving things as they existed. He turned then to Russia's military strength. The regular army numbered about 304,953 and the irregulars about 32,000. Of this number no more than 100,000 men could be deployed. Regiments were never up to full strength. An infantry regiment numbered 2637 men but always lacks 600 to 700 men. The War College holds troop numbers to the minimum in order to save the Treasury money.

The constant passage of army regiments over such a vast country, traversing one province then another, costs many men. There is in addition the Russian's inborn hatred of military service and the difficulty of drafting and transporting recruits. A regiment includes officers, non-commissioned officers, corporals, medics, chaplains, clerks, musicians, carpenters, smiths, orderlies and teamsters. These number from 600 to 700 men in each regiment. The Russian soldier eats bad food, constantly finds himself at hard work, and lacks good surgeons and medicines. Consequently, one fourth of the regiment is laid up in hospitals. A sick soldier may be considered lost because of the poor care he receives. Thus 800 to 900 men remain per regiment.

Russians are not talented militarily and have no skilled generals save some foreigners. During the current war certain foreigners in Russian service were by-passed and neglected. Over the last few years several thousand able and skilled officers were forced to seek discharges and received them without difficulty. The army and navy cadet corps are fruitful gardens, producing able officers.

The fleet consists of 31 ships of the line; with others the number is 42, and when galleys are included, 99. The older ships are in poor repair, so rotten as to be scarcely salvageable. In general, the fleet is sorry because the ships are constructed poorly. The ship *Elizabeth*, built in 1745 and carrying 99 guns, was not seaworthy because it heaved to one side. The oaks of Kazan and the pines of Archangel used for shipbuilding are soft and lack fiber. The harbor of Kronstadt has no salt water. Seven months of snow and ice hurt the ships very much. The Russian fleet will always be mediocre because it lacks skilled sailors. This will last until Russia begins to develop its own merchant fleet.

If Russia knew to exploit the many advantages bestowed on it by nature, it could bring its trade to the highest levels of success. But Russians lack the necessary freedom, knowledge, credit, and capital. Their foremost merchants are the mere agents of foreign merchants, primarily the English. Foreign goods entering Russia are valued at 3,002,715 rubles; those exported at 4.7 million rubles. To escape high duties, imports are listed at least one third under the actual price. Furthermore, many goods enter secretly through customs. The difference between imports and exports therefore cannot be large.

Trade suffers greatly from high customs duties. It is estimated that all goods are charged some forty percent in duties. The current or even permanent Russian trade losses are attributable in part to the government's policy of prohibiting the export of certain goods. When grain from Livonia could be exported, Sweden bought several thousand measures annually. But when Russian grain exports were halted, Sweden developed its own grain production to overcome the loss. Wasteful grain distillation was prohibited and improved agriculture was introduced.

Monopolies are one of the major reasons for the drop in trade. To this must be added bureaucracy, conflicts, inefficiency, and the bribes accepted at all customs houses. When the crown handled customs, the merchants paid their duties at the end of each year in a lump sum. Their capital could be used all year. But when customs collections were farmed out the merchants were forced to pay the duty when goods left customs. Customs agents were to pay three million rubles to the Treasury annually but the higher duties caused trade to fall off, and they became insolvent.

The government is not properly concerned with factories and individuals who lack capital and credit. Factories either deteriorate completely or remain unimproved. Russian craftsmen cannot obtain the best instruments and materials and thus their work is poor. Their labor is cheap but, in all fairness, it can in no way compare to foreign labor.

Ostermann, for his part, reported to the empress the poor state of affairs in Sweden, the lack of money, fearful prices, universal grumblings against the government, and the possibility of convoking an extraordinary Riksdag. Ostermann wrote that general dissatisfaction might cause the return of absolute rule, for he had never heard such embittered comments about the current form of government. The opponents of the court party asserted that its goal was the re-establishment of absolute rule. They pointed to the fact that the queen personally guided this group and that the most influential member of the party, Colonel Sinclair, was totally loyal to the queen.

Ostermann found an opportunity to speak with Sinclair concerning his policies. The latter denied that he wished to bring back the absolute rule. He explained that his single goal was the elimination of the existing disorder. This was impossible without re-evaluation of the existing form of government, resolution of its internal problems, establishment of a fundamental law unalterable by every meeting of the Riksdag, and agreement about the respective powers of the king and the Senate. To Ostermann's question about how this could be achieved given the influence of the French party, which would not allow it, Sinclair replied that it was difficult to do anything without money. If he had a third of the sum the French party spent in Sweden, he could achieve significant results. To the question of what he would do without this money, Sinclair answered that the only alternative was to suffer until such time as the people finally opened their eyes and considered their own salvation themselves. The last Riksdag, wrote Ostermann, adjourned without either the court or the French party seizing a decisive edge.

POLAND AND COURLAND

The affairs of Poland were more important. Under Peter III Count Keyserling served as ambassador to Poland in place of Voeikov. Catherine made no change but kept Keyserling in Petersburg for a while for consultations. The resident, Rzhichevsky, remained in Warsaw in charge of embassy affairs. We have observed that the court of Poland was brought to desperation by the change in Russian policy and by Peter III's close alliance with Frederick. It found solace in rumors that there would be an overthrow in Petersburg soon. In a dispatch of June 16 Benois, the Prussian envoy, relayed to his sovereign that people arriving from Petersburg spoke of the empress's popularity among the Russian people.

The rumors proved true. A change did take place in Russia. But the Polish-Saxon court gained nothing from it. The winner was the Czartoryski party. Rzhichevsky was unable or did not wish to ignore the old Elizabethan instructions directing Russian ministers in Poland to be impartial in dealing with the parties there and to refrain from provoking the court on the question of the Czartoryskis. Furthermore, Rzhichevsky may have been fearful of Bestuzhev, a well-known adherent of the Polish-Saxon house. Besides, Keyserling, Bestuzhev's friend, was named ambassador to Poland.

Even so, the Czartoryskis complained about Rzhichevsky, who was reproved by the chancellor. "From the letters I have received from you and the messages you sent to the court, your actions have not met with approbation here. You were instructed explicitly that in discussions of the Sejm[19] in Poland with the Czartoryski princes you were to convey, in strict confidentiality, our well-meaning intentions. This was to have been clarified prior to the arrival of Ambassador Count Keyserling. Likewise, you were to petition his Polish highness on behalf of our court that he grant Chancellor Prince Czartoryski's request that Lithuanian officials be given the vacant posts of military governor in Vilna [Wilno], and the hetmanship of Lithuania. The hope is that the king will gain the obligation of this family, which previously has displayed so much loyalty and effort in serving the crown and whose circumstances of service had changed.

"Finally, you must inform the chancellor and both candidates of our efforts and request their assistance in furthering our interests. These are tightly interwoven with the welfare of their homeland. You have understood the content of these instructions very poorly and have acted contrary to them. Instead of cultivating proper relations with the Czartoryskis, you have done exactly the opposite. Most of all, you were not to promote discord between the parties and the intrigues of Count Brühl. You were supposed to incline them to moderation and ending hostilities, particularly because it is her imperial majesty's policy not to disappoint the king of Poland because of our protection of the Czartoryski family. When you were forced to bribe Ambassador Tsekhanovsky to disrupt the Sejm, you should not have allowed him to enter comments reproachful of Russia into the proclamation. I must note as well that you may refrain from writing reprehensibly about the good intentions of the Czartoryskis. Their intentions are wellknown here. In the future, act strictly according to instructions. In general, adhere closely to the views and interests of our imperial court."

Rzhichevsky defended himself in a letter to the chancellor. "My abuse of the Czartoryski princes consists in the fact that when I told them of our favor for them, they suggested that I visit the primate, the hetman, and others and inform them of the new attitude of the Russian court toward the Czartoryskis. I was to lead these magnates into an understanding with them. Before I could discuss matters with these nobles, the Czartoryskis had made their imperial favor known. The following day several senators and ministers asked me whether it was true that the empress was prepared to approve the Czartoryskis' policies and assist them in their activities. When I inquired where they obtained this information they said that the Czartoryskis were boasting of receiving this information from the Russian court through me.

"Then I was forced to state that I had made no such declaration and that I had told them only of the empress's desire that the posts they sought be granted thanks to her solicitations. It is true that the Czartoryskis are powerful men. But they are not the majority in the commonwealth. There are many other powerful houses disposed toward Russia that would be honored to receive imperial favor even though they disagreed with the Czartoryskis. I act in the manner I think best in strengthening the Czartoryskis without irritating the others. The Czartoryskis now lament their rashness, which brought them no honor. Their action caused them to quarrel so with Count Brühl that there is no way to reconcile them. They claimed support in the of the Polish nobility [Sejm] but it turned out that the support was on the opposite side. Their proclamation was signed by far fewer people than that of Count Brühl. As old friends, they should not be discarded so that others may hope for Russian aid as well. But to act against Count Brühl and the court, particularly in this affair, would be reprehensible."

This justification did not help as may be observed from Catherine's own comment. "Rzhichevsky, with his dull head, could not understand that if he was ordered to recommend to the court that the Czartoryski's be granted the vacant posts the same could be recommended to the primate and the others. Lest in the future it be not thought we are playing a double role there, he should be instructed to follow Keyserling's instructions. In addition, I see that Rzhichevsky is much taken with Count Brühl. I wish, rather, that business be conducted in conformity with my instructions, not according to someone's whims. He should be informed of this, although without reproof and in a measured tone."

The most difficult task facing Rzhichevsky was to hand the Polish ministry the documents relaying Catherine's decision to restore Biron to the throne of Courland. Rzhichevsky must convey the notion that there now were no reasons to prevent Biron's departure from Russia. Hence there were no obstacles in restoring him to the duchy, his investiture in which had been made to him once and for all time. Justice demanded that all estates given him by Empress Anne, plus those he purchased with his own funds, be returned to him.

The rescript to Rzhichevsky read: "It is natural to assume that while the king is magnanimous and accepts our attitude toward a family that has suffered and has offended neither us nor his crown, as a father he must feel sorrow. We wish to comfort the king to the extent possible and demonstrate our concern for his well-being and that of his house. We enjoin you to reassure him that there is hope that we shall urge just compensation for the devastation Saxony has suffered. We shall also assist in compensating Prince Charles for his loss of Courland. Perhaps this can be done by secularizing some bishoprics, or by other means. For example, he might receive the bishoprics of Münster or the city of Erfurt, the bishop of Mainz to receive an equivalent. In his confidential proposals for peace in 1757 the king of Prussia voiced his inclination for this solution."

Augustus III demanded that Biron advance his claims directly to him. Rzhichevsky received the following note on this point: "There is no need for concern about the justice of his majesty's wish or whether Ernst Johann [Biron] must claim possessions of which no law allows him to be deprived. We direct your attention to the fact that the king's reply was drafted in the Saxon chancellery, which lacks standing in Polish affairs and, consequently, in those of Courland. You are instructed not to accept any further documents dealing with Poland and Courland originating in the Saxon chancellery."

On August 14 Rzhichevsky commented that he had noticed no Polish magnates interceding on Biron's behalf. All said that because the king had been unable to obtain Biron's freedom for such a lengthy period, and because he had received assurances from Empress Elizabeth that Biron and his family would never be freed, the crown and the commonwealth would suffer severely were the king to deprive his son, Prince Charles, of the throne of Courland. He had bestowed on him this principality in accord with the declaration of the Russian court and the pleas of the people of Courland.

That the king's response to the empress was prepared in the ministry of Saxony Rzhichevsky explained in this way. The kings of Poland do not recognize the imperial title of Russian sovereigns. Were it to be drafted in the crown chancellery of Poland, the imperial title could not have been used. There was apprehension that Rzhichevsky would not accept it and it was decided to draft the reply in the Saxon chancellery. "I cannot hide the fact that the king is in great sorrow. He fears that his son will lose Courland to Biron. The court fears that his health might suffer as a result. It is said that after suffering ruin in Saxony he placed his entire hope in the magnanimity of the empress of Russia. Now, with respect to Courland, he has suffered at Russian hands."

Meanwhile, in Petersburg Keyserling and Bestuzhev were preoccupied by various affairs the empress had delegated to them. There is an interesting note on the question of Courland written by Bestuzhev on August 29. "Rzhichevsky's note requesting directions relating to Courland could not be answered until after six this evening as Count Keyserling had no time. He was quite tied up with the affairs of Holstein. The instructions, together with the note, are herein enclosed for imperial approval. As to Prince Charles' letter to her imperial majesty which Count Keyserling showed me, it might be treated as was a similar letter in 1746. At that time the then king of Prussia personally wrote Empress Elizabeth without prior notice. She ordered an imperious reply be prepared. But it was suggested that she follow the Russian proverb 'Appropriate silence is an answer to nothing.' In German this is 'Keine Antwort ist auch eine Antwort' [that is, no answer is also an answer]. The empress then approved this response and now Count Keyserling refrained from correspondence and left him without an answer."

Bestuzhev now was accomplishing his long-held purpose of returning his benefactor, Biron, to the throne of Courland. While chancellor in the reign of Elizabeth he had sought this in vain. On the other hand, Bestuzhev also favored the house of Saxony. Pursuing his preferences, Bestuzhev insisted of Prussia that, at the conclusion of peace, Saxony be compensated in Germany through secularization of religious properties.

But to seek compensation in Germany was unrealistic. In leaving the war Russia lost the right to determine the conditions of peace. In the meantime this very same Russia was seizing Courland from the Saxon house.

The unfortunate Augustus III planned to maintain his son in Courland through the Polish Sejm. But, as noted above, the Sejm had split following Catherine's communication of August 28. "Write to Rzhichevsky to employ every means to disrupt the current Sejm. He is definitely not to allow the election of a marshal. He should confer with the Czartoryskis about this and act even before the arrival of Count Keyserling."

The king demanded that the government and the Senate deal with the matter of Prince Charles. On October 7 the primate summoned some forty senators and in the name of the king proposed that they discuss ways to bar Biron from the duchy of Courland, free Courland as a Polish province from Russian forces, make complaint about Simolin, the Russian official in Mittau, for his imperious behavior in Courland, and send two senators to Mittau to assist Prince Charles. Some senators, hearing the proposals, believed that the conference should meet in the king's presence. In this way he would receive their suggestions personally. During these discussions some senators sat while others walked about the room. Finally, fierce arguments broke out which, as Rzhichevsky wrote, "happily ended the conference without any suggestions."

Count Sternberg, the Austrian ambassador to Warsaw, visited Rzhichevsky and strongly defended Prince Charles. He stated that the policies of a court could not be relied on when sovereigns abandoned the pledges of their predecessors. Count Brühl repeatedly told Rzhichevsky that the allied courts at any future diplomatic congress undoubtedly would intercede on behalf of Prince Charles. All of this Rzhichevsky reported to Petersburg, where it made no impression. The letter of the king to Bestuzhev stirred no reaction either, for reasons familiar to us.

Actually, Bestuzhev had to break ranks on Polish policy with his former friend, Keyserling. The latter fully accepted Catherine's idea of placing a Pole, namely Poniatowski, on the throne. Furthermore, he foresaw the necessity of a Prussian alliance. Panin held the same opinion, helping to pave the road toward his future eminence as Catherine's foremost adviser in all things, although temporarily there was a cooling between them on the question of the establishment of an imperial council. Bestuzhev, despite all his bustle, declined in influence because he steadfastly held to his earlier views of the necessity of keeping the Saxon dynasty on the Polish throne. Hence rumors proliferated that the former chancellor had grown too old and lost his capabilities. There were also rumors of his obstinacy and that he could not deal with new circumstances.

Bestuzhev's memorandum to Catherine of August 29 addressed the issue of stubbornness and collision between two old friends, Bestuzhev and Keyserling. "Most merciful sovereign! Allow me to mention Privy Councillor Gross. Having one foot already in the grave and observing my deepest devotion to your majesty, I am not advancing him. I think that in the current situation he would be useful to you. He knows the three languages, Russian, German, and French equally well, and also Latin. Furthermore, he is familiar with the laws of the Holy Roman empire no less than Count Keyserling and is truly an accomplished minister. If he has been slandered as obstinate, I was in a similar situation under the previous empress. I was accused of denying that the French might attempt, during the last war, to mediate between Russia and Sweden. Later I was vindicated by the communications of Ambassador Count Cantemir, which are in the College of Foreign Affairs. They demonstrate that while urging peace between Sweden and Russia the French court simultaneously was trying to induce the Turks to declare war against Russia. On many occasions I was called stubborn, incapable of accepting the old proverb, 'Do not tell the truth and lose friends.' And now, in my advanced age, I remain your majesty's loyal servant and a son of the fatherland to my dying breath."

Keyserling journeyed to Warsaw enjoying the empress's full favor. "Please give me your advice from afar, just as you have when you were nearby," wrote Catherine. To Poniatowski she wrote: "I cannot release Volkonsky to you. You will have Keyserling, who will serve you excellently." According to news relayed to the English court by Buckingham, its ambassador in Petersburg, Catherine immediately upon her accession sent a message to Poniatowski that he should not visit Petersburg, but that her friendship for him remained constant and that if there were an election of a king in Poland she would intervene on his behalf or, if this was impractical, for one of the Czartoryskis.

The unpleasantries between the two courts were swelling. "Order that it be impressed upon Count Brühl," Catherine wrote Vorontsov on December 10, "that should he take one step contrary to my wishes with respect to Courland I will quit my efforts on behalf of Saxony with the king of Prussia. In Poland I will explore every avenue, some he cannot even imagine, including his enemies, until he is driven from that country. This is to be done through discussion with one of the resident foreign diplomats. You, Mr. Chancellor, may choose the one best suited for this purpose, although I think either the Swedish or the Danish resident would manage. Begin indirectly, then speak with real force of Count Brühl's alleged meddling in the affairs of Courland. Mention that he wished to select two Polish senators to dispatch to Mittau and that every initiative of this sort by Brühl will lead me to support everyone seeking his destruction to the best of my abilities. Try to arrange that this reaches Prasse and my intentions be known. Count Brühl is as leering as a cat and as cowardly as a rabbit."

Keyserling arrived in Warsaw at the end of November and began to "serve excellently." Having informed the empress of the marked dissension between the court party and "our friends," Keyserling posed a question. "Is Russia planning to leave our allies and friends in Poland to decline in influence or not? If not, as the honor and the good of Russia demand, measures must be adopted in advance to avoid lessening their role. When the friends of Russia lose, Russia also loses. If we continue our policy of keeping our friends away from important posts and Russia's enemies, or individuals of no merit other than small brains, riches, and rapacious inclinations, occupy them, our friends will shrink in number and disappear altogether. When we have need, no one will be available. To avoid these unpleasant consequences, will it please your imperial majesty to send me instructions making clear to everyone that your majesty wishes nothing so much as lasting, deep friendship with the king of Poland and the return to Poland of life as it was. Formerly, Russia's friends were never distinguished from friends of the court. They were considered members of the same party, mutual friends.

"We may hope that the king will view the Czartoryskis, Poniatowskis and their friends worthy of his grace when he distributes preferences. We may hope that they are loyal servants of their king, that they seek the well-being and prosperity of their country, that they are friends of Russia because of their concern for their native land and aware that your majesty in following your predecessor is determined to defend the welfare, freedom, and rights of the commonwealth. They shall know as well that your majesty will follow this policy always, will defend always the patriots in Poland and not permit them to be repressed." On this letter Catherine wrote: "Let this be." In addition, she wrote to Vorontsov. "Instruct Count Keyserling not to write here when vacancies occur at the Polish court. He shall recommend people partial to Russia and not lose time in exchanging messages. It is a long distance from Warsaw to here. Also, Count Keyserling is to inform Count Brühl that I observe with considerable surprise that my friends are being denied promotions and favors when, every day, I seek to satisfy the king with respect to Saxony and other matters. An uncharitable act such as this and many others must lead me to consider different measures."

Keyserling forwarded on December 3 and 4 two memoranda he received from both Czartoryski brothers. The first urged formation of a confederation inasmuch as the usual practices were insufficient to destroy the evil plaguing Poland. Numerous younger individuals occupied important positions whence they acted like scourges on the body of the people. The king held no right to remove them once they were invested in office. The serious shortage of money required a new issue of coinage. Only the Sejm was empowered to do this. Because the Sejm could not be counted on for decisive action, a political confederation was the sole, last resort if important offices were to be filled with capable men. Financial and trade losses must be limited and local councils (conseils de la nation) be organized better. The empress of Russia should receive a title worthy of her influence and personal qualities. Amicable relations must prevail eternally between the two sovereigns.

A confederation required money and arms. The assistance made available to loyal leaders by the imperial court of Russia must be sufficient to their aims. There could be no activity until they were specifically informed and assured on this score. A rapid change in rule damages a country least. The stronger it is, the less time it needs to achieve its goal. It cannot be strong if it lacks sufficient resources at the very beginning, and only thereafter receives help gradually.

"If increasing the influence of the Russian party in the country is desired," stated the second memorandum, "it is vitally important to make no mistake in choosing the means to accomplish this. No doubt, one most significant method is the distribution of offices and favors. But this is a way never to be purchased at the expense of public respect. We will lose this respect if we celebrate peace with Count Brühl.

"There are reasons for this. Reconciliation naturally implies discounting and disappearance of indignities suffered. Yet, because the causes of our complaints endure, reconciliation is out of the question. We cannot withhold our complaints because honorable men cannot withdraw charges of impropriety made publicly on firm, proven legal grounds. Count Brühl cannot end his indignities because his errors heretofore requires him to continue the maneuvers which we always must censure and reject.

"Brühl's entire maneuvers have the purpose of preserving his position. Money is the chief means he employs. He is always in need of much money. He must bribe the ordinary individuals surrounding the king. He must maintain spies in all private homes to prevent the king from learning from any source the real reasons for his troubles. His unlimited love of luxury gratifies him not only personally but corresponds to the wishes of the king. Augustus III approves of the impressive appearance of his favorite. He considers it a symbol of his own personal majesty. To provide the king his pleasures, Brühl auctions off favors and corrupts the coinage, and at great profit to himself. The scandal these abuses would cause were they known makes him fear general dissatisfaction, to avoid which he seeks supporters by filling all posts with common and self-interested men, the kind that every country has in abundance.

"Consequently corruption infects the Senate, which is nothing other than an institution of flattery and ignorance. From this source as well flows the sale of judicial offices. These function on the principle of intimidation and readiness to extort silence from anyone daring to object to the lawlessness of Brühl or his chief procurers. Finally, there is the Sejm, the meetings of which accomplish nothing thanks to the mandatory unanimous vote necessary to enact legislation [liberum veto],[20] where someone bribed by Brühl constantly obstructs proceedings. Here is found the link between Count Brühl's mistakes and his requirements. Once he cannot satisfy them he will lose favor. Consequently, he will not change for the better and friendship is inconceivable.

"Brühl's greed is to be held in check solely through fear of juridical evidence that he is not a member of the Polish nobility and thereby illegally enjoys his honors and estates in Poland. An attack on Brühl from this position would be exceedingly dangerous if we were not assured of Russian support. Russian sympathy will yield us as many open adherents as there are already secret friends. Since these supporters must be placed somewhere, as well as paid, we must keep to a middle path. While not withdrawing our charges about Brühl's rights as a Polish noble, and not reconciling with him, we can suspend proceedings against him. Brühl will alternate between hope and fear. He will distribute favors as we desire when the Russian court and its ambassador here adopts a tone appropriate to such a minister. It should be required in no uncertain terms that every favor be awarded to us and our friends."

In this way the Czartoryskis voiced their wants. They asked that Catherine employ diplomatic pressure to force Augustus III and Brühl to be their captives. They would win an opportunity to build a powerful party at the head of which they might venture anything. Or, she might supply funds and arms for an armed uprising. In either event the goal was the same—domestic reform calculated to strengthen Poland, especially transformation of the Sejm through abolition of the liberum veto. Russia was to employ its resources to help Poland become stronger. In reward, Catherine would be awarded the imperial title and an agreement forged between Russia and Poland!

The insolence of these proposals strikes one immediately. But amazement at the Czartoryskis fades when we learn that Keyserling not only forwarded their memoranda to Catherine but supported the confederation they proposed. Why should the Czartoryskis stand upon ceremony after that?

On the other hand Keyserling, while in Warsaw, continued to work for an alliance with Prussia. He informed Benois that the surest path was close ties and identical views among the empress and the king of Prussia, particularly when the question arose of a replacement for the Polish throne. Benois, understandably, agreed. But he disagreed with the Russian ambassador in his opinion of the Czartoryskis' initiative. He sounded alarm and wrote the king that the Sejm must be divided through bribery if it favored activities detrimental to Prussia. Among these would be increases in the armed forces and decisive majority votes. Both of these policies had won many adherents, thanks to the book about them by Konarsky.

Meanwhile against Prince Charles in Courland moves were made. Instructions were forwarded to Simolin on July 5 that all decrees he had received in the preceding reign, such as those about sequestering the duke's income, resisting Prince Charles' orders, and inciting the Courlanders against him in favor of Prince George, were rescinded. He was to support Biron in preference to any other group. On July 22 Catherine wrote to Vorontsov: "Inform Simolin that he is to begin strengthening Biron's party immediately, citing his just rights." Simolin reported that when Biron sent protests to Baron Knieg, his authorized representative, the latter forwarded them to Geiking, the chairman of the organization of Lutheran parishes and also the head of Prince Charles' party, who assembled officers and soldiers, tore up a copy of his protests in front of them and threw them out the window.

Prince Charles was not in Mittau at the time. He was visiting his father in Warsaw. Geiking, his son and their followers acted vigorously on his behalf, trumpeting loudly that the empress personally supported Prince Charles. There were only some ministers who supported Biron, without her consent. Simolin urged that the government prohibit Geiking from making any further such statements. Prince Charles arrived in Mittau at the beginning of August. Geiking, the commandant of Mittau, ordered a reception prepared. Prayers in churches and the illumination of the city would greet the happy traveller. It was announced that failure to illuminate a house would be considered an inhospitable act. Even so, the majority of the residents did not illuminate [their homes].

Prince Charles announced that he would not accept Simolin as the Russian representative because the latter was not accredited to him. He prohibited his courtiers to visit Simolin's home or have any relations with him. In reply, a Russian battalion arrived in Mittau from Riga. Simolin explained that the battalion had been sent to quell disturbances that sometimes occurred in these circumstances. Prince Charles ordered distribution of ammunition and cannon to his force (180 men). He threatened that anyone known to support Biron would be treated as insurrectionaries. The guard in the palace was doubled.

Biron arrived in Riga and many nobles from Courland visited him there. Prince Charles then sent the younger Geiking to Warsaw with a petition in his behalf in the name of all Courland. Simolin informed his court that Courland no longer could endure this impasse, especially in that Russian forces returning from Prussia had entered Courland and that Prince Charles was creating impediments to the procurement of rations. A note from Moscow on October 17 instructed him to announce his accreditation to Biron. The note ended with these words. "Attempt to convoke an extraordinary assembly of their parishes, or some other form of associations, in which sharp divisions can be created. Upon being invited to join them on grounds of the patronage we always have extended to Courland, as invitees we would be in a position to interfere directly in their affairs and confirm the former duke, Ernst Johann."

Simolin called in a number of people from the parish organizations. Some thirty of them responded and, in the presence of the high marshal sent by Biron, discussed how best to fulfill her imperial majesty's wishes. They did not conceal their affection for and devotion to his highness, Duke Ernst Johann. They stated that an extraordinary session of the assembly or a conference of fraternal groups was unthinkable so long as Prince Charles reigned and governed. They recommended drafting a letter to the empress wherein they offered congratulations on her happy coronation and thanks for freeing their old duke. This would demonstrate their favorable disposition toward him. They promised to persuade the parish organizations to sign the letter.

Biron wrote Simolin that negotiations with Poland held no prospects. The court in Warsaw would seize every excuse for delay in order that Prince Charles remain in Courland and enjoy the income thereof. If the empress wished to return Biron to Courland, it must be done without delay and ceremony. Reporting this, Simolin added that nearly the entire nobility and merchants, practically the entire duchy, impatiently awaited Biron's return.

On December 13 Simolin received instructions that he should sequester Prince Charles' income on grounds that he had violated good relations among neighbors by refusing Russian troops winter quarters and provisions. Prince Charles instructed all leaseholders and friends to ignore Simolin's announcement about seizing his revenues. Simolin then sent Russian officers to enforce his orders. The empress's new rescript instructed Biron to enter Courland. Simolin must impress on Prince Charles that the empress had resolved irrevocably to restore Biron to the throne of Courland. Prince Charles therefore must leave Mittau. Her majesty would not neglect her efforts on his behalf but should he prove stubborn in resisting her purposes it was quite possible that he might encounter personal unpleasantries.

In responding the prince noted that the situation depended not on him but on his royal father, of whom he had requested a decision. Meanwhile Charles had moved most of his possessions from Mittau and had sold almost all of his furniture. Biron and his son Peter arrived in Mittau on December 30, 1762 and was greeted by about 200 members of the gentry. Of the officials only the mayor made an appearance. The other officials obeyed Prince Charles' prohibition. After dining at Simolin's quarters Biron signed decrees specifying a public meeting on February 10, 1763 and returned to Riga.

TURKEY AND AUSTRIA

Catherine's accession to the throne made an unfavorable impression in Constantinople. Obrezkov wrote (on August 27) that the Porte, at that time in the best spirits seeing Vienna in an extremely weak position, was thunderstruck by the news of Catherine's accession. The Porte's interpreter who visited Obrezkov with congratulations expressed curiosity: what would be the relations now between the courts of Russia and Austria? Would the truce with Frederick continue? Would the issue of Denmark end peacefully or in extremes?

Obrezkov gave assurances that the relations between the courts had not changed at all and that if indeed the alliance with Austria had weakened because of the former emperor's partiality, its earlier authority now would be reasserted. The return of Chernyshev's army corps demonstrated this. The truce with Prussia would be honored unless the king of Prussia violated it. The issue of Denmark involved no extremes and would be settled peacefully.

This response had the purpose of leading the Porte to abandon any hostile notions with respect to Austria. In the meantime Frederick II informed the Porte that his influence at the court of Catherine II was as strong as it had been under Peter III. In search of clarification the Porte's interpreter visited the French and Russian ambassadors to find out their thoughts about these Prussian assertions. The French ambassador answered that he seriously doubted their accuracy and advised the Porte to be careful. Obrezkov suggested that this was a new example of Prussian cunning. To underline the lack of Prussian influence in Petersburg, Obrezkov cited the formulations in Catherine's manifesto of accession referring to the king of Prussia and to the return of Chernyshev's corps.

News reached Constantinople after much delay. Vienna learned earlier that the events of June 28 would bring no great benefit to Austria. Maria Theresa personally wrote a letter to Catherine to congratulate her on the accession. "In my opinion," wrote Maria Theresa, "after the deceased Empress Elizabeth no one could be more deserving of the throne or more deservingly replace her in my heart than your majesty. I thirst for an occasion to demonstrate my feelings to your majesty. I count so heavily on your acuity and friendship that I depend on you for everything demanded by our mutual interests and which might be expected of your magnanimity."

Catherine replied in a similarly personal communication. "I have entertained always the greatest respect for you. I am sincerely interested in everything that is of concern to you. Here I follow the example of my dear deceased aunt, Empress Elizabeth, whose memory is dear to both of us. Nothing gives me more pleasure than receiving your tender of friendship. I hope, as well, to extend to you that same friendship, the more so that this friendship is strengthened by our mutual interests." On July 6 the Austrian ambassador, Mercy d'Arganto, attended a meeting with the chancellor and vice chancellor. He inquired whether the empress valued retention of Russia's commitments to Austria and magnanimously would proclaim to the world her lasting concern for the welfare of ancient allies. The response was that her majesty would not continue the war because its length had exhausted her people. Nonetheless she was prepared to extend assurance of friendship to the empress-queen. A clear display of this was the recall of Chernyshev's corps from the Prussian army. Meanwhile the empress lacked an opportunity to examine Russia's previous commitments to the empress-queen.

Upon perusal of these commitments Russia extended to Mercy an offer to aid in hastening peace between Austria and Prussia, with the latter of which Russian now was at peace. Mercy then allowed himself an outburst that could lead only to further irritation. At the meeting on August 20 he declared that there was a contradiction between the note given to him and the manifesto published upon the empress's accession to the throne. That is to say, the peace with Prussia was proclaimed to the world in the manifesto as one signed with Russia's most dangerous enemy, and damaging to the glory of Russian arms. Mercy added that the empress-queen was pleased to accept the offer of good offices to help attain peace more quickly. But he wished to know the extent to which the empress intended to exercise her good offices. He was told that her majesty would not rule out mediation if she felt both sides would benefit. Noting Russia's plea that the warring sides withdraw their forces from Saxony, Mercy stated that Maria Theresa would comply the moment the king of Prussia did the same.

At a gathering in Moscow on October 14 Mercy asked for clarification of the empress' policy of meeting the commitments to Austria as defined under Elizabeth, or whether changes were envisaged. The court of Vienna must know St. Petersburg's intentions, particularly since the peace with Prussia signed during the previous reign had been confirmed but not yet communicated to Vienna. It was known that one of the provisions of this agreement nullified all earlier relevant commitments made by the Russian court.

An answer was forthcoming only on November 7. It said that the war still being waged with Prussia, which Russia had left because of domestic considerations, was a European crisis of such dimensions that nations were not able to form alliances nor establish policies with respect to peacemaking. These circumstances make it best to cultivate friendship and agreements reflecting the present, mutual interests, and the states of the governments. Domestic affairs and reasons of state had dictated the empress' withdrawal from the war, but she had conveyed to the court of Vienna that she looked upon its prosperity as her true concern and sincerely desired amity and maintain close ties with it. The court of Vienna had known of the empress' intentions not to participate in the present war. Her majesty felt that her efforts on behalf of European peace therefore now would enjoy a far greater significance. The opposing sides now were certain that Russia had not abandoned its polices and in assisting its natural ally had retained its freedom of action and maintained a considerable army on its borders.

Mercy was not satisfied with this answer. He pointed out its lack of clarity; it did not state whether Catherine intended to honor Elizabeth's obligations in full or whether there would be a change. These commitments, nullified by the recent agreement with Prussia, gave reason to think that the Russian court presently had no alliances other than the Prussian one. Were the empress truly to regard the welfare of the court of Vienna as its essential concern, this court might hope that the empress would communicate this to the enemy and would take actual steps to avoid Austria's precipitate decline and exhaustion from the war.

The treaty with Prussia and the fact that previous commitments to Austria had not been confirmed did not leave Russia's hands untied at all, actually, these factors tied them. Russia's assistance to Austria in a European peace promised little benefit for the latter. The king of Prussia, ignoring the signal services the Russian empress rendered him, which had allowed him to escape utter disaster, paid no heed to Russia's intercession and entreaties. At the very least the king of Prussia should have been informed that Russian forces would not depart his territories until he met the empress's demands. The chancellor replied that in the existing situation Vienna itself ought to realize that Petersburg could not enter into renewed war with Prussia.

At the time that these unpleasant exchanges were taking place in Petersburg and Moscow instructions were sent to Prince Dmitry Golitsyn in Vienna. He was to attempt to learn privately from the Austrian ministry whether Maria Theresa would accept Russian mediation in reaching a truce with Prussia. If this inclination were established, Golitsyn would reveal his authorization to act as mediator and learn the conditions Austria felt necessary for peace.

Golitsyn replied that the court of Vienna was grateful indeed to the empress for her interest in its well-being and greatly praised her humanitarianism in mediating an end to hostilities. He felt reluctant to state his opinions prematurely, fearing that Prussia would make false assumptions by believing Austria too weak to continue the war. Furthermore, the close ties between Austria and France hindered the former from being too frank with another power without France's agreement. "The court here," wrote Golitsyn, "in expressing its sincerest gratitude for the offer of mediation, still feels the need to be careful. It sees, to its regret, that Russia wishes to act jointly with Austria only on matters relating to the Ottoman Porte."

Golitsyn impressed upon Kaunitz that even the appearance of close friendship between Russia and Austria was sufficient to allow the latter to negotiate an advantageous peace. Kaunitz replied that the chief goal of the Prussian court was diminution of Austria's power. Prussia therefore wished to continue the war. It would not end until the king of Prussia was forced to accept peace. Simply the appearance of close relations between Russia and Austria was insufficient. "I must say," Golitsyn reported, "that Count Kaunitz accepted my representations with particular moderation. Nothing could be detected in him other than regret and sorrow that the long-established alliance between the imperial courts had declined to the mere level of amity and agreement."

On December 25 Golitsyn informed his court of the commencement of peace negotiations between Austria and Prussia in Hubertusburg (between Dresden and Meisen). "The initiative in these negotiations," he wrote, "belongs to the house of Saxony. Having no hope of compensation for losses suffered in this war, wishing to repossess its lands and return to Dresden from Warsaw as soon as possible, the house of Saxony convinced this court to seek reconciliation with Prussia. It was agreed to here all the more willingly as the prospects for continuing the war diminished. It became clear that the next campaign must be a defensive one, and even this with difficulty. Not only had they been abandoned by their allies, they knew that the imperial principalities [of the Holy Roman empire] were in no condition to help with troops."

Naturally, France and Austria had to share the despair of dashed hopes. "Your accession to the throne," wrote Chernyshev in Paris to Catherine, "has caused great happiness here, not only at court but among the people as well. They recognize your imperial majesty's power and influence in European affairs. It is felt that your imperial majesty will observe the agreement with this court in contrast to the previous regime when things were moving toward a split. They are impatient for a quick peace since all parts of this country need it. The war cannot continue longer without complete ruin. It is expected that your imperial majesty will assist in this."

FRANCE AND ENGLAND

Together with satisfaction there was some annoyance in connection with the early departure from Petersburg of the French ambassador, Baron Breteuil. There was hostility to Breteuil, particularly because he had been aware of preparations for the coup. Breteuil was sent back to Petersburg and reprimanded for leaving that city too quickly and, when in Warsaw he had learned of the events of June 28, for not hurrying to Petersburg instead of proceeding to Vienna.

Louis XV recognized in Catherine a woman capable of commencing and accomplishing great things. This was the impression made by her secrecy prior to June 28 and the fortitude displayed on that day. But the king recognized the difficulty of her position. "There is no doubt," he wrote to Breteuil, "that the memory of Peter III will have few defenders. Thus we cannot assume that there will be disturbances as a result of the desire for vengeance. But the empress is a foreigner by background and has no ties to Russia. She is also the niece of the king of Sweden. She must exert herself constantly to hold a throne gained not through the love of the citizenry nor through respect for the memory of her father, as Empress Elizabeth had done. No matter how careful she is, there always will be the dissatisfied.

"Despite her strong spirit, Catherine has a weak heart. She will have a favorite, a confidante. It is none of our business who it will be. We must know only those who will be the primary recipients of her trust and seek their good will. Of course, Princess Dashkov must expect many favors from the empress. But can we say that this young woman assisted in the coup solely for the love of her fatherland and for attachment to the sovereign? The tsar's passion for Vorontsova may have excited her jealousy. If this motivation ended with the sovereign's death, Princess Dashkova, romantic and encouraged by success, might feel that she has not been sufficiently rewarded, that she is not trusted enough, and in the end for some reason or other again will create a disturbance. The empress, discovering something, may punish her. This will change the complexion of the court once more. We must expect many cliques, particularly if there is a favorite."

Observing political affairs, Louis XV instructed his envoy to struggle against Austrian influence in Petersburg. The king feared that Mercy would take advantage of Breteuil's absence and step to the forefront. Louis XV spoke plainly about Russia. "You already know, and I will repeat it here in the clearest fashion, that the goal of my policy toward Russia is to keep it as far away from European affairs as possible. Not involving yourself directly, so as not to engender protests against you, you must support each of the parties which surely will form at this court. Russia will have less opportunity to practice policies suggested by other powers the more domestic disturbances prevail.

"At the present moment our influence may work to benefit us in the sense that it may further a happy turn in Polish affairs, which will change the tone of Petersburg's dealings with the commonwealth. Our future influence must be exerted to prevent Russia's participation in a war against me and my allies, and particularly to avoid Russian opposition to my views in the event of a royal election in Poland. You know that Poland is the chief subject of my secret correspondence. Consequently you must pay attention to everything that concerns this country."

Breteuil was very well received by Catherine. She could not refuse herself the pleasure of conversing with a French diplomat who shone among the representatives of other countries like a Petersburger among provincials. But relations were limited to conversation. The duke of Choiseul, from the outset, had to abandon all hopes of holding Russia in the Franco-Austrian alliance.

Chernyshev explained to Choiseul that the Russian empress was the most talented among sovereigns in finding peace. Her majesty acted dispassionately, having only the good of mankind in mind. Choiseul observed that in this event the French court hoped that the empress at least would be more inclined to the side of her true allies. Chernyshev replied that surely this must be so. The word "dispassionate," he continued, should be employed in all clarifications concerning peace as a means of winning the trust of all courts. Choiseul then noted the advantage were the empress, to strengthen her influence in mediations, to permit her forces to remain in the territories won from Prussia. Chernyshev's response was that peace with Prussia was a reality, and that the empress in her solicitude for mankind and for her realm found it desirable to honor the peace and avoid reentanglement in the present war unless forced. Whereas the Russian forces were to return home, they were always prepared to execute their orders until such time as peace returned.

At the time that the court of Versailles was telling Russia that the best way to obtain peace from Frederick II was occupation of Prussian territories, the court in London also wished to turn Russia against Frederick. It suggested that France soon would reach an understanding with Prussia. Elizabeth's earlier alliance between Russia, England, and Austria was not out of date.

It has been observed that after Goltz, the English ambassador, Keith, had been particularly well received by Peter III. This embarrassed him with Catherine on the throne and he requested his recall. Whereas the empress received him kindly he learned from a trusted source that he was more objectionable to her than he had imagined.

Keith's successor was the duke of Buckingham. Count Alexander Vorontsov remained in London as ambassador. Seeing Frederick's reluctance for peace, Petersburg initially wished to act in concert with England. On September 21 Catherine wrote to Chancellor Vorontsov: "Instruct

Count Alexander Vorontsov to communicate in conversations my sincere desire for peace. It is with no little sorrow that I observe the unwillingness of the king of Prussia to accept a policy so beneficial to mankind. His uncharitable views distance me from this sovereign. Each measure calculated to end hostilities therefore pleases me. More helpful than subsidies (England to Prussia) in the cause of peace would be agreement between Russia and England, which I gladly would hasten and strengthen."

Vorontsov forwarded his response to the empress on November 8. "Allow me to convey my loyal respect and happiness with respect to the just and courageous policy of promoting peace in Germany by variously leading the king to sacrifice his love of power. Europe long will be indebted to you. The realization of this purpose will augment in Europe the honor of Russia, inspired by the happy reign of an empress so august. Even here the friends of the court in Berlin are reluctant to approve Prussia's failure to respond to your imperial majesty's proposals for peace. His disposition is such that even his extreme straits cannot induce him to abandon his purposes.

"Who then is more capable of overcoming this obstacle and introducing equilibrium into Germany than a power as forbidding as Russia, inspired by a sovereign well aware of the uses of her influence in advancing the prosperity and honor of her citizens? I did not conceal from the state secretary for northern foreign affairs, Count Halifax, that your imperial majesty properly expected greater flexibility on the part of the king of Prussia with respect to the peace proposals conveyed to him by Prince Repnin. His reluctance could serve only to distance you from him. As discreetly as possible I seek not to allow the dissatisfaction with Berlin noted here to diminish. Even so, nothing is more effective in furthering chances for a complete break between the two courts than his Prussian majesty's continuing policies. We may include his envoys here, whose intemperate reactions will reap their proper rewards."

Vorontsov wrote on November 12 that England's current policy consisted of interfering as little as possible with the continental powers. London could not be expected to assist in firm measures to force Frederick II to peace. Earlier failures had cooled the ardor of the English ministry, which had seen Frederick treat proposals with no respect whatsoever.

London was prepared to practice a firm policy toward Prussia solely in agreement with Russia. On December 19 the chancellor and vice chancellor conferred with Buckingham, the English ambassador. Buckingham stated that his sovereign, prepared firmly to cultivate and to enhance friendship with Russia, requested a frank explanation of unpleasant discussions he recently was requested to hold with the Prussian ruler. The king wished to learn the empress's opinion of the king of Prussia as a means to form a common effort to re-establish the European peace so desired by the two courts. Buckingham later explained that the natural interests of the Russian, English, and Austrian courts suggested a close alliance between them. In contrast, the interests of France involved the salvation of the king Prussia.

Buckingham was certain that relations between Vienna and Versailles soon would cool because their interests conflicted. This opening should be exploited. Vienna should be led toward the idea of restoring the older and only truly natural alliance system. With respect to Franco-Prussian relations these powers, according to Buckingham, may have had temporary differences. But with time, perhaps soon, they would return to their earlier, close ties. It was not without reason that Goltz, the Prussian minister in Petersburg, was quite friendly with Breteuil. Goltz treated Buckingham cooly, and even parted without good-byes. Prior to his departure Goltz held a long conversation with Breteuil, no doubt an important one.

The chancellor and vice chancellor limited themselves to generalities in responding to Buckingham because on November 1 Chancellor Vorontsov received from the empress instructions regarding England. "During the current state of indecision in European affairs our policy must be one of exercising great care in forming new alliances and promoting prosperity domestically. The political situation bars no beneficial commercial agreements. We may negotiate a commercial treaty with England without delay. But we should exercise care that thereby we do not exclude opportunities to make similar agreements elsewhere for competitive as well as for export reasons. To present our policies as honest and firm, we must assure the English court that we find an alliance beneficial and will, of course, eagerly renew it. Yet at the same time tell them confidentially that we are putting it off now only because at present we have declined to renew the old obligations with the court of Vienna, and are content to maintain good accord and friendship on the basis of our natural and unshakeable common interests with them, until we shall see the political posture of this court after peace has been restored."

Buckingham recalled a sad event of the previous reign. According to a memorial of Count Finckenstein, the king of Prussia possessed the originals of a Russian dispatch disclosing British attempts to hinder Prussian negotiations in Petersburg under Peter III. The chancellor and vice chancellor informed the empress that they believed this dispatch to be Golitsyn's, then minister in London. The note allegedly contained a frank conversation by Lord Bute about Prussian relations. The king of Prussia asserted in vain his possession of the original. Actually the intact original was in Petersburg and differed greatly in language from the Prussian version.

The chancellor and vice chancellor informed Buckingham of this, but did not deny that perhaps the former emperor, blind in his loyalty to the king of Prussia, had written the king to this effect or told Goltz personally of the contents of the note. The empress replied to Vorontsov that "a determination about the dispatch can be made later. It is established that no original was or is in the hands of the king of Prussia. The passion of the former emperor was so great that he sometimes interpreted innocent words as harming the king of Prussia. These words he relayed to him, even though not the original words. This may serve to defend Lord Bute against the great multitude of his enemies who seek to find a crime in his conversation with the present vice chancellor."

NOTES

Additional information on personalities and topics found in the text and notes is available in Joseph L. Wieczynski, ed., *The Modern Encyclopedia of Russian and Soviet History* (MERSH); Harry B. Weber, ed., *The Modern Encyclopedia of Russian and Soviet Literatures (Including Non-Russian and Emigre Literatures)* (MERSL); Paul D. Steeves, ed., *The Modern Encyclopedia of Religions in Russia and the Soviet Union* (MERRSU); and David R. Jones, ed., *The Military-Naval Encyclopedia of Russia and the Soviet Union* (MNERSU), all published by Academic International Press.

A comprehensive account of the period immediately preceding the era covered in this volume, with illustrations, an extensive bibliography and background information, is Joseph T. Fuhrmann, *Tsar Alexis. His Reign and His Russia* (Gulf Breeze, Fla., Academic International Press, 1978).

CHAPTER I

1. A voevoda was the chief executive of a district or country; the term originally meant commander.

2. Count Burkhardt Christoph von Münnich served in Russia from the Petrine era. Ernst Johann Biron came to power in the reign of Empress Anne, under whom Münnich headed the army. Both were associated with the supposed "German" party in the government. Münnich overthrew Biron's regency in 1740. *Bironovshchina* refers to the repressions allegedly directed by Biron under Anne.

3. Johann Hermann Lestocq or Lestock was a Franco-German court physician (though he held no medical degree) and one of the organizers of the coup that brought Elizabeth to the throne in 1741. Count Alexis Petrovich Bestuzhev-Riumin was chancellor, that is, the chief of foreign policy for most of Elizabeth's reign. He favored alliance with Austria and Britain against Prussia and France. He was overthrown in 1758 and banished to his estates in 1759 until rehabilitated by Catherine II in 1762.

4. The procurator general chaired the Senate; the senior procurator was his assistant.

5. The Preobrazhensky Regiment was created under Peter I as one of the new guards units. The name comes from the suburban Moscow village of Preobrazhenskoe (literally Transfiguration) where Peter lived as a child and young man.

6. There were three principal Shuvalovs: the brothers Peter (1711-1762) and Alexander (1710-1772) and their cousin Ivan (1727-1797). Under Elizabeth they were prominent in many areas of government, primarily military, diplomatic, financial, and educational affairs.

7. A verst is .63 miles or very close to a kilometer.

8. The Holy Synod, established by Peter I in 1721, was a collegial body that supervised church affairs once the patriarchate had been formally abolished. The senior procurator, a layman, supervised the Synod.

9. The term "service of the nobility" refers to the nobility's obligation to serve the state. This obligation was enforced zealously under Peter I, who created the Table of Ranks to reflect various grades and types of state service, military, civil, and court. After Peter's death these service obligations gradually were relaxed until Peter III decreed the nobility's liberation from compulsory service in time of peace.

10. Lifland/Livland is an archaic usage and has been rendered as Livonia. At this time it referred to an area that is now partly in Latvia, partly in Estonia.

11. The term votchina referred to various patrimonies and hereditary properties, but by the eighteenth century the distinction between them and conditionally held estates largely had eroded.

12. The war actually occurred in 1741-1743 and was fought against Sweden, which had launched it in an attempt to exploit the confusion surrounding Elizabeth's coup and to regain territory in Finland. But Russia emerged victorious and gained further Finnish territory.

13. Autonomous monasteries (few in number) were those not responsible to the Holy Synod, but solely to the sovereign.

14. The term "soul" originally applied to the poll or capitation tax instituted under Peter I. Because it referred especially to the registered male peasant, the two became equated in popular parlance. Payments were made in money and/or other kind annually by the peasants to noble landowners.

15. The schismatics were those religious dissenters who had rejected the established church in protest against reforms in the liturgy introduced by Patriarch Nikon in the 1650s. They became irreconcilable after the repressions of the 1680s and splintered into several factions. The more fanatical groups resorted to self-immolation as the ultimate protest against church and state policies.

16. Vasily Tatishchev (1687-1750) served in the administration of Peter I and his successors. A versatile statesman, official, and intellectual, he is best known for his posthumously published multivolume *History of Russia*, an historiographical and documentary landmark that has remained quite controversial.

17. Peasant uprisings were a constant occurrence in Russian history. They varied greatly in degree and impact, and often involved groups other than the peasantry, itself a broad and vague designation. Soviet historiography has posited the significance of four particularly prominent rebellions, denoted "peasant wars" after Engels' study of the Reformation in Germany, and associated with the cossack leaders Bolotnikov, Razin, Bulavin, and Pugachev.

18. Manorial serfs or domestic servants generally were considered more restricted than village peasants.So it is understandable why the latter might complain about the transfer to domestic status.

19. Military levies, or recruit money, was a tax on peasants to support the military conscripts from their districts or for attendant problems such as the transfer of army units, billeting, feeding and the like.

20. This was the usual way of handling the collection of customs duties and tariffs. A contract was awarded to an individual for a specified period of time, and he would be responsible for all aspects of the operation.The successful bidder was not always guaranteed financial success.

21. The hetman was the military commander and frequently the administrative head of a cossack military force. After the Ukrainian and cossack revolt of 1648-1654 against Poland, and the Pereiaslavl Union of 1654 that united the eastern Ukraine with Muscovy, the hetman assumed both civil and military leadership of the Ukraine.The eighteenth century saw many vicissitudes in this position with respect to Little Russia, the territorial term no longer necessarily restricted to the Ukraine.

22. In Russian the word is *efimok/efimki*. Joachimsthalers were large silver coins mined in Joachimsthal in Bohemia and frequently used in other European countries.

23. The Russian term is *sloboda*, which means settlement or village.

24. Frederick II understates greatly and purposefully here. As Europe's foremost military figure, he was on the verge of a crushing defeat in the Seven Years War. He was spared the consequences of defeat by Elizabeth's death and Peter III's surprising abandonment of Russian territorial gains.

25. The Austro-Russian alliance was particularly the work of Chancellor Bestuzhev-Riumin, who regarded it as the mainstay of Russian foreign policy in Europe. It was signed in 1746. Bestuzhev also courted England to complete the triumvirate. But this broke down when, in dropping France, England signed the Treaty of Westminster (January 1756) with Prussia. In allying with England Prussia dropped France as well. This left France free to seek alliance elsewhere and in May, 1756 it signed a defensive pact with Austria, the first treaty of Versailles. This allowed France again to commence relations with Russia, relations which had been severed since 1748. Thus with Frederick II's ultimatum to Maria Theresa in 1756 and his invasion of Saxony he faced a formidable alliance of Russia, Austria, and France. England was relatively uncooperative with Prussia despite the Treaty of Westminster and the subsidies promised to Frederick II turned out to be few.

26. Duke Charles Peter Ulrich, the future Peter III of Russia, was the son of Elizabeth's older sister Anne (not to be confused with Empress Anne), and Charles Frederick, duke of Holstein-Gottorp. His father was a nephew of King Charles XII of Sweden. Charles Peter Ulrich was under the guardianship of Adolph-Frederick, prince-bishop of Lübeck and later king of Sweden, 1751-1771.

27. The *Szlachta* was the Polish noble class or middle nobility as contrasted to the magnates.

28. Russo-Turkish relations in the eighteenth century were often belligerent, as they had been in the late seventeenth century. The gains of Peter I in the Azov campaigns of 1695-96 were lost to the Turks in the disastrous Pruth campaign of 1711. The Russo-Turkish War of 1736-1739 resulted in the reconquest of Azov but without the right to fortify it or to operate a fleet on the Sea of Azov. Still, this partial Russian victory showed the slippage of Ottoman military might and heralded the much greater gains under Catherine II in the Russo-Turkish wars of 1768-1774 and 1787-1792, which made Russia a Black Sea power and commercial presence.

29. Tartar/Mongol "baskaks" were collectors of tribute in the thirteenth and fourteenth centuries.

30. Latin was the language of instruction in Russian seminaries for most of the eighteenth century, hence its use along with Russian in official church documents, petitions, and letters.

31. The black clergy was the monastic clergy and hierarchs of the Russian Orthodox church. The white clergy was the married parish clergy.

32. The inaccuracy of this judgment will be apparent later in Soloviev's text. It is another example of how easily the overthrow of Peter III was executed. Although the Prussian envoys had their ears sharply tuned to gather secret information, they had scant inkling of the actual conspiracy against Peter III.

33. Ivan VI, a great-grandson of Ivan V, who was the half-brother of Peter I. Born in 1740 and named successor to the throne by Anne shortly before her death and under his mother's regency, Ivan VI was dethroned by Elizabeth in 1741 and spent the rest of his life in prison until killed by his guards in 1764 during an attempt to liberate him.

34. Catherine's astuteness was apparent from the beginning of her career in Russia in 1744. She cultivated good relations with a variety of Russians instead of abusing their values as did Peter III.

35. Oranienbaum, an imperial estate southwest of Petersburg on the Gulf of Finland. Originally built in Peter I's reign, it was altered by the Italian architect Antonio Rinaldi during Elizabeth's reign and was much frequented by the Young Court of Grand Duke Peter and Grand Duchess Catherine.

36. For the Preobrazhensky Regiment, see Note 5. The other two leading guards regiments were the Semenovsky and the Izmailovsky. All three were instrumental in several of the coups in eighteenth-century Russia, most particularly those of Elizabeth in 1741 and Catherine II in 1762.

37. Peterhof was an imperial estate on the Gulf of Finland some five miles east of Oranienbaum and celebrated for its elaborate gardens and fountains.

38. The Chancellery of Posts (prikaz ramskoi) was the administration of posts and roads.

39. The Treasury College (1718-1785) supervised state revenues, particularly the state monopoly on the production and sale of spirits.

CHAPTER II

1. Ivan Shuvalov remained in Europe, primarily in Rome, from 1763 to 1777, when he returned to Russia and resumed prominence in court and cultural affairs. He was famed as a patron of many writers and artists, including Voltaire.

2. Private churches and chapels could be found in the homes of the well-to-do. This was a longstanding Russian practice particularly widespread among the merchant class.

3. A pud equals 36.1 lbs. A *grivna* was a coin usually made of silver which varied in value. In this period it was probably worth about ten copecks.

4. *Kormlenie*, literally "feeding," an administrative term that goes back to medieval Russia; it denoted an assignment of jurisdiction and revenue collection to an official in a particular area.

5. Catherine did not exaggerate much in this statement. Under Elizabeth both commercial and industrial concessions were awarded to individuals and companies in the form of monopolies. Aware of the criticism of this practice, suspicious of its beneficiaries such as the Shuvalovs, and influenced by European notions of promoting free trade, Catherine largely abolished monopolies at the start of her reign.

6. See Note 20 in the previous chapter.

7. A pail was a liquid measure of 12.3 liters.

8. Catherine's concern for timber reserves was quite enlightened for its time and built on Elizabethan precedent. The greatest timber reserves were in the northern Urals and Siberia, regions remote from the empire's main population centers. Depletion was most noticeable around Petersburg and Moscow, both large industrial centers. The issue received some attention at the Legislative Commission of 1767-68, one subcommittee of which investigated the matter.

9. These were laymen who worked in monasteries or in the administration of bishoprics.

10. Catherine II asked Teplov about errors, for her Russian was imperfect and she spelled poorly in all languages. Teplov was a clever man with much experience in Europe.

11. Teplov noted a spelling disparity in the Russian verb for "may."

12. See Note 33, Chapter I. "Ivanuskha" is the Russian diminutive for Ivan and refers to Ivan VI, the imprisoned crown prince killed in 1764.

13. Tsar Ivan Alexeevich (Ivan V), half-brother of Peter I and co- tsar with him from 1682 to 1689, when Sophia's regency was overthrown.

14. The reference is to peasants owned by the crown. By voiding their obligations, the false manifesto was calling for rebellion.

15. The Spiritual Regulation was issued in 1721 and established the Holy Synod.

16. The question of free labor arose more than once as the text demonstrates. Its use had been criticized late in Elizabeth's reign and then again under Peter III. Catherine II further restricted it, reaffirming her late husband's prohibition.

17. For Bironovshchina, see Note 2 of the previous chapter.

18. Empress Anne's accession was accompanied by the attempt of the Supreme Privy Council to curtail her sovereignty by restrictive "conditions." Shortly after her arrival in Moscow to be crowned, Anne tore up the "conditions" in response to petitions from large groups of noblemen who feared an aristocratic powerplay.

19. The Sejm was the general diet, sometimes bi-cameral, in Poland- Lithuania.

20. The "liberum veto" was a rule of the Polish diet whereby one negative vote could block a proposal. It was an extreme manifestation of the notion of noble "liberty" vis-à-vis the crown.

INDEX

FROM ACADEMIC INTERNATIONAL PRESS*

*Request catalogs **OP—out of print